Soul
Psychology

*How to Clear Negative Emotions
and Spiritualize Your Life*

Soul
Psychology

*How to Clear Negative Emotions
and Spiritualize Your Life*

Joshua David Stone, Ph.D.

Ballantine Wellspring™
The Random House Publishing Group • New York

A Ballantine Wellspring™ Book
Published by The Random House Publishing Group

Published in the United States by Ballantine Books, an imprint of The Random House
Publishing Group, a division of Random House, Inc., New York, and simultaneously in
Canada by Random House of Canada Limited, Toronto. A portion of this book was
previously published in different form by Light Technology Publishing in 1994.

Grateful acknowledgment is made to the Lucis Trust for permission to reprint two charts,
"The Rays and Corresponding Professions" and "Ray Methods of Teaching Truth" from
Discipleship in the New Age by Alice Bailey. Reprinted with the permission of the Lucis
Trust, which holds copyright.

www.ballantinebooks.com

Library of Congress Cataloging-in-Publication Data
Stone, Joshua David, 1953–
Soul psychology : how to clear negative emotions and spiritualize your life /
Joshua David Stone. —Rev. ed.
p.   cm.
ISBN 978-0-345-42556-0 (TR : alk. paper)
1. Melchizedek Synthesis Light Academy—Doctrines.
2. Spiritual life Miscellanea.   I. Title.
BP605.M44S76   1999
299'.93—dc21   99-28724

Cover design by Jennifer Blanc
Cover photo by Freydoo Rassouli

Manufactured in the United States of America

First Ballantine Wellspring™ Edition: November 1999

Contents

✴

Tools for Spiritual Development   *vii*

PART I   THE FOUR GOLDEN KEYS   3

Chapter One   *What Is Soul Psychology?*   5
Chapter Two   *Personal Power: The First Golden Key to*
                  Psychological and Spiritual Health   20
Chapter Three   *Unconditional Self-Love: The Second*
                  Golden Key to Psychological and
                  Spiritual Health   34
Chapter Four   *Balancing the Three Minds and the Four*
                  Bodies: The Third Golden Key to
                  Psychological and Spiritual Health   47
Chapter Five   *Christ Consciousness and How to Achieve*
                  It: The Fourth Golden Key to
                  Psychological and Spiritual Health   59

PART II   HOW TO SPIRITUALIZE THE
                  NEGATIVE EGO   91

Chapter Six   *Tools for Healing the Emotions*   93
Chapter Seven   *Reprogramming the Subconscious Mind*   120
Chapter Eight   *The Human Aura and the Seven Bodies*   137
Chapter Nine   *The Twenty-Two Chakras*   147
Chapter Ten   *Pitfalls and Traps on the Path of Ascension*   159
Chapter Eleven   *The Laws of Manifestation*   166
Chapter Twelve   *The Laws of Karma*   179

PART III **ESOTERIC PSYCHOLOGY** 187

Chapter Thirteen *Psychoepistemology* 189
Chapter Fourteen *How to Clear the Negative Ego*
  Through the Science of the Rays 210
Chapter Fifteen *How to Clear the Negative Ego*
  Through the Science of the Archetypes 235
Chapter Sixteen *The Fifteen Major Tests of the Spiritual*
  Path 264
Chapter Seventeen *How to Clear Negative Psychic Energies* 276
Chapter Eighteen *Transcendence of Negative Ego and the*
  Living Bardo 299

Afterword 307
Appendix 311
Index 313

Tools for Spiritual Development

✴

SPIRITUAL AFFIRMATIONS

Disidentification	31
Personal Power and Becoming a Creative Cause	32
Emotional Invulnerability	32
Self-Love	42
Affirmations of Faith, Trust, and Patience	134

ACTIVITIES AND EXERCISES

Self-Love Visualization	44
Identity Visualization	46
The Red Ladder Visualization	52
The Golden Bubble Visualization	52
Six-Step Process for Spiritualizing Your Emotions	93
Yin Self-Control Method	96
Yin Acceptance Method	96
Yin Catharsis Method	97
Yin Indulgence Method	98
Yin Secondary Communication Method	98
Writing a Letter to Your Subconscious Mind	100
Dialoguing	101
Twenty-One-Day Psychological Foundation Logging Charts	105
Tools for Contacting Your Higher Self	117
Attracting Money Visualization	126
Self-Empowerment Trip	128
Variations on The Golden Bubble	129
Revitalizing the Subconscious Garden	132
Cosmic Healing Visualization	207

Dialoguing with Glamours   233
Voice Dialoguing with the Archetypes   239
Journal Dialoguing with the Archetypes   241
Beginning the Psychic Healing and Clearing Process   277
Requesting Dispensation from the Lords of Karma   292

Notice

✳

Much of the information in this book has been channeled through communication with the Ascended Masters. As with all types of information, it is subject to the lens of the individual who is receiving the information. Any application of the material set forth in the following pages is at the reader's discretion and is the reader's sole responsibility.

The spiritual healing techniques presented in this book are a source of important information, but if you suspect any medical problems, you must seek out a qualified health care professional and/or medical doctor.

Soul Psychology

How to Clear Negative Emotions
and Spiritualize Your Life

Part I

The Four Golden Keys

Chapter 1

✴

What Is Soul Psychology?

God equals man minus ego.
—SAI BABA

We are living in an extraordinary time in the history of the earth's evolution. Extraordinary advances have been made within this last millennium. In the last hundred years alone, we have witnessed startling breakthroughs in technology, medicine, and communications. We have landed on other planets, put a space station in orbit, grown test-tube babies, and cloned sheep. In the midst of these incredible achievements, mankind has never been more at odds with itself and so lacking in inner peace. Why is this?

To say that there is one answer would merely oversimplify complex issues. While there are many aspects to consider, there are two main patterns woven through this tapestry of answers. The first is humanity's obsession with material expansion and accelerated change at the expense of focusing on psychospiritual development. The second thread is failing to take into account the degree to which an individual's relationship to the psychological self affects his or her spiritual life. Simply put, if we are not right with ourselves, then every relationship in our lives, including our relation to God, will be compromised.

I have spent my life studying psychology or sharing my days with those who work in the field, including my parents, my stepmother, and my sister, who are all professionals in this area. This early and frequent exposure hasn't given me all the answers to life's problems; however, I do feel that my personal and professional background, including my many years of experience in working as a licensed marriage, family, and child counselor, and as a licensed minister and spiritual teacher, has given me some valuable insights. Most particularly, it has helped me to understand, and to experience firsthand, the limited means traditional forms of psychology have used to deal with these two crucial issues.

I have a great deal of respect for traditional psychology and for those well-intentioned individuals who practice it. And I feel fortunate that I underwent traditional psychological training. It provided me with the solid foundation on which I've based my explorations of alternative methods and models, which eventually led me to establish my practice based on the principles of soul psychology. As you can probably gather from the very words themselves, soul psychology takes us out of the realm of traditional psychology by dealing with elements of human existence that traditional psychology often ignores completely or makes only passing mention of.

While traditional forms of psychology are primarily concerned with helping individuals deal with crises and helping them make adjustments to their personality, soul psychology expands upon the work with the individual's personality to integrate the metaphysical aspects of human existence. Regardless of our spiritual or religious orientation, most of us would agree that *soul* is a convenient term to use for that part of human experience that is beyond body, mind, and emotion.

The purpose of this book is to build a bridge that spans the wonderful work being done in the field of personality-level psychology (traditional psychology) and the new tradition of soul-based psychology. What amazed me as I sat through lecture after lecture and read textbook after textbook in my traditional training was that few if any of the psychological theories I encountered even mentioned one of the most important aspects of human life — our relationship to God in whatever form we perceive him/her/it. I was doing my spiritual work at the time, and I simply couldn't understand why none of the most highly regarded psychological theorists dealt directly with our spiritual side. Perhaps their need to guard psychology's tenuous position as a rational science prevented them from doing so. The prevailing belief that being "correct" scientifically was more important than helping people become fully human troubled me as a student and well after.

When I went through my B.A., M.A., and Ph.D. programs, professors taught psychology by throwing many different psychological theories at us, without guiding us to an understanding of which ones were valid and which ones were not. That was because no one teaching the classes could tell us this with any certainty. Every professor had a favorite theory. Our job as students was to try to develop some understanding of all of them and, on our own, select the one we preferred. This became the foundation for how we practiced and how we lived. My problem was that I couldn't really accept any single theory by itself. They all contained what I would call "slivers of truth." Maybe if you put them all together you would have a half-truth. But each theorist asserted that he or she had discovered the whole truth.

That's not to say that these slivers of truth can't help some of the people some of the time. Nevertheless, if you were to construct a horizontal graph with numbers at the endpoints of 0 and 100 (with 0 representing the lowest level of consciousness and 100 being the highest level—the realm of the Ascended Masters), then traditional psychology might be able to help some people attain level 30. It could never take you any higher. Even if you visited a traditional psychologist five times a week for the next fifty years, you wouldn't be able to get past 30. Why? Because traditional psychology is 98 percent devoid of spirituality.

In my first book, *The Ascension Handbook*, I spoke of the three levels of self-actualization—the personality level, the soul level, and the monadic level. At traditional psychology's absolute best (and even this is debatable), it can help you to achieve personality level self-actualization. That is the 30 percent level of consciousness I credit it with. Some people would say that 30 percent consciousness is acceptable. Many others aspire to something higher. If you are reading this book, you probably belong to that second group, and you intuitively understand that traditional psychology cannot help you to gain the soul self that you are working toward.

Of the many theories that I studied in school, I can recall only three that acknowledged spiritual reality—the theories of Carl Jung, Abraham Maslow, and Roberto Assagioli. Most people, including many students of traditional psychology, have probably never heard of Roberto Assagioli. He was an Italian psychologist who developed the theory of psychosynthesis and was an early practitioner of what we would today call transpersonal psychology. Because this is a comparatively new field in this country, his work has had little effect on traditional psychological theory. Assagioli believed that in the aftermath of turbulent wars, humankind could no longer safely identify with the groups we once sought to help establish our identity—family, tribe, clan, class, or nation. As a result, people had to turn back to themselves as individuals.

Unlike Freud's psychoanalytic theory, which relied on analysis (literally, a breaking down into parts), psychosynthesis seeks to expand our awareness so that we can integrate all parts of our personality, including the spiritual components, into a more cohesive self. It is founded on the principle that life has purpose and meaning and we are a part of this ordered universe.

Abraham Maslow, who is probably most well known for elaborating on the concept of humans' hierarchy of needs, mentions the value of a spiritual aspect of life, but he wrote very little directly about the subject. When one interviewer asked him if he believed in God, Maslow replied that he didn't need to believe; he knew. What most interests me about his work was his belief that the body, and to an extent the psyche, operates under the principle of homeostasis, or balance. Finally, it was Maslow who coined the term *self-actualization*. He stated that this was mankind's highest-order need, and that unless our other needs were fulfilled first, we could never attain self-actualization. His theory falls short, however, because it deals only with personality-level self-actualization.

Carl Jung was one of the few famous traditional psychologists to break away from the pack and integrate spirituality into his theories. He was truly a great catalyst in depth psychology and the field known as adult development theory. He recognized the ideal of the self, and broke away from Freud's fixation on sexuality. He was a master interpreter of dreams and believed in reincarnation, although he was reluctant to let this belief be known. Among his many contributions are the concepts of introversion and extroversion, synchronicity, archetype, and collective unconscious. He taught us that by confronting honestly the everyday personal conflicts we all encounter, we also face the challenges presented by the most fundamental spiritual problems of universal concern. I have great respect for Jung's work and recommend that you read it. Unfortunately, although Jung was a great catalyst to the field, even his work was quite limited when compared to the fuller understanding of Soul Psychology that is developing today.

Besides traditional psychology's lack of a spiritual component, traditional psychology and soul psychology differ in several other important ways. One of the basic beliefs underlying soul psychology is that we can choose between two ways of thinking in the world. We can think from the negative ego mind—self-centered and dualistic, separated from the Divine, and based on fear—or we can think from the spiritual mind. Traditional psychology tries to heal us from *within* the negative ego's web. In fact, we cannot truly heal ourselves until we fully transcend the negative ego.

It is essential to understand that the negative ego is the one real problem that all people on earth make themselves suffer from. The negative ego does not interpret experiences in our lives as lessons, challenges, or gifts. Rather, it curses or gets angry when its attachments/expectations are not met. The negative ego is the root of all negative emotions, all negative thoughts, all negative behaviors, all relationship problems, and poverty consciousness, (lack of money and real success). In essence, it is the negative ego that is blocking you from God-realization. As one of the great spiritual teachers of India, Sai Baba, says, "God is hidden by the mountain range of ego."

Anytime we get out of balance, the negative ego is the cause. We have to decide which voice we are going to listen to. Will we listen to the voice of fear and separation or the voice of perfect love and union? Will we listen to the voice of self-centeredness or that of selfless love? Every moment of our lives we are choosing either God or the negative ego. I offer you a challenge. I ask you to take a vow to choose only God from this day forward. Don't worry about making mistakes. Perfection doesn't mean not ever making a mistake; it means not ever making a *conscious* mistake. Ideally, we learn from each mistake and make a conscious decision to try to avoid repeating it. We do not fall out of favor with God, nor do we need to punish ourselves—or, worse yet, others—because of our shortcomings. We simply have to decide to choose rightly, love unconditionally, and move on.

Whether or not to listen to the voice of the negative ego is not the only choice we make, nor is the role of the negative ego the only difference between soul psychology and traditional psychology. Traditional psychology also does not address the concept that our thoughts create our reality. This is the second main thesis that underlies soul psychology. Our thoughts create our emotions, our behaviors, and what we magnetize into our lives. If we allow the negative ego to dominate us, then we will create a negative reality for ourselves, we

will attract negative elements into our lives, and all these negative influences will only make us feel and believe and behave more and
more negatively. That is what people mean when they talk about a vicious circle.

Traditional psychology does not account for the fact that our
thoughts create our reality, our emotions, and our behavior. Traditional psychology believes that forces outside ourselves (environment,
family, biochemistry) create our reality for us. In their view, negative
emotions are unavoidable and a normal part of living. As a result, traditional psychology teaches victim consciousness.

Again, I want to emphasize that I am not saying that traditional psychology has no value. It does have some initial value. If it can lead a
person to personality-level self-actualization, that is wonderful. The
problem is that very few forms of traditional psychology do lead to this
point, and many people stay stuck in traditional psychology for years
upon years, never really progressing beyond what they achieved in
their first year's work. They can't, because it is not within the theory
they are working with or within the consciousness of the therapist to
take them any farther.

The most fundamental difference between soul psychology and traditional forms of psychology is how they differ in their belief about the
application of the concept of balance in our lives. Even those of you
who have not investigated any of the traditional forms of psychological
therapy are familiar with this concept. We hear about it all the time:
eat balanced meals; balance work and recreation; balance mind, body,
and spirit. All of these are very well-intentioned bits of advice. But as
with many principles that work, we sometimes apply this principle of
balance too liberally.

Because many people either are reluctant to seek therapy or have
had unsatisfactory experiences with traditional psychology, they create
their own theories and coping strategies. They hope to take the best of
what seems to work from many different systems and combine them
into what they hope will be an effective tool. This is what I call the
False Sense of Balance Theory. Practitioners of this therapeutic model
believe that psychological health means balancing the light and dark
aspects within ourselves.

Many of you are probably nodding and saying, "That sounds all
right. I think we are supposed to do that." To a certain extent, you are
right. Yes, you are here to balance the feminine and masculine parts of

yourself. And you are here to balance the heavenly and earthly aspects of yourself. You are also here to balance all your chakras and your four bodies and your three minds, as well as many other components of your self that I will discuss later in this book.

There is only one thing that you are not here to balance, however. This is the key point that every few people in this world understand. You are here to get rid of and die to the negative ego. That is why Sai Baba, in defining God, says, "God equals man minus ego." This is the essence of Sai Baba's teachings and the fundamental principle of *A Course in Miracles*, Buddha's teaching, and in truth all the teachings of all the Self-Realized Masters.

Many people who are caught in the False Sense of Balance Theory think that they have to balance every aspect of the self. They fear that if they disown some negative portion of self, then it will come back and bite them on some level. That is not true. Remember, it is your thoughts that create your reality.

We are not here to balance fear and love. Does not the Bible say, "Perfect love casts out fear"?

We are not here to balance separation and oneness. We are here to live in the oneness.

The negative ego creates negative qualities such as hatred, revenge, jealousy, lack of self-worth, false pride, depression, low self-esteem, inferiority complex, and all the other ills that plague us.

We are not here to balance hatred and love. We are not here to balance our inferiority complex with high self-esteem. We are not here to balance lack of self-worth with self-worth. God created us in his image and likeness, so we are filled with worth. Our true identity is the monad, the Eternal Self, the Mighty I Am Presence. As the Bible says, "Ye are gods and know it not."

Does God experience hatred, revenge, jealousy, lack of self-worth, false pride, and depression? Of course not. If God created us in His image and likeness, then where do these qualities come from? They come from misthinking on humanity's part. They come from thinking with your separated, fear-based mind, instead of your united-in-oneness, love-based Christ mind. The Bible says, "Let this mind be in you that was in Christ Jesus."

To realize your Christ consciousness, you have to get rid of your negative ego consciousness. When you achieve this state of thinking and perception of reality, you are loving, joyous, happy, even-minded, and peaceful all the time. Did not Buddha say, "All suffering comes from your attachments"? God does not suffer, so why should we? We are here to become the light, to become the love, to realize God.

As Sai Baba says, you will not achieve God realization unless you die to your negative ego, which is fear, separation, materialism, and selfishness. If you die to this lower-self type of thinking, then you will be reborn to your higher-self way of thinking and you will realize God. This is the main curriculum of the spiritual path, regardless of which path or teacher you choose to follow. Contrary to what other people will tell you, you do not need negative emotions. They are created by your mind. They do not come from outside of yourself or from your instincts. They come from your interpretation, perception, and beliefs about reality.

Your life is like a movie projected on a screen. You are the writer and director of it. You have a choice about how each and every frame of this movie will turn out, and you have a choice about how to view it. The Buddha said in the four noble truths that all suffering comes from "wrong points of view." Think with your God mind, which is light. That is why it is called en*light*enment.

We are not here to balance happiness and suffering. We are here to live in happiness and the light all the time. This is the mastery over what the Ascended Master Djwhal Khul has called "the dweller on the threshold." The dweller on the threshold embodies glamour, maya, illusion, and negative ego. The dweller on the threshold will forever remain an outsider, existing in the weak light that falls through the doorway, but never able or willing to leave behind the negative ego and stand in the full brightness of right living.

Much of humanity still longs for inner peace, happiness, and success because they have not been instructed on how to become masters of their subconscious minds, achieve self-love, properly guide their child consciousness, and transcend the negative ego. Nor do they understand how to integrate the conscious, subconscious, and superconscious minds, balance their four bodies (spiritual, mental, emotional, and physical), transcend lower-self desires, and fail to live as a cause and not as an effect. In short, they do not know how their particular piece fits into the Divine Plan.

Humanity has often fallen short of this mark because what we most need to learn is not taught in schools, at home, or in our churches and synagogues. Most counselors, psychologists, psychiatrists, and social workers don't yet fully understand the basic principles of soul psychology. Most of them are doing great work and should be commended; however, they have not moved into the realm of soul psychology. Because of this, many of their clients remain stuck in the negative ego, are still run by the emotional body, succumb to lower-self desire, and are filled with negative emotions. Worse, they are taught that they cannot transcend this state but must adjust to it. It is simply not true that you cannot transcend the negative ego. This book will show you how.

Unfortunately, much of what can be said about traditional psychology also applies to many spiritual movements. In this case, however, there is an overidentification with the spiritual body at the expense of the psychological self. Doing this is like building an enormous structure on top of a fragile foundation: It is doomed to collapse eventually. We see evidence of this faulty construction both in spiritual movements and in traditional religions, in spiritual leaders and in their seemingly most devout initiates. Each time a spiritual or religious leader falls victim to the failure to master the negative ego, it is as though another crack in the foundation is revealed. This book has been written as a means to shore up this foundation so that our real work can begin. We need to clean up our act, purify our mental and emotional bodies, and learn to integrate at the heart level.

If you are currently evaluating your value systems and belief systems, this book is for you.

If you are wondering why your personal relationships sometimes feel like they're being conducted more on a field of battle than on a field of unconditional love in a Christed state, then this book is for you.

If your emotional and mental bodies have you swinging like a pendulum instead of resting on a rock-steady platform of inner peace and contentment, then this book is for you.

If you're eager to become a fully integrated human ready to don the mantle of spiritual leadership and world service, then this book is for you.

This book is for all those who wish to properly integrate and synthesize the spiritual, psychological, and physical aspects of self into a comprehensive, unified whole, as God would have you.

What you must realize is that you can work out in a gym every day, eat healthfully, and run three times a week, but until you are the master of your subconscious mind, emotional body, and negative ego, you are still at risk. You cannot truly be healthy by concentrating on just one level, whether it's the physical, the spiritual, or the psychological. You must address and work with each on a daily basis. Synthesis and integration are the keys. This book will help you identify and overcome the many traps and pitfalls that can hinder you along the way. Having counseled individuals for over twenty years, I have developed great insight into the dynamics of the processes that will lead you to this integrated state of being.

As many of you know, the subconscious mind exerts control over much of our reality. One purpose of this book is to help us open our soul's eyes so that we can see the unconscious aspects of self that lead to inappropriate actions and put us on the merry-go-round of unsatisfactorily patterned and programmed behavior. Also, this book will help us to heal the split between our conscious and unconscious minds. Even among the most advanced lightworkers on the planet, this rift still prevails. Very few of us have mastery over the subconscious mind.

To regain control over our nonreasoning subconscious, we must retain our personal power and resist using it in service of the negative ego. This is one of the most important processes to employ while on our spiritual path. We can never truly realize God until the conscious mind masters the subconscious mind. Part I of this book will provide you with guidance, techniques, and exercises for addressing this schism between the conscious and unconscious minds. Please remember that whenever you allow your subconscious mind to control you, you have handed over the reins to the negative ego.

For example, a spiritual teacher who believes that he is totally clear of the negative ego but performs his work because of the acclaim he can receive and not the service he can do for others is under the control of the negative ego. A mother who wants to treat her child with respect and unconditional love but resorts to ranting and raving has surrendered herself to the negative ego. Someone who joins a gym but doesn't work out, starts a diet but eats the wrong foods, or claims to forgive a wrong done to him but still holds a grudge is within the negative ego's grasp. These splits among the subconscious, conscious, and superconscious minds afflict many people, from those oblivious to the spiritual path to the most advanced and sincere lightworkers. In fact, the more advanced we become, the more our unconscious surfaces and the more our negative ego needs to be purified.

Where did the negative ego come from? In the beginning, prior to and just after creation, there was no negative ego mind. God didn't create the negative ego; humanity did. It developed as a result of God's sons and daughters coming into matter, existing in human bodies, and then overidentifying with these physical bodies. In that moment, when the sons and daughters of God thought they were physical bodies rather than children of God who merely temporarily inhabited physical bodies, the negative ego developed.

The Bible relates this as the story of Adam and Eve. The pair ate the forbidden fruit, having been lured by the serpent, which symbolically represents the negative ego mind or lower self. These two competing philosophies (listening to God or listening to the serpent/negative ego) could be called the philosophies of the lower self and the higher self. If you listen to the lower self, you live a "low life existence," meaning that you are primarily concerned with the life and material needs of the physical body. If you listen to the philosophy of the higher self, Holy Spirit, soul, monad, Mighty I Am Presence, or Christ mind, you live a "high life existence" because you are striving to integrate the three minds and the four subtle bodies. To realize God, you must remove your attention from the lower-self interpretations and perceptions of life, and instead keep interpreting and perceiving life from the higher self.

Since our thoughts create our reality, which philosophy we choose will determine what we see. In truth, we see not with our eyes, but with our minds. This is why Sai Baba has said, "Your mind creates bondage, or your mind creates liberation." We will have negative emotions if we think with our negative ego mind. We will have positive emotions if we think with our spiritual mind. Our thoughts create our feelings, emotions, behavior, and physical health or lack of health. Psychological health is nothing more than maintaining a good mental diet. As the Master Jesus revealed through Helen Schulman in *A Course in Miracles*, the key is not to allow any thought that is not of God to enter our minds. We must be vigilant for God and His Kingdom at all times and never go on automatic pilot.

Whenever a negative ego thought tries to enter your mind, just deny it entrance and push it out. Switch your mind like a channel changer to a positive and/or more spiritual thought. This is the concept of denial and affirmation. You use this tactic literally hundreds of times a day. You are the executive director of your personality and thus you choose what to think. God and the Ascended Masters will not do this for you no matter how often you ask. This is your job. By denying the negative thoughts and keeping your mind steadily in the light at all times, the negative thoughts will die from lack of energy, and a new positive habit will be formed in your subconscious mind, making it easier to be positive.

Developing this positive habit is difficult only in the beginning, although we must remain vigilant regardless of our level of development. The essence of negative ego is fear, separation, and self-centeredness. As strange as it may seem, the truth is that the negative ego doesn't really exist. As Jesus revealed in A Course in Miracles, "The Fall never really happened, we just think it did." In other words, we have all always been one with God and have always been the Christ, or sons and daughters of God. But if we give in to negative ego thinking in our own minds, we will believe in the fall from grace, and live in that negative state of consciousness even though it is not true that we have fallen.

This is much like living in a negative hypnosis, or like dreaming. When we dream at night, we really believe and feel that the dream is real. When we wake up in the morning from a nightmare, we are relieved and say to ourselves, "I am so glad that was just a dream." This is what I am trying to say to you now about your normal waking life. You have been dreaming with your eyes open, living in a dream of the negative ego's interpretation of life, rather than interpreting life from your Christ mind.

It is much like the glass that is either half empty or half full. This simple analogy applies to every moment of life. There is a way of interpreting life that will bring you inner peace, calmness, joy, happiness, unconditional love, even-mindedness, and equanimity all the time regardless of what is going on outside of the self. There is another way of interpreting life that will make you angry, impatient, moody, unstable, and depressed. Which of the two is your reality has absolutely nothing to do with what is going on outside yourself. It has everything to do with how you are interpreting life.

To illustrate this, let's discuss how to flow with the universe instead of fighting it. This is called the Blessing Method. The Holy Spirit and the Masters would have us bless and give thanks for everything that happens in our lives. This is like saying, as in the Bible, "Not my will but thine" and offering thanks for the lesson.

The negative ego cannot bless and give thanks because it does not interpret things as lessons, challenges, or gifts. It curses and gets angry when its attachments and/or expectations are not met. The Christ mind, having only preferences and not attachments, is happy either way; its inner peace is a state of mind rather than an attachment to something outside of self. Bless everything that comes into your life and welcome adversity, as Sai Baba has said, for everything that comes into your area of influence happens for a reason and is God teaching you something you need to learn.

Do you see my point now? Lightworkers have been focusing on the spiritual level and making great progress, but if this core psychological level is not mastered, there is a threat of a kind of cancer. If we do not attend to the disease of our psychological self, then eventually our symptoms won't allow us to do our spiritual work. This kind of cancer can be healed very quickly through the science of "attitudinal healing."

Attitudinal healing involves the corollary lessons that are also required that emanate from this initial lesson of denying the negative ego and choosing the Christ consciousness. The main corollary lessons are learning to balance the four bodies (physical, emotional, mental, and spiritual), learning to integrate the three minds (conscious, subconscious, and superconscious), learning to properly parent our child consciousness, developing self-love and self-worth, learning to own your personal power at all times, learning to reprogram the subconscious mind, proper control of sexual energy, psychic self-defense, right human relationships, proper care of the physical vehicle, and mastery of the desire body.

Imbalances in any of these areas are a result of the negative ego programming still present in us. A friend provided me with a very good metaphor for balancing the four bodies. She suggested that we look at the four-body system as four tubes filled with water and stacked on top of one another. The water actually is energy, but it is easier to understand how that energy works if you see it as water. Many lightworkers are top-heavy. They filter a great deal of their water into the spiritual tube, which leaves the mental, emotional, and physical tubes depleted. This creates imbalances and overflows and a whole host of problems.

The same potential for imbalance can be seen in the chakra system. When certain chakras are overemphasized, causing overactivity in some and underactivity in others, this affects the glandular system and causes another manifestation of lessons, which I will explore in great detail later in this book. The idea here is to keep the amount of water flowing freely in all four tubes. Other lightworkers may be more mental, others too emotional, some even too fixated on the physical body.

All the attitudinal healing lessons must be mastered to truly achieve soul-level self-realization. Although one can achieve the seven levels of initiation prior to fully addressing the psychological level, you cannot fully actualize ascension until you integrate the three minds and the four bodies.

One final word that describes the negative ego is *duality*. To transcend the negative ego in its fullest extent, one must learn to transcend the world of duality. Another reason this is important is that as we ascend in consciousness and move through the seven levels of initiation, we begin clearing not only individual karma but also the mass planetary karma.

As we begin to clear karma from all our soul extensions and from our oversoul, our higher self, we continue to evolve until we can affect the group soul level, the group monadic level, and eventually clearing on universal levels. If we haven't completed this work in our selves, how can we possibly consider doing it on these more expansive levels? In this most accelerated period in the earth's history, we are now receiving a fuller understanding of what the ascension process is really about.

HOW DO YOU KNOW WHEN YOU ARE OUT OF BALANCE AND IN BALANCE?

On the physical level, being out of balance may manifest as fatigue or improper diet. On the emotional level, it may show up as mood swings or negative emotions. On the mental level, it may come out as negative thinking. On the spiritual level, it may manifest as meditating too much or too little. A balanced person is a calm person, one who has inner peace. A balanced person has detachment but is also very responsive to self, other people, and life. Balancing the four bodies should not lead you to a point of stillness. Being in balance is more like being on a gentle teeter-totter or making subtle adjustments while driving a car. When we are balanced, we can feel ourselves going out of that subtle appropriate range and will then be vigilant and make the appropriate correction, within our individual body.

In a sense, we live within a group consciousness within our own being. We must strike a balance between our four bodies, three minds, child consciousness, parent consciousness, seven major chakras, soul, monad, and personality. Each part, except for the negative ego, has a voice and a place in the ideal state, which allows for the full merger with the soul and monad. All these other parts form a vast communication system within us which we must stay attuned to, and honor. When we don't, imbalance occurs and, like dominoes falling, can lead to a whole host of other problems.

We must be right with ourselves before we can be right with God and right with other people. As the conscious mind, each of us must be like an orchestra leader bringing all of the elements of the group consciousness together in balance every day to create a beautiful symphony, which is called God-realization. It is a good idea to do a quick inventory of all these parts to make sure everything is in harmony. All these elements really want to be part of the team. Sometimes they can get a little greedy, so it is the job of the orchestra leader, conscious mind, or parent consciousness to demonstrate tough love or to be a strong, loving commander in chief, so to speak, to let all these parts know who is in charge.

Even though the conscious mind is in charge, it and the whole team are totally subservient to the dictates of the soul and the Mighty I Am Presence. So I ask you now, my brothers and sisters, are you willing in this moment to make a commitment to maintaining this subtle synergistic balance in service of the soul and monad for the purpose of demonstrating God-realization on earth? This is the challenge. This is the Mantle of the Christ, which God wishes us all to put on in this moment as a tribute of our love and devotion to Him on earth. Are you willing to dedicate your life to such a noble purpose? This is the path of all religions, all schools of mystery, and all spiritual traditions. God is awaiting your answer!

Before such things as levitation, teleportation, and materialization can even be approached, this other aspect must be 100 percent committed to and demonstrated in your daily life. This has been called in some circles "practicing the Presence of God" in our daily life. Can there be a more noble purpose for us all? Is there anything else in the infinite universe we should be focusing our energies upon? As the Master Jesus said, "Be ye faithful unto death, and I will give thee a crown of life."

Chapter 2

*

Personal Power: The First Golden Key to Psychological and Spiritual Health

This one thing I do, forgetting those things which are behind, and reaching forth unto those things which are before, I press toward the mark.
—COLOSSIANS 3:13–14

The single most effective means to achieving psychological and spiritual health is learning to own your personal power. By understanding how the conscious and subconscious minds work, you're taking the first steps toward personal power.

The conscious mind allows us to reason, whereas the subconscious mind operates at a more basic, instinctive level. The superconscious mind is the all-knowing mind. A metaphor that illustrates how these first two work is to think of the conscious mind as the captain of the ship. If the conscious mind is the captain, then the subconscious mind is the shipmate belowdecks who follows whatever orders the captain gives.

Another way to describe this relationship is to think of the conscious mind as a gardener. The gardener plants the seeds (thoughts), and the soil (the subconscious mind) grows whatever kind of seed is planted, be it a weed or a beautiful flower. The subconscious mind will store information and follow orders whether the orders are rational or irrational. The subconscious mind doesn't care because it has absolutely no reasoning ability.

The subconscious mind is an amazing paradox. It has no powers of reason on its own, yet it has an incredible number of abilities and in-

The Three Minds

The
Superconscious
Mind

or

Higher Self

The
Conscious
Mind

or

Middle Self

The
Subconscious
Mind

or

Lower Self

The Spiritual Mind
1. Can be contacted through:
    a. Meditation
    b. Dreams
    c. Journaling
    d. Intuition
2. Can help us only if we ask for assistance. Does not interfere with our free choice on a conscious level.

The Reasoning Mind
1. Executive Director
2. President of the personality
3. Captain of the ship
4. Computer programmer
5. Gardener
6. Decision-maker
    a. Willpower, discipline, discernment, discrimination, concentration, reasoning.

The Non-Reasoning Mind
1. Works on impressions, stimulus/response.
2. Is a memory bank and file of thoughts, feelings, memories, imagination, habit patterns, impulses, desires, instincts.
3. Operates physical body.
4. Creates most dreams.
5. Creates vital force.
6. Works twenty-four hours a day.
7. Functions according to the law of attraction.
8. Examines, classifies, stores information.
9. In metaphorical terms is the computer, garden, engine room.
10. Plays a key role in the prayer process.
11. Controls the inner senses (visualization).
12. Radiates senses.
13. Creates threads of energy that contact both objects and other people.
    a. Can leave body and follow those threads (as in the use of pendulums, psychometry, psychokinesis).
    b. Can send vital force and thought forms along these threads (as in telepathy and prayer).

telligence factors. The best illustration for understanding this is the computer analogy. A computer is an astonishing piece of equipment, capable of performing millions of computations per second, yet it doesn't care whether it's programmed to solve the problem of world hunger or to create a nuclear war. It has the capability to do either job efficiently, but it doesn't have the reasoning power not to want to create nuclear war. It is this difference between intelligence and reason that we are primarily concerned with.

The subconscious does whatever it is programmed to do, no matter what. For example, the subconscious mind completely operates the physical body. Hypnosis offers some insight into how this works, for example, when posthypnotic suggestions are being used to control a person's physiological craving for nicotine. Unfortunately, our subconscious mind is as happy to destroy the body as it is to create perfect health. The subconscious mind has the intelligence to create perfect health or create cancer. It will create whatever it has been programmed to do.

Certainly no one consciously programs himself or herself to develop a cancer, but many people unconsciously program cancer into their bodies through self-hatred, victim consciousness, revenge, giving up, and so on. The key, then, is to constantly program your subconscious mind for perfect, radiant health.

INTELLIGENCE FACTOR OF THE SUBCONSCIOUS MIND

Another basic function of the subconscious mind is to store information. It is the warehouse and memory bank of all our thoughts, feelings, emotions, imaginings, habit patterns, impulses, and desires. From our infancy we have been programmed by our parents, grandparents, peers, teachers, ministers, and extended family, not to mention television. All those exchanges of information have been stored in our subconscious.

Little children are all in a sense victims. By this I mean that children's reasoning minds have not developed enough to be able to discriminate and protect themselves from negative programming. As small children, we were totally open. As a result, our subconscious minds are filled with mental poisons, faulty thinking, and faulty beliefs. Just as the body can be filled with physical toxins from poor eating, the subconscious can be filled with mental toxins from improper programming and education.

The subconscious mind also creates our dreams every night. There are occasions when the superconsciousness creates dreams. However, most dreams originate in the subconscious mind. A dream is basically a mirror of the way we think, feel, and act during our conscious daily life. A dream is like a newspaper we receive every night, depicting the organization and dynamics of our internal energies.

Dreams are in the universal language of symbols. To understand our dreams, we must first accept that every part of every dream is, in reality, a part of us. By examining the relationship among the symbols, we can gain insight into and understanding of the thought patterns that are manifesting themselves in our lives through our actions. A dream is an automatic process that the subconscious mind brings to us as feedback. This feedback is essential because very often we are all manifesting patterns in our lives that we are not consciously aware of.

The subconscious mind can also be termed the habit mind. It stores all of our habits, both positive and negative. A lot of people think habits are bad. This is not true. We want to get rid of only bad habits. Ideally we want to create good habits.

A good example of this is learning to drive a stick-shift car. When we first learn how, it takes a lot of conscious effort and willpower. After we learn how, it requires little conscious thought. If we didn't have a subconscious mind to store our developed abilities, every activity would always take great focus and concentration. The subconscious mind's ability to store habits allows us to grow continually and develop new abilities without worrying about old ones. You can learn something in a day, but there is a basic psychological or metaphysical law that states that it takes twenty-one days to cement a new habit into the subconscious mind.

The subconscious mind is where the Law of Magnetism and Attraction operates as well. The subconscious mind continually attracts and repels things according to what has been programmed into it. A Master is someone who uses this law to his own conscious benefit. Let's take the example of money and prosperity. If you have the subconscious belief that you will never have money, you won't. If, on the other hand, you think you will, the subconscious mind will attract those opportunities and possibilities to you. Whatever you want in life, you have to affirm or visualize this into the subconscious mind, and the subconscious mind will attract it to you.

Carl Jung spoke of this when he talked about the collective unconscious. Your subconscious mind is interconnected to all other subconscious minds. You might say that all the sons and daughters of God have one great collective subconscious mind. You can learn to tap into the power of that collective.

The subconscious mind has the ability to sense radiations of energy. We all automatically use this ability in our daily lives. The practical application of this ability can be specifically used in areas such as water dowsing, also called water witching. The subconscious can sense the radiation of energy of any substance, not just water, and so it can be programmed to search for any physical substance.

The subconscious mind is also the seat of our psychic abilities. The subconscious has five inner senses that are the subtler counterparts of our five external senses: inner sight (clairvoyance), inner hearing (clairaudience), inner smell, inner taste, and inner touch.

Have you ever noticed that when you dream you have your five senses available to you? How can this be if you are sleeping? This is because you are utilizing your five inner senses of the subconscious mind. All people have psychic abilities and can develop them further. It is just a matter of practice and proper training, as with any external ability.

HOW THE CONSCIOUS MIND WORKS

The key function of the conscious mind is to be the programmer, protector, and master of the subconscious mind. The subconscious mind is meant to be the servant or servomechanism of the conscious mind. Most people, not understanding how these psychological laws operate, let their subconscious mind run them. When this happens, we become victims.

The subconscious mind was never meant to direct our life. It will run us into oblivion if we let it, not because it is bad, but because it has no reasoning. For example, your car has a number of computer systems that help manage specific systems such as air-fuel mixture, anti-lock brakes, and so on. Just because these computer chips can perform these functions, that doesn't mean they can drive your car. In and of itself the subconscious mind is divine; however, why would anyone let a nonreasoning mind run his or her life? Strangely enough, this is what most people do.

You might also imagine the conscious mind as an inner gate or inner bubble that protects us from our own subconscious mind. When a thought or feeling or impulse arises, it is the conscious mind's task to use its powers of reasoning, discernment, and discrimination to check that thought at the gate. If the thought or impulse is positive and spiritual, we let it into our mind. If it is negative, we push it out.

Psychological health is the process of letting positive, spiritually balanced thoughts into our minds. Psychological health is like physical health. If we want to be physically healthy, we put good, healthful food into our bodies. If we want to be psychologically healthy, we put good, healthful thoughts into our minds.

By pushing the negative thoughts out of our minds, we are refusing them energy. This is much like not watering a plant. The plant eventually withers and dies from lack of water (attention and focus). Once we have pushed the negative thought out, the second step is to affirm the opposite positive thought or spiritual thought. This is called positive thinking through positive affirmation.

By continually disregarding the negative thought and affirming the positive thought, we can form a new habit in the subconscious mind within twenty-one days. The old habit dies because we are not giving it energy, and the new habit takes its place because we are continually affirming and thinking positively.

Remember that the subconscious is filled with all sorts of old tapes that our parents and other people programmed into us when we were young. If the conscious mind isn't making choices, then all this old programming from early childhood is controlling our present life.

DEVELOPING AN OUTER BUBBLE OR
SHIELD OF PROTECTION

Just as it is essential to develop an *inner bubble* to protect us from our own subconscious minds, it is also essential to develop an outer bubble or shield to protect ourselves from other people's negative energy. The ideal is for us to be the programmer of the subconscious mind. In a sense, the outer bubble acts like virus protection software on a home computer. It screens out any potentially dangerous outside codes.

Always remember that if we don't take responsibility for our own programming and protection, then the subconscious mind or other people will run our lives. The ideal is to be the cause, creator, and master of our own lives. If these psychological laws aren't clearly understood, then other people will be our programmers.

Let's take the example of someone criticizing or judging you. The ideal is to have an imaginary bubble or shield around you so that when criticism comes toward you, it hits the bubble or shield and bounces or slides off, like water off a duck's back. It must be understood that this bubble is *semipermeable*. In other words, it allows in positive energy but keeps out negative energy. You make a conscious choice or discrimination as to whether to let others' energy into your subconscious mind or not.

If you don't have this bubble of protection available to you at all times, then you can be victimized by another person's comments, statements, or energy. There is a time to be open and a time to be closed. It is necessary to close down and protect yourself if other people are being negative. If someone threw a real spear at you, I am sure you would physically try to get out of the way if you could.

The same thing is true when other people are directing negative energy toward you like a psychological spear. You will be wounded if you let it in. You wouldn't let a person shove physical poison down your physical mouth. So don't let people shove mental poison into your mind. You don't want the subconscious mind to run your life, and you don't want other people to run your life, either.

Another way of saying this is that you want to respond instead of react. A response is a product of the conscious mind, when you choose how to deal with the incoming energy. A reaction is a product of the subconscious mind. If someone judges or attacks you and you let the incoming energy go right into your subconscious mind, solar plexus, or emotional body, you will either be hurt, withdraw and cry, or lash back. You are letting another person be the cause of your emotions.

Another way to think about this is that if your inner and outer bubbles are not functioning properly, you are letting yourself be hypnotized. I am licensed as a hypnotist as well as a counselor. However, most of my work as a counselor is really not about hypnotizing people but about dehypnotizing them. Victims are in a sort of hypnotic state, letting another person program their emotions in a waking state. Many people live their lives this way, and I am trying to get them out of it.

We are hypersuggestible when we don't make a choice about how to respond. In reality, we all are invulnerable psychologically. This is a very profound statement. To be invulnerable means that we can't get emotionally hurt unless we choose to be.

MY FAVORITE METAPHOR

My favorite image likens psychological health to physical health. If a person we know catches a cold or the flu, we certainly don't want to get it. We do everything in our power not to get it. We stay away from that person. We take extra vitamin C. We tell ourselves we are not going to get sick. We eat well and try to get enough sleep. In other words, we build up our resistance. If we keep our resistance up, we don't get sick.

Doctors and nurses don't get all their patients' sicknesses. Why is that? The reason is that there is no such thing as a contagious disease. There are only people with low resistance.

This analogy is exactly the same on the psychological level. There is no such thing as a contagious psychological disease. There are only people with low resistance. How do we keep up our psychological resistance so that we don't catch the infectious diseases of anger, depression, jealousy, hatred, and so on? We keep our psychological resistance up by maintaining a *positive mental attitude*.

Developing and maintaining the protective bubble is one basic way to foster a positive attitude. Other key techniques are maintaining our personal power, unconditional self-love and self-worth, and faith and trust in God.

These are a few of the main techniques. In following chapters I will explore some of the others. The main point is that we are here in this world to set a better example. We are here to bring other people up, not to let ourselves be sucked down. So in essence the earth is like a hospital that is run by the patients. There are very few healers or doctors. Our life purpose is to be a healer or doctor.

When we allow other people to victimize us, we have become patients again, and now we need healing. This is okay if it happens.

The lesson is to get back to our centered selves and be the doctors and healers again as soon as we can.

THE DEVELOPMENT OF PERSONAL POWER: THE FIRST GOLDEN KEY

Of all the attitudes and qualities we need to develop in our healthy personality, none is more important than personal power or the development of will. I cannot emphasize this point enough. Everything I have spoken of so far in this book will not work without personal power. Personal power is the engine that drives this theory. Personal power, or willpower, is the first golden key.

What is personal power? Personal power or will is the guiding force of the healthy personality. Personal power is first an attitude. We can choose to hold an attitude of weakness or of strength as we begin each day. Our power is the energy that we use to enforce our decisions.

For example, let's say you plan to exercise at three o'clock. When three o'clock comes, it is a good bet that you will need your power to make yourself do what you have committed yourself to do. You also need your power to control your subconscious mind. Your subconscious mind will push you around unless you own your own power, so personal power is the enforcing agent of the conscious mind. It is the energy that the mind musters to command and direct that personality. Personal power is expressed externally as assertiveness.

Personal power is also very much tied in with decisiveness. Decisiveness is intrinsic in the attitude "fish or cut bait." If you are not decisive, then the subconscious mind or other people will make your decisions for you. Remember, the subconscious mind has no reasoning power, and other people's decisions are not always in your best interest. Consequently, if you are not decisive and assertive, you let others overpower you.

How can you be the master of yourself and your life if you do not have personal power? If you don't own your power, then you end up giving it to the subconscious or to other people. We know that God has power. The fact is that you are a cocreator, so you have power, too. God helps those who help themselves. You can't help yourself if you don't own your power.

There is and has always been total personal power available to you.

Personal power is nothing more than channeling the energy in your physical body and subconscious mind to control your life. Part of owning your power is being a spiritual warrior in your life. Never giving up and having the will to live is really possessing the will to fight.

Yoga teaches that life is not only a school but also a battlefield. You are trying to get to the top of a mountain. Progress many times entails taking three steps forward and slipping back two, again and again, until you reach the top. This is the nature of life for everyone on the spiritual path. The most important thing is not to quit.

Paramahansa Yogananda, the great Indian sage, said, "A saint is a sinner who never gave up." Part of owning your power is to keep plugging away. It is also having faith in God's power as well as your own personal power. When all of your outer security is stripped away, you always know that you have your power and God's power available to you all the time. This is true safety and security.

Your power fuels your risk taking. If you don't own your power, you are going to have a hard time keeping your bubble of protection inflated. Your power is what allows you to "fake it until you make it." When you own your personal power, you feel more centered.

When you use your power over a long period of time, you develop what is called discipline. Owning your power allows the conscious reasoning mind to stay in control and not to be overwhelmed by subconscious or environmental forces. When you don't own your power, you get depressed. Anyone who is depressed is not owning his power.

There are two opposing forces in life: good and evil, light and darkness, positive and negative, illusion and truth, egotistical thinking and spiritual thinking. Your power is your weapon with which to fight the negative and align yourself with the positive. As Egar Cayce, the great "sleeping prophet," said, "There is no force in the universe more powerful than your will or power."

The conscious reasoning mind, with the will or power, directs all the incoming forces. If you don't have will or power, you can be overwhelmed. People in the extreme state of giving up their power, control, and mastery have become psychotic. The conscious mind has abdicated all responsibility for control, orchestration, and analysis. The subconscious mind and the environment completely take over.

HOW DO YOU CLAIM YOUR POWER?

Every morning, the second you get up, you claim your power by choosing to affirm the attitude in your mind that you possess it. The diagram at the end of this chapter lists some personal power affirmations that you can say to yourself to cultivate and build this energy. I have also included some emotional invulnerability affirmations to build your protective bubble, since this is so much involved with owning your power.

Edgar Cayce made another very important statement involving power. He talked about the importance of developing positive anger. I emphasize the term *positive*. Positive anger is controlled anger that is not directed at other people or yourself but rather at the dark force that is trying to push you down. It is used to catapult you toward the light and positivity.

Anger has enormous power. The idea is to channel this power constructively and creatively. When one of Jesus' disciples started to complain, Jesus turned to him and said, "Get thee behind me, Satan." Rather than attack the man, He chose to do battle with the force behind the man. He also spoke with great emotion and power.

When you say the affirmations to yourself, say them with emotional intensity and real power or they won't work. As soon as you mean business, the subconscious will become your servant. You have to *make* it serve you, not *ask* it to serve you. It should also be noted here that God is not going to control your subconscious mind for you, no matter how much you pray. That is not His job. That is your job.

Every morning when you get up, claim your power and commit yourself to becoming the master of your life. Be loving, serve God, and have a great day, and let nothing in this universe stop you from your appointed task. This is how to live properly. Once you have established your power, then pray for God's help and do some affirmations and visualizations to program your subconscious mind the way you want it to work for you. This is the ultimate power in the universe.

Do you realize the power that is at your disposal? How can you not win this war? How can you not eventually get to the top of the mountain? How can you not be successful with all this power? Add to this the fact that each of us is a son or daughter of God and is *one* with God. Can God and the sons and daughters of God lose a battle with Satan, which is another name for ego, illusion, and negative thinking?

Spiritual Affirmations
MY TWO PERSONAL FAVORITES

God, my personal power, and the power of my subconscious mind are an unbeatable team.

Be still and know that I am God.

Visual imagery is a powerful addition to affirmations. Visualize that you are holding a symbol full of power—a sword, a scepter, a baseball bat, a beautiful red rose—when you repeat your affirmations and you will feel even more power.

Disidentification Affirmations

Every morning and every night for twenty-one days repeat these affirmations out loud three times until they fully sink into your conscious and subconscious mind.

I have a body, but I am not my body. My body may find itself in different conditions of health or sickness. This has nothing to do with my real self, or the real "I."

I have behavior, but I am not my behavior. All my behavior comes from my thoughts. If I have not developed self-mastery and I am operating on automatic pilot, I sometimes behave inappropriately. Even though I behave well or poorly, I am not my behavior. This has nothing to do with my real self, my real "I."

I have feelings and emotions, but I am not my feelings and emotions. If I have not yet developed self-mastery, my feelings and emotions are sometimes negative and sometimes positive. As I become more of a cause, creator, chooser, and master of my life, this will change. Though a wave of feelings and emotions may overtake me, I know I am not my feelings and emotions. My true nature will not change. "I" remain the same.

I have a mind but I am not my mind. My mind is my tool for creating my feelings, emotions, and behavior, as well as what I attract into my life. If I have not developed self-mastery, my mind sometimes runs me, instead of me running my mind. My mind is my most valuable tool, but it is not who "I" am.

AFFIRMATIONS

Personal Power and Becoming a Creative Cause

I am the power, the master, and the cause of my attitudes, feelings, emotions, and behavior.

I am 100 percent powerful, loving, and balanced at all times.

I am powerful, whole, and complete within myself. I have preferences but not attachments.

I am 100 percent powerful and decisive in everything I do.

I have perfect mastery and control over all my energies in service of a loving spiritual purpose.

I am the master and director of my life, and my subconscious mind is my friend and servant.

I am a center of pure self-consciousness and will, with the ability to direct my energies wherever I would have them go.

I am powerful, centered, and loving at all times.

I am powerful and centered at all times and I will allow nothing in this external universe to knock me off balance or off center.

I have 100 percent personal power and I vow never to give it to my subconscious mind or other people again.

I have perfect self-control and self-mastery in everything I do.

Emotional Invulnerability

I am 100 percent invulnerable to other people's negative energy. Other people's negative energy slides off me like water off a duck's back.

I am the cause of my feelings and emotions, not other people. I will not give them this power over me ever again.

Other people's negative energy bounces off me as if I were a rubber pillow.

I hear what other people have to say to me. However, I internalize only what I choose to internalize.

The only effect other people's negative energy has on me is the effect I let it have. I choose not to be affected ever again.

Chapter 3

✦

Unconditional Self-Love: The Second Golden Key to Psychological and Spiritual Health

If there is a panacea or cure-all to life, it is self-love.
—PAUL SOLOMON, SPIRITUAL TEACHER AND UNIVERSAL MIND CHANNEL

If the development of personal power is the first golden key to psychological and spiritual health, then unconditional self-love is most definitely the second golden key.

Personal power and self-love are the building blocks of a healthy self-concept and self-image. The most important relationship in our lives is our relationship to ourselves. If we are wrong with ourselves, we will be wrong with all other relationships. If we are off center in ourselves, how can we be on center with others?

Self-love begins with the understanding that there are two types of love in the world: *conditional love* and *unconditional love*. Conditional love is egotistical, personality-based love. Unconditional love is spiritual or transpersonal love.

The first key question we must ask ourselves is whether we love ourselves conditionally or unconditionally. Unconditional self-love is based on the understanding that we have worth and we are lovable because God created us. We are sons and daughters of God, and God doesn't make junk. Of course we have worth! If we don't have worth, then God doesn't have worth. In other words, our worth and lovableness are a spiritual inheritance.

But the ego says our worth and lovableness are based on meeting certain conditions. We have to have a certain kind of physical body. We have to go to college, have a high-paying job, be spiritual, meditate, exercise, have a relationship, be perfect, and so on.

Now, a lot of these things are very noble goals to strive for. *However, they have nothing to do with your self-love and self-worth.*

Self-love and self-worth come from who we are, not what we do. There are no conditions we have to meet. We can do everything in our lives right or everything wrong, and our worth and lovableness are the same. I cannot say this more emphatically.

A good metaphor for understanding this is to imagine a baby. Does this baby have to do anything to have worth or value? Does it have to look a certain way? Isn't there an inherent value in the spark of life? Of course a baby is of value and lovable. Don't we continue to love that child as it grows older, even if he or she gets into trouble or fails a first-grade spelling test?

The point is that there is a difference between the soul that is that child and the child's behavior. The soul is always lovable and worthy. The behavior may not always be so. This is an extremely important discrimination to make with others and with yourself.

Take this analogy a step further. We are God's children. He gave birth to us. Don't you think He loves us as we love our children? He continues to love us even though we make mistakes in the spiritual school called earth life. We need to love ourselves as God loves us — unconditionally! Jesus said, "You shall love your neighbor as yourself." Notice he didn't say to love our neighbor and hate ourselves.

We can determine where we are on our spiritual path by seeing how much we love our neighbor and how much we love ourselves. We also need to learn to allow ourselves to feel God's love. God's love is like the sun. It is always shining. It is just a matter of whether we are going to give ourselves permission to step out of the darkness to receive it.

I've heard it said that we are diamonds splattered with mud. God created us, so we are diamonds. Our faulty, egotistical negative thinking has put mud on us. This book is my attempt to get out the hose and wash off the illusions of faulty thinking so that we can see our true selves. Our true identity is the Christ, the perfect creation of God. It is only the ego's false, negative, pessimistic interpretation of us that makes us feel unworthy or unlovable.

Earth is a school. Our mistakes are not held against us. There are no sins, only mistakes. Some believe that a sin is like some stain on our character that cannot be removed. This is absurd. In truth, mistakes are positive. We don't go out of our way to make them. But if they happen, we learn from them.

Every mistake is a blessing in disguise because there is always a golden nugget of wisdom to be learned from it. We learn the easy way or in the school of hard knocks. We are in this school to know ourselves and hence know God. God's universe is governed by knowable laws—physical laws, psychological laws, and spiritual laws. We learn by making mistakes and then making adjustments.

The spiritual path up the mountain consists of five steps forward, then four backward; seven forward, then six backward. Don't buy into the ego's game of creating this impossible perfectionistic standard where mistakes are unacceptable. The spirit believes in striving for perfection but looks at mistakes as positive and unavoidable.

LIFE AS A DREAM

When you go to sleep at night and have a nightmare, you wake up and say to yourself, "Boy, am I glad that was just a dream; it seemed so real while I was sleeping!" Well, that is what I am saying to you right now: Wake up from that bad dream, that negative hypnosis you have been experiencing.

It's time to wake up! Wash the mud off your diamond and see who you really are. You are the most precious thing in all creation. Do you think God loves a rock or a tree more than His own children, who are made in His image?

Now comes the key to the whole process. Remember that your thoughts create your reality. Your thoughts don't create truth. Thoughts merely create the reality of the people who are thinking them. In other words, if you think you are unworthy, then you are going to live in the nightmare and self-created hell of your own thought's creation.

You will live in your own nightmare, even though it really isn't true. Because you are what you think, your task is to push these false attitudes of unworthiness and unlovableness out of your mind and to start affirming the truth about yourself. By doing this you will record a new message into your subconscious.

SELFISH-SELFLESS BALANCE

Another aspect of self-love is what I call the selfish-selfless balance. This means that there is a time to be selfish and there is a time to be selfless. To be selfless is to direct your energies toward helping others. To be selfish is to take care of yourself. Walking the spiritual path requires balance. We are not here to be martyrs and completely sacrifice ourselves for others. We must learn to be spiritually selfish.

Many very sincere and good spiritual people misunderstand this. I am not saying you shouldn't help others; the greatest among you is the servant of all. I am saying that you have to take care of yourself also. You are a part of God. You are a son or daughter of God.

Not to be spiritually selfish at times is to reject a part of God. If you are too selfless, you will probably be resentful. The great lesson is that when you are selfish, don't feel guilty, and when you are selfless, give and don't feel resentful. Be decisive in whatever choice you make.

THE CHILD CONSCIOUSNESS

We all have a relationship to ourselves. What is this self I am talking about? Another name for this self is the inner child or child consciousness.

As the following diagram illustrates, there are two ways of parenting either ourselves or a real external child—the spiritual way or the egotistical way. The spiritual way of parenting is to be firm but loving, so yin and yang are balanced.

The wrong way to parent is to be too firm or too permissive. A

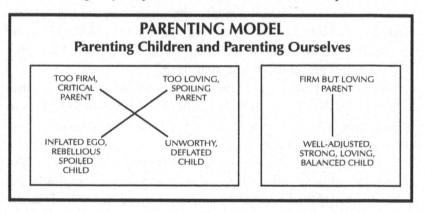

PARENTING MODEL
Parenting Children and Parenting Ourselves

TOO FIRM, CRITICAL PARENT	TOO LOVING, SPOILING PARENT	FIRM BUT LOVING PARENT
INFLATED EGO, REBELLIOUS SPOILED CHILD	UNWORTHY, DEFLATED CHILD	WELL-ADJUSTED, STRONG, LOVING, BALANCED CHILD

parent who is too firm is excessively critical. As the diagram indicates, when a parent is too critical the child feels unworthy or unloved. When a parent is too lenient the child can become spoiled or rebellious. A firm and loving parent helps the child become balanced and well adjusted.

The first step in understanding this whole process is to look at the way you were raised. Were your parents critical or firm and loving? It is very likely that you treat yourself the same way your parents treated you. Now look at how you have raised your children. And finally look at how you are currently guiding your own child consciousness.

The child consciousness is a psychic reality. Learning to raise the child within you properly is one of the most important skills you can possibly learn. You will also be a much better parent to your real children when you learn to parent yourself properly.

INNER PARENTING SKILLS

When we are being too critical of ourselves, what is really happening is "child abuse." If you saw child abuse occurring at the supermarket or at your neighbor's house, you would step in and say something to stop it. Well, that is what you need to start doing with your inner child.

The critical parent is like a mean baby-sitter with whom you have unwittingly left your child. Now you are returning (waking up) to reclaim your child as your own. You need to start by giving your child the protection he or she needs.

What this means psychologically is that when you become aware that the critical inner parent has started beating your child consciousness, you must stop him! It doesn't matter how. You can put up your protective bubble and say, "I am not going to let the child within me get beaten or abused any longer. I am going to protect it. I love that child and will not let it continue to be hurt."

When the overindulgent parent steps in and wants to be permissive, you can say, "No. I give up this extremism. I don't want to be too yin or too yang. I want balance. Get out!" Push the permissive parent thought out of your mind.

The second step, after pushing the critical or permissive parent out of your mind, is to affirm that you are going to be firm and loving toward yourself from now on. Continually doing this will allow the critical or permissive parent to fade from lack of attention, and the firm and loving parent will grow stronger. It will take practice and vigilance. Just remember that if you choose to forget to pay attention, you are allowing child abuse to take place in your own mental home.

What you must also consider here is that if improper parenting has taken place, then your child consciousness is going to be in need of healing, just as a real child would be after being abused. The child who has had a critical parent is going to need a lot of extra love and nurturing. The child who has had a permissive, spoiling parent is going to need "tough love." A child who is acting out needs to be sat on a little bit, but without excessive criticism.

In many cases, the child has had more power than the parent. This needs to change. The parent is in charge, and the child consciousness needs to be told this. You may have to get real tough in the beginning to get the point across, just as you would with a real child. The child will get the message if he sees that you mean business. The child doesn't really like being out of control anyway, and will appreciate the care and attention you are paying to him.

Your child consciousness desperately wants your unconditional love, just as a real child does. Down deep, your inner child wants firmness and limits, just as a real child does. If you are firm and loving, then both the child within you and your flesh-and-blood children will develop self-control, personal power, and self-love.

DIALOGUING

A very helpful tool in developing the proper relationships is to dialogue with these different parts of yourself in your journal. Talk to your child consciousness and see how it is doing. Then let the child within you talk back as you imagine he would respond. Dialogue with the critical parent and with the permissive parent, then with the firm and loving parent. Get more deeply in touch with how these dynamics are operating within you. You might even add your higher self into the dialogue and see what it has to add to the whole process.

The Huna teachings from Hawaii call the higher self the "utterly trustworthy parental self." I find that fascinating. In other words, we need to learn to parent ourselves as our higher selves parent us. Don't our higher selves parent us with firmness and tough love?

VICTORY LOG

This suggestion is absolutely essential for fully stabilizing self-love and self-worth. So far I have talked about self-love on the essence level, the level on which we have worth and receive love because we are sons and daughters of God.

There is also the form level. In other words, besides feeling good about who we are, we also need to feel good about what we are doing and creating in our lives. The critical parent spends all of its time being a perfectionist in a negative sense, looking for what we are doing wrong. In a given day we may be doing things 98 percent well, but the critical parent will spend the entire day focusing on the 2 percent we are doing wrong. This doesn't make sense. We should be 98 percent happy that day and 2 percent depressed, seeing the glass half full instead of half empty. The purpose of a victory log is to look at what we are doing well, not at what we are doing poorly.

Developing a proper victory log is a two-step process. First go over your entire life with a fine-toothed comb and list all the things that you have done well in. List all your fine attributes and qualities. Write down everything, no matter how minute. By doing this you will automatically feel good about yourself. Your perspective changes, and you see things the way your higher self wants you to see them.

The second step in the victory log is this: Every night before bed and every morning after you wake up, add to the list and review the victories of that day and that week. By doing this you are giving strokes, a positive reinforcement, to your child consciousness. You are telling the child within you how much you appreciate his cooperation and teamwork. You might tell your higher self the same thing. Together you are an unbeatable team.

MAKING BIG MISTAKES

When you do make mistakes, it is important to keep the critical parent out. It is okay to make *observations* about yourself or others; this is called spiritual discernment because it is done in unconditional love.

Whatever the mistake is, gain the golden nugget of wisdom from the experience; it then becomes a positive experience. If you truly learn from a mistake, you will never have to go through similar suffering again. Tell yourself that you are worthy and lovable even though you made a mistake or error in judgment. Mistakes are positive and unavoidable. Pick yourself up and get on with it.

A crucial part of self-love is forgiveness. You have a choice of subscribing to a philosophy of forgiveness or holding grudges. This applies to yourself also. Remember that if you hold a grudge, you are holding it against your child consciousness. Would you hold the same kind of grudge against a real child? If you want to be forgiven by God, is it reasonable to give the same energy in return to yourself and others?

WHAT HAPPENS IF YOU DON'T HAVE SELF-LOVE?

If you don't have unconditional self-love within yourself, then automatically you end up seeking it outside yourself. Love is a survival need; children in institutions have been known to die from lack of love.

The ideal is to give love to yourself and to allow yourself to receive God's unchanging, unconditional love. If you don't do this, you end up seeking love, approval, and acceptance from other people. This puts you in a compromised position. Other people become your programmers and the creators of your reality. Your worth is then in their hands. Do you really want other people to hold this power over you? Also, not having self-love puts a hole in your protective bubble, so when people criticize you, you can't protect yourself.

Ideally, you will give yourself so much love, and allow yourself to feel so much of God's love, that you will go into each day feeling totally powerful and totally loved before you encounter another human being. You feel full and complete within yourself, and feel at one with God. You are so filled with love that you can give love to others even if they don't love you. In essence, you *want* love, but you don't *need* love. You prefer loving relationships but are not attached to getting love. When you are a self-actualized person, you first form a right relationship with yourself and a right relationship with God before seeking relationships with others.

These are the two most important relationships in your life. You can then move into life as a whole, masterful, independent person who is in the world to give rather than to get, and who does not need to fill an empty void within the self. This is the work of the spiritual path.

We actually have it all right now. The only problem is that we think we don't. We live in the nightmare of self-inflicted limitations, even though they aren't real. We can get rid of these limitations anytime we want by owning our power and taking command over our minds.

SELF-LOVE AFFIRMATIONS

The following are self-love affirmations for reprogramming your conscious and subconscious thinking.

1. I love and forgive myself totally for all my mistakes, for I now recognize that mistakes are positive, not negative.

2. I now fully recognize that I have worth because God created me, and I do not have to do anything to have it.

3. I now recognize that I am a diamond, not the mud on the diamond.

4. My worth is unchangingly positive because it is a spiritual inheritance. It is not increased by my success nor decreased by my mistakes.

5. I realize now that I have total worth and value as a person whether I learn my lessons in life or not.

6. I now recognize that everything that has ever happened in my life has been positive, because it all contained lessons I needed to learn.

7. I choose to live in the now and not hold the past against myself.

8. I hereby choose to approve of myself, so I do not have to go around seeking approval from others.

9. I deserve love because God created me, and my mistakes are not held against me.

10. I realize that everything that happens in life is a teaching, a lesson, a challenge, and an opportunity to grow.

11. I now realize that I am the "I" person, chooser, consciousness, and spiritual being, and that this part of me deserves unconditional love at all times.

12. I am the light and not the lamp shade over the light.

13. I deserve love because my true identity is not what I do in life. I am the chooser of what I do.

14. I now understand that I am here to learn lessons and grow in life, but if I make mistakes, I am still totally lovable and unchangingly worthy.

15. I hereby choose the attitude of being very firm with myself and unconditionally loving.

16. I am the master of my life, and I choose to be my own best friend instead of my own worst enemy.

17. I choose to love me as God loves me—unconditionally.

18. I now choose truly to understand that I want to be perfect, with the understanding that mistakes are positive and part and parcel of the growing process.

19. I now realize on the level of my true identity being—the "I," the chooser, the person, the spiritual being, the soul—I am a perfect equal with every other person in the world.

20. I now choose to awaken and recognize that it was only the faulty thinking of my ego that has caused me not to love myself.

21. I now choose to undo all the faulty thinking society has programmed into me and replace it with self-love.

22. I choose to recognize that I deserve love and so do other people.

23. I choose to recognize that I am guiltless and sinless, because all mistakes are just lessons and opportunities to grow. Mistakes, in reality, are golden nuggets of wisdom and are positive.

24. I now realize that God does not hold my misuse of free choice against me, so why should I?

25. I love me. I forgive me. I approve of me. I commit myself from this moment onward to treating myself in a spiritual manner rather than in an egotistical manner. I now fully realize that the way in which I think is the reality in which I live. I have been living in my own self-created hell of faulty thinking. I now choose to and will live in my self-created heavenly state of consciousness. It is really that simple.

26. I unconditionally love me because I am a son/daughter of God, and my misuse of free choice or faulty thinking is not held against me.

27. Could what God created not be lovable and worthy?

28. I love me because I am innocent and not guilty.

29. The only thing in this infinite universe that says I do not deserve love is my ego. I hereby reject my ego and its false attitude and get back in tune with my true spiritual attitude and self.

30. I now, once and for all, release the ego's game of "having to do" in order to deserve love and worth. I now fully recognize I have always been lovable and worthy and will always be so.

PERSONAL POWER, EMOTIONAL INVULNERABILITY, AND SELF-LOVE VISUALIZATIONS

Self-Love Visualization

Begin by imagining a beautiful natural scene. Visualize yourself as smiling, happy, joyous, loving, and at peace with yourself and the world. Look around you and enjoy the colors, smells, and sounds and the feeling of being in harmony with nature.

Next, imagine one of your favorite animals being with you in your natural scene. See the animal come up to you and give you love and affection. Then imagine that your best friend is walking toward you from the distance and is carrying a six-month-old infant. See yourself greeting your friend and sharing a hug and conversation.

Your friend asks you to baby-sit this infant for a couple of hours. He or she carefully and gently hands you the infant. See your friend leaving and promising to return within two hours. See yourself holding, rocking, and giving love to this beautiful baby.

Next, realize that this infant is really the child within you. You have not only a child within you, but also a parent within. You have a choice as to how to parent this child. How you are going to raise this infant that is you?

If you are too permissive, this child will grow up spoiled and inflated. If you are too critical, the child will grow up feeling unworthy, incapable, and unloved. The key question is: How do you want yourself to grow up? Make this choice now. Give this infant firm and unconditional love to help your child become well adjusted.

Now imagine that five years have gone by and this little child that is you is playing in your natural setting. Tell the child how you feel about it.

Now imagine that ten more years have passed and this child that is you is an adolescent of fifteen. Be the parent you want to be to this teenager.

Imagine next that this adolescent has grown to be the adult you. Now that this child is an adult, have you thrown unconditional love and firmness out the window?

Make a choice right now to communicate with yourself, to get back to the right relationship with yourself. Go up to yourself and give yourself a big hug, recognizing that you are, in truth, your best friend. Apologize to yourself for being so hard on yourself in the past. Forgive your parental self for its mistakes and forgive the adult-child self for its mistakes.

Let the child tell you what kind of relationship it wants to have from now on. Make a choice to love in the now and get a fresh start from this moment forward. Make a choice to look at the past as a series of positive experiences, because you now choose to look at everything that happened as opportunities to grow. Give yourself approval and acceptance because you now recognize that mistakes are positive, not negative.

Tell your adult-child self that you will love him unconditionally instead of conditionally from now on. Tell him that you are not going to base your love on what he does but rather on the fact that he was created by God, so of course he has value and worth regardless of mistakes or successes.

See the consciousness, the "I," the person, the spiritual being now, as differentiated from behavior, mistakes, successes, personality, physical body, thoughts, feelings, or content of consciousness. Make a commitment to yourself from this moment forward to form this right relationship with yourself.

Take time now to have a heart-to-heart talk with yourself to come to a place of treating yourself spiritually and with love. Take the time now to talk out all unfinished business, lack of clarity, faulty thinking, or incompleteness, so that when this meditation is over, there is a fresh start and rebirth in your relationship to yourself.

YOUR TRUE SELF: THE CASUAL CONSCIOUSNESS

Even though you have both parent and child selves within you, the real you is neither the parent nor the child. The real you is the consciousness or "I" that is choosing what kind of parent-child dynamic you are creating within yourself.

The real you is the *observer self*, who controls, directs, chooses, and causes. The key to being the director is understanding the need to differentiate yourself from the content of your consciousness. You are not your thoughts, emotions, body, actions, personality, mistakes, successes, abilities, or beliefs. You are the essence and not the form. You are the consciousness, not the creation. You can direct and control only what you do not identify yourself with. Whatever you, as the consciousness or "I," are identified with will be your master. Unfortunately, living in this world, we must deal with form. This is why it is essential that you consciously choose the form of parenting you are going to provide yourself.

Identity Visualization

You can now do a visualization, putting all the things you have thought were you (the content of consciousness) into a big metal pot that is in the middle of your natural setting. Put everything in it until are you stripped of all mental, emotional, or physical form. All that is left is a center of pure awareness with nothing in it.

Practice trying on qualities, attitudes, feelings, beliefs, abilities, and nonabilities as you would a role in a play and then throwing them back in the pot. Practice identifying, then disidentifying. Practice being the controller, cause, and creator of your life. Always remember what your real self is and who and what you are.

Now that you understand the importance of owning your personal power and loving yourself unconditionally, it is time to take the next steps in your quest to fully integrate yourself.

Chapter 4

✳

Balancing the Three Minds and the Four Bodies: The Third Golden Key to Psychological and Spiritual Health

Be moderate in all things.
—THE BUDDHA

One of the most important keys to becoming a self-realized or God-realized being is learning to balance and integrate our three minds and four bodies. However, for the purpose of this discussion the soul and the monad are combined into the same category, since they serve similar functions.

With respect to our discussion of the subtle bodies, we will discuss the first four bodies—the physical, emotional, mental, and spiritual bodies. In actuality, the spiritual body can be further divided into many other bodies, including the causal body, the buddhic body, the light body, and on and on into cosmic levels of consciousness.

We work with these higher spiritual bodies in stages as we go through the initiation. For the purpose of this discussion, I am combining these higher spiritual bodies into what I am now going to call the spiritual body or spiritual vehicle.

Let's begin this discussion of the need for balance and integration by talking about our three minds. Each mind is a level of mentation, or thinking. The ideal is for the subconscious to become subservient to the conscious mind and for the conscious mind to become subservient to the superconscious mind, or soul.

Another way to say this is that our conscious self is meant to become the master of the subconscious mind, with the soul or higher self acting as our master teacher or guide. The Kahunas of Hawaii had a very eloquent way of explaining this. They call the higher self or soul the *aumakua*. The *aumakua* is defined as the "utterly trustworthy parental self." As the higher self or soul is our utterly trustworthy parental self, so the conscious mind is meant to be the utterly trustworthy parental self to our subconscious mind and child consciousness. We learn how to raise ourselves properly by following the example of how our soul or higher self raises us.

God is a Trinity, and since we are made in God's image, then we must be a trinity also. The Bible states very clearly that we are made in God's image: the Father, the Son, and the Holy Spirit. In Hinduism they call this Brahma, Shiva, and Vishnu. In the Huna teachings of Hawaii this is termed Ku, Kane, and Kanaloa. Our trinity is that of the superconscious, conscious, and subconscious minds.

God, Christ, and the Holy Spirit are different levels of Divinity; however, they function as one consciousness. Our goal is to get our three minds to function as one consciousness. The problem is that for most people, the three minds are not in balance. Some people don't even know they have a soul or higher self guiding them, and most people let the subconscious, or lower self, rule the conscious mind. When the subconscious mind runs our lives, the negative ego becomes our director, and our emotional bodies usually end up directing our lives.

The first step toward becoming balanced and integrated is to recognize that we have three minds. The second step is to begin the process of learning to own our personal power and take control of our subconscious mind and the three lower vehicles. The third step is to begin attuning to and asking for help from our soul and higher self.

The three minds can be compared to large metal rings. In the earlier stages of a person's evolution, the rings are very separate. As we evolve and begin to develop self-mastery and attunement to the soul, the rings start to link up.

At the time of the third initiation, or soul merge, these rings become interlocked and start to function as one mind. This is because self-mastery has been achieved to a great extent over the threefold personality (physical, emotional, and mental vehicles), and because at least 51 percent of the personality has become merged with soul consciousness.

As the soul-merge state continues to stabilize, the three minds function in greater and greater harmony and balance. As we continue to evolve, the monad or spiritual mind, as opposed to soul, begins to guide us. At the fourth initiation the soul merges back into the monad, or spirit, and the monad, or Father in Heaven, becomes the full director from then on in the person's evolution. At the fifth initiation, called monadic merge, a similar integration and balancing of the three minds takes place in that the evolving person now merges completely with the monad.

The three rings in this metaphor have come together in an even higher union. At ascension the monad or Mighty I Am Presence descends completely into the evolving person on earth and into the four bodies and is transformed into light. Even the physical body merges completely with the light. In this stage we have achieved perfect integration and balance of the three minds and four bodies.

THE BALANCING OF OUR FOUR BODIES

To achieve the ultimate union, integration, and balance, we must learn to balance the four bodies. Every one of us has four distinct and separate energy bodies, each with a different and unique perspective: a physical body, an emotional body, a mental body, and a spiritual body. The ideal is to greatly respect and listen to all four simultaneously. What happens more often than not is that we tend to overidentify with one or two to the detriment of the others. More than half the people in the world respond to life through an emotional body focus.

Some people *feel* life as their main function. Other people *think* about life and are less concerned with their feelings. Still others may be so involved with their spiritual body that they don't take care of their physical body, or may not even care about thoughts or feelings either.

Others are so caught up in their physical body that they are completely cut off from their spiritual body, and possibly even intellectual pursuits or thoughts. We are likely to over- or underidentify with one or two bodies in particular. When this over- or underidentification occurs, the energy flowing down from the Creator does not flow properly or efficiently. If this continues, it will ultimately manifest as disease in one of the four bodies.

The physical body usually ends up being the mirror of these psychological imbalances. This is based on the Hermetic law "As within, so without. As above, so below." By seeing where we are having health problems in our physical body, we can then find the mental, emotional, or spiritual cause.

Most of us don't think about our four bodies until we feel discomfort, but the goal is to integrate the four bodies and to align their differing points of view so as to use them all to be fully creative and to fulfill our potential and divine purpose for being here. We are all like cells in the body of God. When cells in our body don't work properly and reproduce uncontrollably, this is called cancer. When we don't work in harmony with God's Divine Plan, then in a sense God has cancer. Part of the lesson of the four-body system is to get all the bodies working for the same purpose, which is to grow spiritually and to realize God.

When the four bodies are balanced and integrated, there is no restriction or limitation and we are free-flowing. When the four bodies are balanced, we are fully able to realize God. Many of us understand this with our mental body but haven't yet aligned the other bodies with this truth.

The same thing very often happens in balancing of the three minds. For example, sometimes the conscious mind might not want to worry or be depressed anymore, yet the subconscious mind might not be cooperating. The mental body might understand the ideal, but implementing or experiencing it fully with all four bodies may take a little more work and practice.

Each of the four bodies and three minds has a unique and special gift of information and guidance to give us. The soul, or monad, may give us intuitive perceptions, and it may be the voice of our conscience, which gives us our morals and ethics. The conscious mind is the site of analytical thinking, logic, and deductive reasoning. The subconscious mind is responsible for feelings and emotional reactions to things. The physical body reacts instinctively and senses. The emotional body, which is connected to the subconscious mind, focuses on how we feel in any given moment or situation and might provide psychic impressions. The mental body gives us a logical perspective regarding what is going on. The spiritual body, which is intimately connected with the soul and monad, gives us intuition, conscience, and God's guidance.

When we over- or underidentify with one body or one mind, we are losing invaluable information. It is the nature of the ego to tell us that the way that it processes reality is the best. I am here to say that God's understanding of what is the best way to process reality is to use all levels of guidance.

If, in doing business, you would tune into your three-mind and four-body system when you make major decisions, I am sure that your business would be much more successful and you would make fewer costly mistakes. Your spiritual vehicle would tell you one thing, your mind another, your feelings something else, and your physical body and instincts yet another thing. You limit yourself by focusing on just one kind of input. Why not access all levels of information and guidance that God has provided?

As you become more and more balanced you will find your three minds and four bodies working in harmony toward the three-part goal of success on all levels, God-realization, and fulfilling your mission and Divine Plan on earth.

THE EMOTIONAL BODY

An emotional focus upon life can be very beneficial. It makes us very sensitive to beauty, the arts, nature, music, and dance. Yet an emotional body focus in its negative aspects often causes us to be on an emotional roller coaster, being constantly tossed around by the instability of the emotional body.

We can learn to use our personal power and will to pull ourselves out of this focus. This can be done through attitudinal healing, because it is our thoughts that are creating our feelings. This can be difficult to do if we have an emotional focus, because we are so habituated to accessing just the emotional body.

So we must learn to better analyze and logically process what we experience. A helpful visualization to use when the emotional body is in crisis is to imagine a red ladder, which is symbolic of the will. In the visualization, climb the red ladder to get out of the negative feeling or emotion. Another tool is to immediately do some affirmations, or chant the name of God and visualize His form. We need to use our mental faculties to balance the emotional overidentification.

There are several visualizations you can do when your emotional body is in crisis and you wish to restore balance.

The Red Ladder

Sit quietly for a few minutes and focus on your breath. Now begin to visualize a red ladder, which symbolizes your will, as a tool to climb up out of the grip of your negative emotions.

Start at the bottom, and climb slowly, rung by rung. With each step leave behind you all the negative emotions that you have been feeling—doubt, anxiety, fear, anger, insecurity, self-judgment. Feel yourself growing stronger and stronger, and more and more light-filled as you ascend the red ladder. With each step, you might want to repeat a helpful affirmation or chant the name of God. Use your mental faculties to help balance the pull of your emotions.

At the top, take a deep breath, feel the new, cleansed space within you, and all the possibilities that surround you. Step off the red ladder knowing that you have reached a new level of being.

The Golden Bubble

This is an excellent visualization for when you are feeling overwhelmed with life and assailed by negative thoughts. In times of high stress, you may want to start every morning with this protective, strengthening visualization for your mind and spirit.

Sit quietly and focus on your breath for a few minutes. Allow the negative energies from other people and the outer world to drop away from your consciousness as you tune into the love and guidance radiating from God and the Ascended Masters.

Visualize yourself sitting inside a beautiful protective bubble of golden light. It is exactly the right size, neither cramped and restricting nor vast and lonely. Feel the skin of the protective golden bubble, its tensile strength, and its permeability—keeping out all negative energy but allowing in love and positive thoughts and feelings.

The next step is to clear away all the negativity you were carrying when you spun the protective golden bubble around you. Very gently, open a small hole in the skin of the bubble, as though you were dilating the iris of a camera lens. Feel all the negative energy, thoughts, and feelings that may still be inside the bubble rushing out as though being pulled by a vacuum. Breathe out all the darkness and heaviness within you. When this energy has completely cleared, visualize the skin of the golden bubble resealing itself.

Now you're going to breathe in golden white light from the depths of your soul. Feel God's love pouring in, filling the inside of the protective golden bubble with positive energy and positive loving feelings and emotions. Feel yourself becoming balanced, even-minded, peaceful, and joyous. And when you're ready, step out into your day, knowing that the protective golden bubble will surround and support you wherever you go and whatever you do.

The earth also has an emotional body; it has the same four bodies we ourselves have, and they are interrelated. What does the feeling body of the earth look like? It has to do with its relationship to water. Think about the contrast between a torrential rainstorm and a placid lake at sunrise. In the earth's four-body system, the mental body of the earth might be considered the man-made structures, such as pyramids or skyscrapers or cathedrals. From another perspective, the element of air is part of the mental structure of the earth, as water is for the emotional body of the earth.

Understanding the four-body system can help us greatly to understand both romantic relationships and friendships. If we think about our relationships with those people to whom we are closest, we can determine if they are emotionally focused, mentally focused, physically focused, spiritually focused, or a combination. By understanding this, we can avoid imposing our focus of identification on them. Very often in marriages and romantic relationships, the man tends to be more mentally focused and the woman more emotionally focused. A lot of disagreements occur because neither appreciates the gift he or she is bringing to the other. It could be said that each is the disowned self of each other.

In reality it is the soul that is really learning when we are working with the four-body system. What I mean by this is that the soul incarnates twelve personalities, or soul extensions, into physical incarnation. The soul experiences each of these extensions in simultaneous time, not in sequential time. If in one particular extension the soul is trying to work out a particular emotional area and isn't succeeding, then it will work out that lesson through another personality.

The soul might focus on a man in the Mayan civilization, a woman in Lemuria, and another woman living in Los Angeles in the twenty-first century to work through this lesson. The soul learns through all twelve soul extensions simultaneously to achieve the soul realization it is looking for. Through all the experiences of all twelve soul extensions, the four bodies finally become properly balanced and developed, so one soul extension accepts the full expression of the soul, which is called the soul merge or third initiation. This same process occurs at a higher level when one soul extension merges completely with the monad at ascension.

To view spiritual growth from the perspective of the soul or the monad rather than from the personality is quite an interesting process. From the perspective of the soul, beings on earth are the soul's extensions, like the fingers on the soul's hand. If one isn't working properly, it will just use another finger that is working. All the fingers belong to the same body, so it doesn't really matter which finger it uses to learn its necessary lessons.

THE MENTAL BODY

Mass consciousness on earth is in the process of achieving complete development of the mental body. This is because we are currently in the Aryan root race cycle, whose focus is mental attunement. Two previous root race cycles focused on other bodies. Atlantis was focused on emotional attunement and Lemuria on physical attunement. Advanced humans have already developed the mental body and are now working on the future Aquarian cycle, with its development of the spiritual body.

Those of us who identify with a mental focus very often get so absorbed in this focus that we pay no attention to the emotional one. We can be like the stereotypical college professor who pays attention solely to intellectual pursuits. If we pay attention to the mental and spiritual bodies, we might become highly developed occultists but lack sufficient focus on love and human relationships. Very often, if we are mentally focused, we will be less developed psychically and intuitively. These of us with a mental focus will seek to study everything, finding life interesting and always seeking greater knowledge. This is fine as long as we balance that mental focus with the other three bodies. Great scholars often forget their physical needs and become depleted physically as a result. If we are overidentified with the mental focus, we need to use our will to shift our focus and balance it with love, address the needs of the child consciousness, and engage in play and recreation time. If we overidentify with the mental focus, it is easy to fall into the trap of feeling superior to the person who is emotionally focused. It is essential to realize that the four bodies are all equal. The same is true for all the chakras. The higher ones are not better than the lower ones. The ideal is for all the chakras to be balanced. Being in balance and integrated is the state of God-realization.

To climb the ladder of awareness, evolve spiritually, and fulfill your potential, you must use all four bodies. Relying on the mental body will limit your perspective. One helpful exercise to achieve a better balance and more complete integration is to let the mental and emotional bodies talk to each other, either out loud or in your journal writing. After this dialoguing, let the spiritual body guide the two of them while also giving the physical body a voice. Each body needs to be instructed as to its divine role and its proper balanced relationship to the other bodies. All your four bodies will be happy to cooperate as long as each of them knows that it has its place in service of the Divine Plan.

When a problem or challenge arises, decide whether it is a physical, emotional, mental, or spiritual problem, or a combination. Assess whether the communication links between the four bodies are operating effectively. Try to determine how the four bodies can work together as one team to solve the problem and attune themselves to the soul's purpose.

THE PHYSICAL BODY

The physical body is the part of self that carries out functions necessary to maintain life here on earth. This vehicle, as with other bodies, performs only as well as it is cared for. If we don't feed it properly and give it exercise, sunshine, fresh air, and recreation, it will develop problems.

Another thing the physical body needs is love. Very often we take the physical body for granted and do not recognize it as the divine being that it is. We might forget to thank it enough for the wonderful service it performs for us.

Many people choose to experience their spiritual lessons in life through the physical body in the form of illnesses and other types of dysfunctions. When this happens, the body is trying to send a message that there is an imbalance somewhere. This is a gift and a teaching.

As mentioned earlier, the physical body reflects or mirrors the state of functioning of our other bodies. If we have stomach problems, this usually has to do with some emotional imbalance. If we have foot problems, this has to do with our understanding. Headaches have to do with issues of control, either being too controlling or having other people controlling us too much.

When we truly learn to be balanced in our four bodies and learn to be guided and merged with our soul, and later our monad, the physical body literally will live forever. An Ascended Master can live indefinitely on earth, as many of them have proven.

It is very important to make sure that the energy intake valve at the top of your head is always open. We can visualize this as a funnel. If this funnel is blocked, we will be tired or fatigued. When the four bodies aren't balanced, it takes a toll on the physical body, for the proper flow of energy is not feeding it.

Very often subconscious patterns get embedded into the physical vehicle. Just clearing our thoughts is not enough; physical exercise and body work also help move the pattern. We must work on all levels to clear ourselves, not just from the spiritual or mental level.

The physical body provides a point of focus on the earth through which the soul can experience. It is a means for the soul to enter school and learn an entirely new set of lessons, which can greatly accelerate spiritual growth. When a soul is not in a physical body, spiritual growth is much slower. When we understand what a great demand there is in the spiritual world for physical bodies, we will respect the ones we have much more.

The physical body also provides a grounding place for the soul from which to explore and to integrate what is learned on other levels. A person cannot go through the initiation process without being in a physical body.

We must learn to treat the physical body as the divine being and partner that it is. It has intelligence and can communicate. It desires to be of service to us and the Divine Plan as long as we will give it the respect of an equal partner.

The four bodies are like musical instruments, each with a different vibration and tone. We must learn to weave these bodies together into a beautiful symphony. To always play just one instrument would be boring and monotonous. To play them all together in perfect balance and harmony, in service of the soul and God's Divine Plan, is what the Masters have referred to as the music of the spheres.

It is okay to emphasize one of the four bodies in a more focused manner for a short time, such as when writing a book, going on a vacation, going to a meditation retreat, or running and training to run in a marathon. This is fine as long as the overall context of life is one of balance and integration.

SPIRITUAL BODY

The spiritual vehicle, or body, is the means by which we experience ourselves as an individualized portion of the Creator. It is the vehicle in which we begin our experience and in which we are destined to complete our experience.

As we grow and evolve we ultimately shed the physical vehicle, then the emotional vehicle, and finally the mental vehicle, eventually returning to our spiritual vehicle. We drop these other bodies one by one until we return to the essence of our self, our soul, and then our monad—the ultimate goal of ascension. In order to achieve this goal, the four bodies must be balanced and integrated properly in daily life on the earth plane in service of God's Divine Plan.

To become a master mechanic one must know how to take a car apart and put it back together almost blindfolded. As future cocreators with God at the highest level, we must know how to take our four bodies apart and put them back together in perfect harmony and balance before we can ascend and become a Master. As we learn these lessons, this knowledge is absorbed back into the spiritual body. We are then thrust forward into a higher level of awareness and spiritual expansion.

The spiritual vehicle, on whatever level of awareness we perceive it, is forever attuned to God. When we reach that level there is no more pain, because there is never a point when we lose focus on God. By contrast, we suffer in our four bodies whenever we are out of harmony with God and God's laws.

As long as we stay in harmony with God's laws on this plane we will not suffer. When we do suffer it is just a sign that we need to seek truth and have broken one of God's laws. This is not a punishment but a gift. If we didn't suffer, I don't think very many people would be likely to seek God. They would be satisfied being in a rut, thinking they would be happy for eternity, not realizing what they are missing. The small amount of joy that the personality can obtain through earth life is infinitesimally small compared to the joy and love found in God and the spiritual path. Suffering is like a gentle kick from God to keep us on the straight and narrow path toward the realization of God and service to mankind. This is what we really want anyway. The suffering is just a safeguard to keep us moving in the right direction.

The spiritual body encompasses all of the potential we are not yet able to use. The spiritual body is like a ladder we climb by interacting with the other bodies. Another way to put it is that we use our other bodies to climb the ladder of awareness to our full spiritual potential.

Each time we achieve a realization, we let more light into our spiritual body, or light body. A person who is clairvoyant can tell where any given person is in his or her evolution by looking at the amount of light that person allows into the physical, mental, emotional, and spiritual bodies.

Ideally the three other bodies work toward the goal of the spiritual body, and of the soul and monad. As the soul merges into the four-body system it brings even more balance. The soul, and later the monad, is incapable of any other response. It is only the negative ego that causes us to be out of balance. This is why the soul merge, or third initiation, is such a significant achievement in our evolution. It means we have balanced our four bodies enough to achieve this merger, which helps to create even greater stabilization of the four-body relationship. After the soul merge there is more energy and life force present on the physical level.

Chapter 5

✦

Christ Consciousness and How to Achieve It: The Fourth Golden Key to Psychological and Spiritual Health

Forgiveness is the key to happiness.
—A COURSE IN MIRACLES

A *Course in Miracles* is essentially a course in attitudinal healing. The basic premise of these books is that there are two and only two ways of thinking or philosophies of life. Every person in the world falls into one or the other group. There is the voice of the spirit or of the Christ, and then there is the voice of the ego. This could also be stated as the voice of your higher self or the voice of your lower self; the voice of the big "I" or the voice of the little "i,"; the voice of the Holy Spirit or the voice of glamour, maya, and illusion; the voice of the self or the voice of the not-self; the voice of the Holy Spirit or the voice of the negative ego.

As children, we are conditioned by society to think and interpret life from the negative ego's perspective. This is why so many people are filled with so many negative feelings and lack inner peace. A *Course in Miracles* teaches a very systematic way to undo the negative ego's thinking and instead think with the Christ mind. The Bible says, "Let this mind be in you that was in Christ Jesus." Jesus, as we know, was a human being just like you and me who became the embodiment of the Christ by becoming one with the Christ consciousness.

CHRIST CONSCIOUSNESS—NOT JUST FOR CHRISTIANS

The Christ consciousness is not just for Christians. The Christ consciousness, the Buddha consciousness, the Krishna consciousness, God consciousness, and the consciousness of all religions are all the same thing. Many people have been negatively programmed by their religious upbringing. It is important here not to get caught up in the words, or semantics; all religions or spiritual paths are fine. The new religion of the future is the one that honors and recognizes all religions and all spiritual paths, for they all lead to the same place. The introduction to A *Course in Miracles* states:

> This is a *Course in Miracles*. It is a required course. Only the time you take it is voluntary. Free will does not mean that you can establish the curriculum. It means only that you can elect what you want to take at a given time. The Course does not aim at teaching the meaning of love for that is beyond what can be taught. It does aim, however, at removing the blocks to the awareness of love's presence, which is your natural inheritance. The opposite of love is fear, but what is all-encompassing can have no opposite.

The Course can be summed up very simply in this way:

> Nothing real can be threatened.
> Nothing unreal exists.
> Herein lies the Peace of God.

For most people, A *Course in Miracles* is a very difficult book to understand. One of my main purposes in writing this particular chapter is to take the essence of the Course's teaching and make it very easy to understand. Even if you have never read A *Course in Miracles*, its essence will become clear by the end of this chapter.

My personal spiritual evolution would have benefited from a clear explanation of the Course in simple language. In this chapter, I expand on the Course's teachings to make them more universal to all religions and all spiritual paths. I have also added many of my own ideas of what "Christ consciousness" really means.

The Course is required, the introductions says. What this means is not that everyone has to study A *Course in Miracles*, but rather that everyone has to learn to think with their Christ consciousness, or God mind.

You cannot go through your spiritual initiations and realize God without transcending the selfish, materialistic, fear-based mind of your ego. The curriculum is set, and *A Course in Miracles* is just one way of learning these lessons.

The core of *A Course in Miracles* instructs us that God created us, and our true identity is the Christ. In other words, we are all sons and daughters of God, made in God's image. God is love, so we are love. We don't have to become love; love is what we are. It is only the negative ego programming and conditioning—the mud on the diamond—that hides this awareness from us. Even Jesus said, "Everything that I can do, you can do and more."

The Christian church has misinterpreted His message. Certainly Jesus was the child of God, but so are we. Or you could say that we each are the Buddha, the Hindu atman, or Eternal Self. Since most of us are more familiar with the Western Christian tradition, we will use Christ as the identifying term for the sake of convenience. Feel free to substitute another term you like better throughout. In the Old Testament the Jewish prophets said, "Ye are gods and children of the Most High." David, in the Psalms, said, "Be still and know, I am God."

This is why the introduction to *A Course in Miracles* says, "Nothing real can be threatened. Nothing unreal exists. Herein lies the Peace of God." Your true identity as the Christ cannot be changed. That is how God created you. You can think you are something other than this, but that does not change reality. You are the Christ, whether you like it or not.

The reason you have no choice is that you didn't create yourself, God created you. The spiritual path is really not about trying to get anyplace. It is just reawakening to who you are. Another way to think of it is that we are not leaving on a journey but returning to where we started. The second step along the way is the practice of being your self in daily life.

Ramana Maharishi, the great saint from India, said that the spiritual path is like a person who came to him asking his help in finding a necklace she lost forty years before. Ramana Maharishi said, "What's that you are wearing around your neck?" The woman suddenly realized that she had been wearing the necklace all along. Well, that is how the spiritual path is. We don't have to find God; we already *are*

God and have been all the time. It is the insane voice of the negative ego that keeps us lost in glamour, maya, and illusion.

WHERE DID THE NEGATIVE EGO COME FROM?

The negative ego did not come from God, it came from man's misuse of free choice. Man is the only creature that has the ability to think out of harmony with God. The fall that the Bible refers to occurred when we as monads, or individualized sparks of God, chose to come into matter. It wasn't the coming into matter that caused the fall but the overidentification with matter. It was that moment when we thought we were a physical body rather than a God-being inhabiting or using this physical body.

In thinking we were a physical body, we fell prey to the illusion of separation from God and separation from our brothers and sisters. Then came selfishness, fear, and real death. From these faulty premises a whole thought system developed that was based on illusion, maya, and glamour.

We have spent hundreds of incarnations caught up in this illusion. The amazing thing *A Course in Miracles* teaches is that the fall never really happened. We just think it did. The basic law of our minds is that it is our thoughts that create our reality. Our feelings, emotions, behavior, and what we attract and magnetize into our lives all come from our thoughts.

Is the glass half empty or half full? Are you optimistic or pessimistic? Do you look at what happens in life as teachings, lessons, challenges, and opportunities to grow, or do you look at things as bummers, problems, aggravations, irritations, and upsets? It is how you think, interpret, and perceive that will determine how you feel in any given situation.

We have always been the Christ, the Buddha, the atman, the Eternal Self, and have always been one with God. All of our negative egotistical thinking has not changed this one single bit.

Well, I say to you now in this holy instant, wake up! Wake up from the negative hypnosis you have been living in, thinking you are unworthy, unlovable, inferior, separate from God, powerless. In this holy instant, wake and realize that you are the Christ, the Buddha, the atman, the Eternal Self. You have always been and always will be.

Sai Baba says, "Your mind creates bondage, or your mind creates liberation." A lot of people downplay the mind as though it were not important. As Sai Baba says, it is your mind, and how you manage it will determine if you achieve liberation or remain in bondage.

Heaven and hell are places, but first they are states of mind. When the negative ego is your guide and teacher, you are in hell. When the spirit and soul consciousness is your teacher, you are in heaven. The Buddha, in His four noble truths, said that all suffering comes from wrong points of view.

It is important to understand that we don't just see with our eyes; we also see with our mind, through our belief systems. We can interpret life from the negative ego's viewpoint, or we can see things from the Buddha's or Christ's. The major work of the spiritual path is clearing out all the negative egotistical beliefs from the conscious and subconscious mind, and to replace them with the spiritual pattern of the Christ.

THE AUTHORITY PROBLEM

The authority problem has to do with the core issue of who is the ultimate authority in life. The ultimate authority is God, and it is God who created us. The negative ego tells us, however, that God doesn't exist because we can't see Him with our physical eyes; hence the ego is the ultimate authority. The ego tells us that each of us is just a physical body, not the Christ living in a physical body.

The ludicrousness of the ego is quite obvious. God created us, and we created the ego; however, we have been letting the ego be the ultimate authority. It is time to recognize and own our personal power and authority over our selves. It is time for us to gain mastery over our mind, our emotions, our physical body, and our ego.

It is not God's job to get rid of our ego, it is our job. We created it, so we can get rid of it. God could do it, but this would be like giving birth to a child and doing everything for the child. If we did that, the child would grow up to be completely incapable and there would be no reason to incarnate into this school called earth life. God doesn't need to learn these lessons—we do. One of the lessons of *A Course in Miracles* is: "My salvation is up to me."

God has already given us everything. It is we who have separated ourselves from God by listening to the voice of the ego. In reality, we have never been separated from God; however, in our consciousness, or perception of reality, we are. We can easily remedy this situation by changing our thoughts. The Bible says, "Be transformed by the renewal of your mind" and "As a man thinks, so is he." Abraham Lincoln said, "A man is as happy as he makes up his mind to be." Ralph Waldo Emerson said, "A man is what he thinks about all day long."

It is time for us to wake up and snap out of this self-created hell of our own negative thinking. It is time to get in control of our subconscious mind and stop letting it push us around. It is meant to be our servant, not our master.

HOW IS ATTITUDINAL HEALING ACCOMPLISHED?

The process of accomplishing this attitudinal healing is actually very simple. What I would recommend is that you imagine that you are surrounded by a golden bubble that protects you from the outside world and other people, and also protects you from your own subconscious mind. In other words, I would like you to imagine that all of your thoughts, feelings, impulses, desires, and images are outside your golden bubble. All of what is termed the content of consciousness is outside the bubble.

The idea, then, is that every time a thought, feeling, or impulse arises from your subconscious mind, you stop it at the gate of the bubble, almost as if there were a guard there checking its passport. If the thought or feeling or impulse is positive, loving, spiritual, balanced, Christ-like, of God, then let it through the bubble and into your mind. If the thought, feeling, impulse, or desire is negative, selfish, fear-based, imbalanced, and not of God, then push it out of your mind. A *Course in Miracles* states, "Deny any thought that is not of God to enter your mind."

Remember that it takes twenty-one days to cement any new habit into the subconscious mind. After twenty-one days it will be automatic to think with your Christ mind. It will not even be difficult. It will be a habit. The idea is to fill the subconscious mind with positive Christ-like habits and get rid of the egotistical ones.

ARE YOU A MASTER OR A VICTIM?

What we think and image within our conscious and subconscious minds will manifest its mirror likeness in our external circumstances. The outer world is a mirror of the inner world. The microcosm is like the macrocosm. As we learn to get control of our minds, we learn to get control of our feelings and emotions. Feelings and emotions do not just happen to us; we create them by how we think. Remember that we are cocreators with God, made in His image. God is not a victim, and neither are we.

There are particular beliefs that cause certain feelings and emotions. When we learn to think with our Christ mind, all of our negative feelings and emotions begin to disappear. It is a way of thinking that will bring us inner peace, unconditional love, and joy all the time.

Nothing outside of us causes us to think or feel anything. It is our interpretation, our belief, our perception of this situation that causes us to feel the way we do. For example, in the 1929 stock market crash, one person might have jumped out the window of a building to commit suicide, but another person who lost a similar fortune might have said, "Easy come, easy go." In another example, two people come to work only to find that the elevator is broken and they have to walk up ten flights of stairs. One person curses and swears, but the other says, "Great! An opportunity to get some physical exercise."

Walking down the street, we can see other people as just other meaningless physical bodies, or as brothers and sisters in a much larger spiritual family. As I said previously, we see with our minds, not just our physical eyes.

Our behavior is also caused by our thoughts and feelings. We never do anything that does not have an antecedent as some thought or feeling in either our conscious or subconscious mind. The idea is to completely clean out the subconscious mind of all negative programming. Later in this book I will dedicate an entire chapter to tools and methods for doing that.

As we achieve mastery over what Djwhal Khul has called the three lower vehicles (the mental, emotional, and physical bodies) and control over the negative ego, we will eventually merge with the soul. The soul brings us a Midas touch, where everything we do turns to gold, because we are in harmony with God's laws. As we continue to evolve, our attunement moves from the soul up to the spirit, or monad. As we achieve this mastery, we can program the subconscious mind to attract to us anything we need. The idea is to consciously program the subconscious with nothing but positive, Christ-like thoughts that attract only positive things from the outside world. Most people don't utilize the incredible power of the subconscious mind, as I pointed out in the chapter on integrating and balancing the three minds. This reprogramming is achieved through the process of denial and affirmation. The idea is to deny the negative thoughts and to constantly affirm the positive spiritual thoughts. In the chapter on how to reprogram the subconscious mind you will find many positive affirmations and visualizations to work with to achieve whatever it is you want to create in your life.

SICKNESS IS A DEFENSE AGAINST THE TRUTH

The subconscious mind runs the physical body; this can be clearly proved in the use of hypnosis. If our true identity is the Christ, then how can we get sick? If God isn't sick, then in reality we can't be sick, either.

We get sick because we believe in and indulge in our negative thoughts. Sickness is a defense against the truth because the truth is that we are the Christ and can't be sick. If we held this thought, then the subconscious mind, which does whatever we order it to do, would keep us healthy.

This applies to the aging process also. If we didn't believe we had to age, we wouldn't. Ascended Masters prove this; they can live in the same physical body indefinitely. Saint Germain did it for 350 years in Europe. In the same way, Djwhal Khul, the inner plane Ascended Master whose guidance I follow, lived as the Chinese sage Confucius, one of the three holy men who visited Master Jesus at his birth and had his teachings channeled through Alice Bailey in the 1940s. Physical immortality is achievable because we are God.

Still, it is important to eat well, exercise, and follow God's physical laws until we reach that ascended state of consciousness at the sixth initiation. Many younger souls try to defy God's physical laws at a stage in their spiritual evolution where they are not yet able to walk on water. They will get to this point; however, until they do, it is most wise to respect God's laws on the physical, emotional, mental, and spiritual levels.

The spiritual path is a process. We do not reach our goal in one instant. In one holy instant you can fully realize that you are the Christ and you are God; however, you must demonstrate this illumination and ground it on the earthly plane to share with others. That all takes time.

The spiritual path does not go straight up to God. Rather, it involves attuning upward and then bringing that consciousness back down to earth. God's Divine Plan is to create heaven on earth. You are here as a bridge between spirit and matter. You are here to spiritualize the material plane.

THE HOLY ENCOUNTER

The holy encounter is an exquisite idea presented in *A Course in Miracles*. It is the understanding that every time we meet another person in the world, it is a holy encounter. Each encounter with another person is, in reality, Christ meeting Christ, God meeting God. Every person we meet, whether we know him or not, is God visiting us in physical form.

This concept applies to the animal, plant, and mineral kingdoms also. There is only one Being in the infinite universe, and that is God. God has incarnated into an infinite number of forms. He is incarnated as you and as me, as the animals, plants, minerals—everything.

Sai Baba has said that the fastest way to realize God is to see Him in everything and everyone, to see Him in our brothers and sisters because He *is* our brothers and sisters. This can be clearly demonstrated through language. When you say, "I feel this way" or "I am going to the market," have you ever thought about what the "I" is? The "I" is the God self, or the Christ. No matter what words we speak in any given sentence, the "I" is the same for everybody. The "I" underlies the mental, emotional, and physical vehicles, or bodies. God is incarnated as the Eternal "I" in everything and everyone.

When we see a person on the street as just a stranger, we are seeing him or her through the negative ego's eyes. The truth is that whether we believe it or not, this person is the Christ. If we don't see him that way, we are removing the possibility of finding God for ourselves. We are not merely doing that person a service by seeing them in their true form; we are doing ourselves the greatest service, for the world is a mirror of our own state of consciousness. By seeing our brothers and sisters as strangers, we have lost contact with God in ourselves.

Jesus Christ said the whole law could be summed up in the statement "Love the Lord thy God with all thy heart and soul and mind and might, and love thy neighbor as thyself." I would go so far as to say that your neighbor *is* yourself, for God has only one child, and we are all part of that relationship. We all share the same "I." How we see our brothers and sisters is literally how we are treating God and our self.

Imagine that you are walking down the street and there before you is your favorite spiritual Master. It could be Jesus Christ, Sai Baba, Djwhal Khul, the Lord Maitreya, the Virgin Mary, the Buddha, Quan Yin, whoever. How would you treat that Master when you approach him or her on the street? Well, if you treat every person you meet in your life, be it a street person, a grocery store clerk, your mother-in-law, or your husband or wife, any differently, you are missing the mark and have more focusing of your consciousness to do. There is absolutely no difference between these Masters and so-called ordinary people, nor is there any difference between these Masters and yourself.

Jesus made this point when he said, "Everything I can do, you can do and more." Our identity is exactly the same. The only difference is that the Masters are doing a little better than we are at demonstrating it. Never give up, for as the great Paramahansa Yogananda said, "A saint is a sinner that never gave up." The Ascended Masters had to work through exactly the same challenges and lessons we are struggling with now.

THE OUTCOME IS INEVITABLE

It is inevitable that all of God's sons and daughters will eventually return home. Can God and the Christ lose against illusion and maya? If ever you get discouraged, you should ask yourself this. Can God and the Christ lose this battle? It is impossible!

Never forget that the negative ego doesn't really exist. It is even ridiculous to get angry at it, for in reality it is not there. It is nothing more than a bad dream, which you can wake up from anytime you like. Remember: "Nothing real can be threatened. Nothing unreal exists. Herein lies the peace of God."

The outcome for all souls in this journey is inevitably a return to the Godhead. When is just a matter of time. Even Hitler will eventually return home. He will have to balance his karma first, but he will return home also. The purpose of my book is to help shorten the time it takes to return home.

We are living in a period of history where what formerly took fourteen years can be done in fourteen months. Never in the history of this planet has there been a greater opportunity for spiritual growth. The key is to commit yourself 100 percent to your spiritual path with all your personal power and concentration. The transformation that will take place will amaze you. Why wait for a future incarnation to do what you can do now?

SIN VERSUS MISTAKES

There are no such things as sins, only mistakes. The true definition of sin is "missing the mark." Please understand that mistakes are positive, not negative. We shouldn't go out of our way to make them, but when they happen, we learn from them. When we make a mistake, we can stop and gain the golden nugget of wisdom, learn the lesson, forgive ourselves, and go forward.

Some religions look at sin as a stain on our character, or attribute some kind of original sin to us. This is ludicrous. We have no sin, for each of us is the Christ, the Eternal Self.

A *Course in Miracles* states, "Forgiveness is the key to happiness." God has already forgiven everything. It is we who need to learn to forgive ourselves and our brothers and sisters. It is important to remember that no one has ever done anything to us, we have allowed it to be done to us. And if it happened, we attracted it or needed it for soul growth.

UNCONDITIONAL LOVE VERSUS CONDITIONAL LOVE

God would always have us practice unconditional love. The rationale for this is that each person, in reality, is the Christ even if their thoughts, feelings, and behavior are not demonstrating that. Jesus said, "Love your enemies." This is one of the true tests and initiations of the spiritual path. It is our lesson to be bigger, to practice innocent perception, to practice forgiveness, for what we give is what we get back. *If we want God, we must give God, otherwise we will not realize Him.*

Everyone is God; however, not everyone realizes God in thought, feeling, and action. Earth is a school to practice realizing God in our daily life. So much of the spiritual path is the small things, like how we treat our neighbor when we walk outside to start our day. Conditional love means that another person must meet some requirement to deserve our love. Ego tells us that we are hurting that person and helping ourselves by doing this. In reality we are hurting both the other person and ourselves.

One of the basic principles of *A Course in Miracles* is to give up our attack thoughts. We are either loving or attacking—there are no neutral thoughts. When we are demonstrating conditional love, we are unconsciously attacking, and the other person experiences that attack on an energetic level. It is like an arrow piercing his aura. If he is weak or a victim, this can affect him quite adversely. We must remember that all minds are joined. Our thoughts are not contained in our physical bodies as though behind a fence. In reality it is quite the opposite. The second we think about another person, whether in a positive or negative way, that thought or feeling hits his energy field.

Conditional love also separates us from God. We are not separated in reality. We are only separated within our own state of consciousness. Always remember that in every situation in life there is an appropriate response and an inappropriate response. How we respond will determine if we realize God or do not realize God in that moment. If we make a mistake, we can stop, gain the golden nugget of wisdom, learn the lesson, forgive ourselves, and choose once again.

By staying vigilant and focused over time, we will develop the habit of being unconditionally loving. In every situation of life we can ask ourselves, "Do I want God or my ego in this situation?" If we sincerely ask ourselves this, who could choose the ego? Practice makes perfect!

TOP DOG/UNDERDOG VERSUS EQUALITY

The negative ego tells us that we are superior to everyone else, inferior to everyone else, or both. This is truly a hellish state of mind to exist in, and it is amazing how many people are unconsciously trapped in the negative ego's game. Spirit says that we all are equals because we all are the Christ. People may be at different levels of demonstrating this truth; however, the "I" in you is the same as the "I" in me.

Whenever we compare ourselves to another person, the negative ego is gripping us. We never want to make comparisons to other people; we want only to compare ourselves to ourselves. If we look at the progress we have made within ourselves only and not against others, it is easy to feel good. Whenever the top dog/underdog dynamic comes up in the mind, do what Fritz Perls, the German psychologist and author of *Ego, Hunger, and Aggression*, who coined these terms, said to do: "Laugh it off the stage."

THE MEANING OF THE CRUCIFIXION

In the text of *A Course in Miracles* Jesus gives a fascinating account of the true meaning of the Crucifixion. What He says is that the Crucifixion was nothing more than an extreme lesson of love and forgiveness. He was not dying for our sins, because we do not have any sins.

What He was demonstrating was that in even the most extreme lessons, in which a person is being beaten, tortured, crucified, and killed, it is possible to remain loving and forgiving. Jesus said, "Forgive them, Father, they know not what they do." He went through this most extreme challenge to prove to us that forgiveness is possible even under the most extreme circumstances. If Jesus the Christ could do it under these circumstances, then certainly we can forgive our mother-in-law, boss, parent, friend, or business partner.

LOVE FINDER OR FAULT FINDER

Spirit would have us see the positive, the good, and the innocent in people. Negative ego as guide and teacher has us seek and see the bad. The ego does this to put other persons down in order to make itself feel good. The spirit's philosophy is a win/win philosophy, not a win/lose philosophy. Why can't we all win? Isn't this a better way to live?

We will see what we look for; we will see where we put our attention. When we see fault and judgment, we are in reality faulting and judging ourselves, for what we see in another is just a mirror of our own state of mind. When we see only God, love, and blessings, that is what we give to ourselves. Whether we see it or not, that is what is there, for that is what God created.

Faulty perception doesn't create truth; it just creates the reality we live in. We can see the glory of what God would have us see. If we see fault, then we are creating separation from ourselves, from God, and our brothers and sisters. Spirit would guide us to remain in a state of oneness at all times, for all is God.

In the New Testament Jesus said, "Judge not, that you not be judged"; "He that has no sin, cast the first stone"; "Don't try to take the speck out of your brother's eye when you have a log in your own eye." The log that Jesus speaks of is the log of ego and the lower self, which so many of us are afflicted with.

All forms of perception, according to A Course in Miracles, are a type of dream. God would guide us, however, to live and experience the happy dream of the Christ consciousness, which is a perfect mirror of the state that Jesus calls knowledge. By living the Christ dream or perception, Jesus says, a translation into pure knowledge will inevitably take place.

TEACHINGS AND LESSONS VERSUS DIFFICULTIES AND PROBLEMS

It is important to realize that everything that happens in life is a teaching, a lesson, a challenge, and an opportunity to grow. Edgar Cayce referred to this when he said that everything that happens is a stepping stone for soul growth.

Paul Solomon, a spiritual leader who channeled the Universal Mind, said that the proper attitude toward everything that happens in life is "Not my will, but thine. Thank you for the lesson." Everything that happens in life is a gift. It wouldn't be coming to us if we didn't have something to learn. Everything that comes to us is our own personal karma and is something that we have set in motion either in this lifetime or in a past lifetime. Our lesson is to welcome it, own our personal power, and deal with it appropriately.

Many spiritual practices teach atonement. Atonement (note that the word contains within it the word one) is the process of undoing the ego and returning it to the oneness of spirit. The Holy Spirit and/or soul serves as our guide, along with the Ascended Masters.

PERSONAL POWER VERSUS POWERLESSNESS

A spiritual Master and God-realized being remains in a state of personal power all the time. Maybe you own your power only in an emergency, or when you have to go to work. If you don't own your power, you give it to other people or to your subconscious mind.

As I've stated before, there are two keys to psychological health. One is to own your personal power, and the second is to practice self-love. If we don't own our power, we can be run by almost anything in the universe. This includes disincarnate spirits, other people, the Dark Brotherhood, ego, thoughts, desires, impulses, physical body, past life karma, and mass consciousness.

It is clearly dangerous not to own one's personal power. Edgar Cayce has said that will or power is the strongest force in this universe. You have heard the saying "An idle mind is the devil's workshop." Most people have consciousness but don't have personal power. The extended use of personal power is self-discipline, which a lot of people don't have, either. You will never progress on the spiritual path without personal power and self-discipline.

Cayce occasionally referred to personal power as positive anger. Anger is ego; however, there is enormous power in anger, which should be channeled into positive anger, or positive personal power. Earth is a difficult school, and we must be very tough in life or we can easily get overwhelmed. We must be like spiritual warriors.

In the Bhagavad Gita, part of the great epic the Mahabharata, Krishna (the Lord Maitreya) and Arjuna, Krishna's disciple, are on the battlefield about to fight the evil enemy's army, when Arjuna comes apart psychologically and falls victim to his negative ego. Arjuna is the head of the army of righteous men, and they are all depending on him. Krishna, Arjuna's charioteer and spiritual Master, begins to lecture Arjuna on the folly of his ways in giving in to his negative ego and losing his power and control over his energies. Krishna is guiding Arjuna into the spiritual mysteries, much as I am attempting to do in this book, when he makes my favorite statement in the entire Bhagavad Gita. Krishna says, after his long speech to Arjuna, "Get up now, and give up your unmanliness. Get up and fight. This self-pity and self-indulgence is unbecoming of the great soul that you are."

Arjuna was awakened by Krishna's spiritual discourse and this statement, and he reclaimed his personal power and led his men victoriously into battle. Krishna's statement applies to each and every one of us in our daily lives.

TO HAVE ALL AND GIVE ALL TO ALL

To have all and give all to all is a message of A *Course of Miracles*, for what we have is what we give. What we are holding back from our brother is what we are holding back from God and ourselves. To have all we must give all, for in reality we already are and already have everything. We have always been this and always will be this. It is only our belief in the ego as our guide and teacher that has made us believe otherwise.

ONLY TWO EMOTIONS

The Course teaches that there are only two emotions, love and fear. All other emotions return to this basic core. Fear is of the ego, and love is of the spirit. When we indulge in attack thoughts, then by the law of karma we operate within our own minds and live in fear. If we attack, we will be fearful, because we will expect other people to attack us, which makes us afraid. If we live in love, then by the law of karma we will expect love in return, and have nothing to fear.

The Course teaches that when we are attacked, it is really a call for love. We need to see beyond or through the attack to the fact that the person who is attacking us is really living in fear. Fear is an indicator of a lack of love—both a lack of self-love and a lack of allowing our-selves to experience God's love. As the Bible says, "Perfect love casts out fear."

THE PAST AND FUTURE VERSUS THE ETERNAL NOW

One of the profound realizations I had in studying A *Course in Mira-cles* was understanding what the past and future really are. Think about the past. What is it? It is a memory. What is a memory? A memory is an image in our minds. What is an image? An image is a thought. So what this means is that the past is totally under our control, for it is nothing more than images or thoughts in our minds.

The same applies to the future. The future is nothing more than thoughts and images in our minds. They are of a positive or negative nature, which determines whether we are worried or excited about it. This means that our future is totally under our control.

All that really exists is the now. We no longer have to be victimized by our past or by a worrisome future because it is all within our own mind. The proper attitude toward the past is to gain the golden nuggets of wisdom from the mistakes and from what we have done well, bring forth the positive memories we choose to keep, and release the rest.

In terms of the future, the proper perspective is to create a plan for the future that serves us, and then leave the rest to God. Edgar Cayce said, "Why worry when we can pray?" I would add to this and say, "Why worry when we can pray, own our personal power, and do affirmations and visualizations to attract everything we need?"

In this holy instant I am the Christ and you are the Christ. We are one with each other, and we are one with God. Remember this: the fall never really happened; we just thought it did. We have and are everything, for we are God. The prodigal son and daughter have returned home, for God never took anything away. We are and always have been as God created us, perfect Christs. He has just been waiting for us to reclaim our inheritance, which has always been our own.

THE TWO MOST IMPORTANT RELATIONSHIPS

The two most important relationships in our lives are our relationship to self and our relationship to God. In actuality, our relationship to self is even more important than our relationship to God. If we are wrong with ourselves and allow ourselves to be run by ego, then we will project this wrong relationship to self onto everything in our lives, including our relationship to God.

This lack of a right relationship with self is the cause of the angry Old Testament God. It is also the cause of concepts such as original sin, the idea that we are lowly, sinful worms, and the judgmental and self-righteous qualities of some fundamentalist religions. This is what happens when the negative ego is allowed to interpret scripture. It is like the game of telephone, played for over two thousand years. The Masters, such as Jesus, Mohammed, and Moses, said one thing, and over the course of the next two thousand years, their disciples (who were not at their level) have completely distorted what they said originally. There is no judgment in this; it is just a simple statement of fact.

ATTACHMENT VERSUS PREFERENCE

The negative ego causes us to become attached to everything. As the Buddha said, "All suffering comes from our attachments." What He is saying is that if we give up all our attachments, we no longer have to experience suffering at all. It isn't anything external that causes the suffering; it is our attachment and addiction to outside things that causes our suffering.

Spirit guides us to have preferences rather than attachments. An attachment is an attitude that causes us to get depressed or angry or upset if our expectations aren't met. A preference is an attitude that lets us be happy no matter the outcome. I prefer to go to the movies, but if that doesn't work out, I will be happy to stay home. This is a profound concept. If we release our attachments, we will find instantaneous peace of mind.

Some spiritual people believe that they are not allowed to have preferences. I would say that this is a faulty belief on their part. It is very important in life that we have our preferences and that we go after our preferences with all our heart and soul and mind and might. However, if they don't come about, it is important to prepare to be happy anyway. By doing this, happiness becomes a state of mind rather than a condition outside of self. The happiness that so many of us are seeking lies in developing a certain perspective toward life. We are born with it, but the negative ego programming blocks the awareness of our natural state, which is joy.

THE TRANSCENDENCE OF DUALITY

One of the basic teachings of all Eastern religions is the transcendence of duality. Duality could be another way to describe negative ego. It also means believing that our reality offers us only an either/or option.

The ideal is to maintain even-mindedness regardless of profit or loss, pleasure or pain, sickness or health, victory or defeat, praise or criticism, good weather or bad weather. Again, it is fine to have a preference, but if it isn't realized, we can still have joy and inner peace.

THE JOB INITIATION

The Job initiation is a test everyone goes through at some point in their spiritual journey. It is really the ultimate test of our spiritual faith and righteousness in God.

Job was a righteous man of God who had a family and children, a big ranch, and material wealth. One day Satan came to God and said, "Sure, Job is a righteous man. You have given him everything. Take away his wealth and let's see if he remains so righteous." God said, "I have confidence in Job. Take away his wealth." Satan did so, and to Satan's consternation, Job remained righteous.

Then Satan sheepishly came back to God and said, "I am impressed! However, let's take away his wife and children and see if he remains so righteous." God said, "So be it." Job's wife and children left him. Amazingly enough, Job remained righteous. Satan was astounded now. He returned to God and said, "Let me try one more test. If he passes this, I will give up and declare that you were right all along. For this final test let me take away his physical health." God said, "Okay, you can take away his physical health, but you can't kill him." Satan agreed, and took Job's health away. He had terrible boils and was tired. He didn't feel well at all. This was the straw that broke the camel's back for Job, and he completely lost his righteousness. He became angry and bitter and depressed. His friends tried to cheer him up, but he would have none of it. Job's attitude was that he was a righteous man of God and a good person, and look at the trials and tribulations he was going through. This state of affairs lasted for a number of years.

One day, in a quiet moment, a whirlwind of light came to Job and entered his crown chakra. Through this God spoke to Job and shared with him that this had all been a test of character, virtue, and righteousness in God. He explained that anyone can believe in and worship God when things are going well, but how about when things are not going well and all outer supports have been stripped away?

Job heard the truth of what God was saying, just as Arjuna had been awakened by Krishna in the story related in the Bhagavad Gita. Then Job made one of the most moving statements in the entire Bible:

> Naked I came from my mother's womb,
> Naked shall I leave,
> The Lord gives and the Lord takes away,
> Blessed be the name of the Lord!

Job had regained his righteousness. His health returned. His wife and children returned. His wealth returned increased by a hundred-fold. Job went on to say, "Even if I should die, I will remain righteous in the Lord."

The meaning of this story is quite obvious. Many of you reading this book have gone through some form of the Job initiation. Remember, too, what Jesus went through. Never forget that what happens to you in life is a spiritual test of your character and righteousness in the Lord.

No matter what your situation, I challenge you to keep your faith and righteousness, whether you face health challenges, money challenges, a death, the end of a relationship, or mental or emotional problems. Hold on to your personal power and your ideals and your faith, for did not Jesus say, "Be faithful unto death and I will give you a crown of life"?

OPTIMISM VERSUS PESSIMISM

The spiritual attitude toward life is to remain optimistic at all times. You can take a person with a good attitude and put him in the worst situation and he may be disheartened for a little while, but he is going to become happy again. On the other side of the coin, if you take someone with a bad attitude and put him in the best outer situation possible, he will be happy for a little while, but he will soon feel despair again.

Part of the purpose of life is to spread joy and happiness. Sickness can be contagious if people are victims and have low resistance. Since so many people live in a victim consciousness, why not "victimize" them into joy and happiness? The purpose of life is to spread joy, happiness, love, goodwill, and blessings everywhere you go so that when you leave the world, it will be a better place for your having been here.

THE EGO'S PURPOSE VERSUS THE SPIRIT'S PURPOSE

The negative ego's purpose in life is essentially hedonistic—it seeks pleasure, gratification of carnal desires, power in a top-dog sense, material wealth, and control over others rather than control over self. The spirit's answer to this is the biblical statement "For what profit is it to a man if he gains the whole world, and loses his own soul?" (Matthew 16:26).

The spiritual purpose of life is to achieve liberation from the cycle of rebirth, to realize God, to become an Ascended Master, and to be of service to humankind. Did not Jesus say, "The greatest among you is the servant of all"? The spiritual purpose in life is also to be happy and to enjoy oneself, in balance with our spiritual growth.

A *Course in Miracles* states that true pleasure is serving God. I know that this is true for me. As long as I am serving God, I am happy. To me everything is serving God, as long as I do whatever I do with the intention of manifesting my spark of God's divinity.

POVERTY CONSCIOUSNESS VERSUS PROSPERITY CONSCIOUSNESS

The negative ego's interpretation of life is that we never have enough. The negative ego also teaches both that money is the root of all evil and the contradictory premise that money is the answer to all our problems. The negative ego is quite hateful by nature, so it sends a message making us feel guilty about, and undeserving of, our prosperity. In contrast, spirit sees the universe as abundant, with plenty for everybody and no need for negative competition.

Spirit's attitude is that you can be the richest person in the world and the most spiritual simultaneously. Money, in and of itself, is divine. It is how you use it that determines whether it is good or bad. Spirit guides people to love money and to make as much as possible, so that it can be used to make physical changes in the earthly world for a spiritual purpose.

The more money you have, the more you can give to charities; you can start more spiritual centers and institutions. If you have prosperity consciousness, you know you can get a job or manifest a business and opportunities whenever and wherever needed. There are also millionaires who have a total poverty consciousness and risk losing their prosperity because of it.

Who is more prosperous, a woman who lives in the ghetto with seven children and has total faith in God to provide her with everything she truly needs, or a stingy multimillionaire who worries about money constantly and makes a habit of stabbing clients and competitors in the back? Millionaires who have prosperity consciousness might talk about losing all their wealth, but they don't worry about it because they know that they could earn it all back again.

You are prosperous when you truly know that God, your personal power, and the power of your subconscious mind are your true source of financial security. Who cannot find a job or make money even during a recession when God, the creator of the infinite universe, is helping you and when you are helping yourself with your full personal power and the power of your subconscious mind?

Can God and the Christ, who is you, not win every battle? As the Bible says, "If God is for you, who can be against you?" "I can do all things with God and Christ, who strengthen me." With this power and faith you can manifest whatever it is you need. You are prosperous because your power is in God and you can apply God's laws for your benefit.

DEATH VERSUS ETERNAL LIFE

The negative ego believes in death because it believes you are your physical body rather than the soul inhabitating the physical body. The negative ego is right about one thing, and that is that the physical body will die. But you are *not* that physical body; you are the Christ and the Eternal Self residing in the physical body.

The physical body is your temple and instrument for you to communicate with on this earthly plane. When you are done with it, you will immediately translate into another dimension of reality. What dimension you translate to will be determined by how much soul growth you achieve in this lifetime. Death is an illusion, just as everything the negative ego says is an illusion.

ANGER AND DEPRESSION VERSUS PEACE OF MIND

Anger stems from the negative ego's interpretation of life. In my experience, it is usually caused by one of four attitudes. The first faulty attitude that causes anger and depression is attachment. When your attachment isn't met, you feel upset and angry. Second, anger and depression are caused by not looking at what is happening to you as a lesson, teaching, gift, and spiritual test. Third, people get angry and depressed when they don't have their bubble of protection up and hence allow another person's negative energy to victimize them. The fourth cause of anger and depression is based on something I learned from Paul Solomon, who defined anger as a loss of control and the attempt to regain it. Whenever you lose your personal power and mastery over yourself, you fall into what I call an underdog or victimized state of consciousness, because you have listened to the voice of your negative ego. Your negative ego will then switch from the underdog position back into the top dog (or anger) spot to get back into control.

As I have already mentioned, there is a lot of power in anger and ideally, instead of blocking this angry energy, it should be channeled into personal power and beneficial activities. When this is done properly, it is called positive anger.

Depression is the state of consciousness in which you surrender your will. Whenever you give up in life, you court depression. Of all the negative attitudes of the ego, giving up is probably the most dangerous. If you give in to this evil game of the ego, all defenses of the conscious mind are laid down and the ego is able to gain total control.

You must have spiritual tenacity and be what Cayce called "longsuffering," if necessary. There is no need to suffer endlessly in life, however; if you are suffering, keep praying and affirming and visualizing what you want. Keep powering it out and seeking an answer. Doesn't the Bible say, "Seek and ye shall find. Knock and the door shall be opened"? God helps those who help themselves. God will do His part; however, we must do our part. Together God, our personal power, and the power of the subconscious mind are an unbeatable team.

The most important thing in life is never to give up. As the I Ching constantly says, "Perseverance furthers success."

GRATITUDE VERSUS TAKING LIFE FOR GRANTED

The negative ego's attitude is to take people and life for granted. The spiritual attitude is constant gratitude and thanksgiving. The spiritual attitude is humility. It can be summed up in the biblical statement "There but for the grace of God go I."

The Bible also says, "Pride comes before disaster and arrogance before a fall." (Proverbs 16:18). You have so much to be grateful for every day. All you have to do is watch the news and see all the terrible things that are going on around the world and see how incredibly blessed you are.

If you currently have handicaps and limitations, the spiritual attitude is to focus on what you can do instead of what you can't do. I have always been moved by Saint Francis, who apparently had terrible physical health problems he had to overcome, and yet he became one of the most revered Christian saints.

Mother Teresa had terrible heart problems and yet she spent her life serving and helping others. Every person on the planet has a weak spot of some kind. For some it is physical, for some emotional, for others mental or spiritual. You are here to valiantly try to overcome these challenges and be grateful for the grace God has bestowed upon you. Remember, even the bad things that happen are really gifts and spiritual tests—blessings in disguise.

God will never give you more than you can handle. Change your attitude; welcome your lessons and challenges with a smile and with strength. When a challenge comes, make yourself bigger than it instead of allowing yourself to grow smaller. Thank God for it and pray for His help in overcoming it.

REJECTION VERSUS NOT MEANT TO BE

The negative ego can't conceive of blessings in disguise. It will have you interpret the end of a friendship or relationship as one person winning and one person losing. Consequently, there must be a rejecter and a rejected. This is not the spiritual interpretation. There are no winners and losers, only winners. If a relationship ends, the spiritual attitude is just that it is not meant to be any longer, and you both leave winners in forgiveness and unconditional love.

GUILT VERSUS INNOCENCE

The negative ego tries to make you feel guilty for your mistakes, or sins, as it tries to call them. The spiritual attitude to take is that you are instantly forgiven. There is no need to hold the past against yourself in punishment. There is no need to punish yourself. The idea is just to recognize that you made a mistake and learn from it. The spiritual attitude states that you are always innocent. The Course suggests that when you make a mistake of some consequence, pray to the Holy Spirit and/or your soul or God to undo the consequences and results of that mistake.

PERSONAL SURRENDER VERSUS OWNING PERSONAL POWER AND SURRENDERING SIMULTANEOUSLY

The negative ego's attitude is to either own the power and control and never surrender to God or to totally surrender to God, avoiding all responsibility and ownership of power. The spiritual attitude is to own one's power and to surrender simultaneously. It is imperative to own your power, otherwise you are going to be overwhelmed by the subconscious mind. It is also essential to surrender to God and the soul as our teacher.

In doing both simultaneously, the three minds begin to function as one mind in perfect integration and harmony.

NEGATIVE EGO SENSITIVITY VERSUS A CENTERED SPIRITUAL ATTITUDE

Negative ego sensitivity is a tendency to feel hurt, rejected, put down, or inferior at times when there is no discernible reason to be experiencing these feelings. It occurs because of a person's lack of personal power, lack of self-love, absence of a bubble of protection, and not having a right relationship with self and with God.

When you are run by your negative ego, you tend to project motives onto others that are not really there. A good example of this is the life of Jesus Christ. All He did was love and heal people, yet so many wanted to crucify and kill Him. Their negative egos interpreted Jesus' acts as attacks when in reality that was not the case. Jesus was the embodiment of love. But their victim consciousness caused them to feel put down or defensive, and they attacked Him.

You know people like this—people who get defensive or hurt or feel put down even when no one has done anything to them. Such a person needs to be treated with extra love and tact until his or her self-concept can be rebuilt on a sturdier foundation.

It is important to realize that when you are centered, you can't be hurt, because you let the other person's attack slide off your bubble. You respond instead of react. You are more detached. You don't let other people cause your emotions, just as you wouldn't drink poison if someone gave it to you. The same is true psychologically. You don't take the mental or emotional poison into your system.

You still may communicate your feelings to the other person; however, you do it as an observation rather than a lashing out. You don't want to let other people be the programmers of your emotions. You want to be the programmer of your own emotions.

No one can make you think, feel, or behave in any way you don't choose to. You are not an effect, you are a cause. You are not a victim, you are a master and a cocreator with God. You can simply decide to feel good, and since your thoughts create your feelings and emotions, you immediately feel good.

Since it is your thoughts that create your reality, why would you want to create anything but joy, happiness, unconditional life, and inner peace? When you think with your Christ mind as opposed to your ego mind, this is exactly what happens.

SECURITY VERSUS INSECURITY

The negative ego creates insecurity because it teaches you to find your security outside of yourself in other people, possessions, houses, money, and so on. The only true security that cannot be taken away from you is security that is grounded in your personal power, in God, in the power of your subconscious mind, and in God's laws.

LONELINESS VERSUS BEING ALONE

The negative ego causes you to feel loneliness because it has you seek your wholeness in another person rather than find your wholeness within yourself and in your relationship to God. You are never really lonely when you are in your spiritual attitude, because you are whole within your self and one with God.

You will never be lonely if you are in proper relationship to your child consciousness. This proper relationship means the child within is given the most beneficial ratio of firmness and love. As a result, the child feels loved and protected. Loneliness is a sign you have fallen into the underdog state of consciousness and are seeking to fill this space with another person instead of with self and God, which is what is really needed.

The same thing is true regarding feelings of abandonment. If you are whole within self and one with God, and if your child consciousness is taken care of before you bond with another person, then the feeling of abandonment won't be there if the other person leaves.

Jealousy occurs when you form a bond with another person because of your lack of wholeness and right relationship to self and God. You then struggle with a known or unknown competitor. The spiritual attitude is to state your preference in your relationship and surrender it to God. If it is meant to be, it will happen; if not, it was not meant to be.

Also, when you bond with another person from the state of consciousness of being right with self and right with God, issues of cheating and infidelity and commitment cannot arise in the same way because of the integrity of the individuals involved. If they do, it probably means you are with the wrong individual, for he or she doesn't experience the sanctity of the bond you have.

The following chart presents the Psychological Centering Model of soul psychology. In the very center of the chart is the Centered Spiritual Self. Radiating out from the Centered Spiritual Self like the rays of the sun are all the Christ-like or spiritual or buddhic qualities. Above the Centered Spiritual Self are the top dog and superior qualities of the ego. Below the Centered Spiritual Self are the underdog, inferior, victim qualities. Meditating upon your daily life experiences and observing where you are polarized into these positions will help you shift your consciousness and behavior.

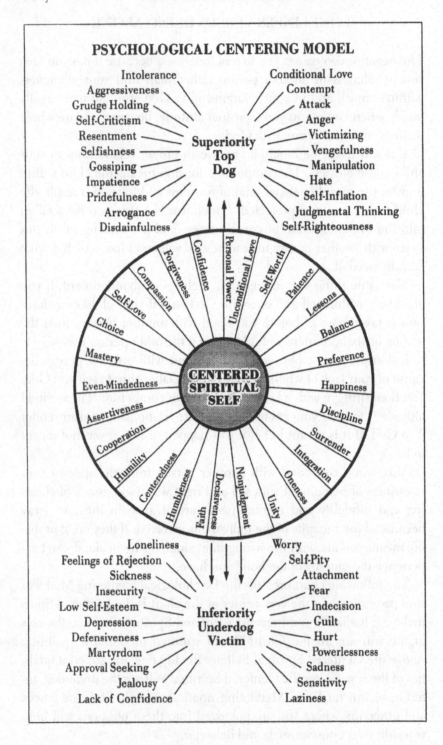

PSYCHOLOGICAL CENTERING MODEL

Intolerance
Aggressiveness
Grudge Holding
Self-Criticism
Resentment
Selfishness
Gossiping
Impatience
Pridefulness
Arrogance
Disdainfulness

Conditional Love
Contempt
Attack
Anger
Victimizing
Vengefulness
Manipulation
Hate
Self-Inflation
Judgmental Thinking
Self-Righteousness

Superiority
Top
Dog

Confidence
Forgiveness
Compassion
Self-Love
Choice
Mastery
Even-Mindedness
Assertiveness
Cooperation
Humility
Centeredness
Humbleness
Faith
Decisiveness
Nonjudgment
Unity
Oneness
Integration
Surrender
Discipline
Happiness
Preference
Balance
Lessons
Patience
Self-Worth
Unconditional Love
Personal Power

CENTERED
SPIRITUAL
SELF

Loneliness
Feelings of Rejection
Sickness
Insecurity
Low Self-Esteem
Depression
Defensiveness
Martyrdom
Approval Seeking
Jealousy
Lack of Confidence

Worry
Self-Pity
Attachment
Fear
Indecision
Guilt
Hurt
Powerlessness
Sadness
Sensitivity
Laziness

Inferiority
Underdog
Victim

Whenever the negative ego has been triggered, the following list of all of the spiritually centered attitudes and qualities, counterposed with the negative ego's attitudes and qualities, will prove to be a very helpful set of checks and balances.

Negative Ego's Attitude	Spiritually Centered Attitude
Attack . . . Fear	Love
Selfish	Selfish-Selfless Balance
Holds Grudge	Forgiveness
Top Dog/Underdog	Equality
Competition	Cooperation
Judgment	Spiritual Discernment
Guilt	Innocence
Self-Righteousness	Personal Opinion
Fights Universe	Teaching/Lessons/Challenges
Pessimistic	Opportunity to Grow/Optimistic
Insecurity/Self-Doubt	Self-Confidence
Powerless/Loss of Control	Personal Power/Self Mastery
Anger/Depression	Lessons/Emotional Invulnerability
Attack/Defensive or Hurt	Love
Neediness, Dependency	Preference/Want
Victim/Effect	Master/Cause/Chooser/Creator
Self-Pity	Takes Responsibility
War	School
Learns karmically,	*Grows by state of grace*
through hard knocks	*the easy way*
Subconsciously Run	Consciously Run
Impatient	Patient
Suffering	Joyous and Happy
Reacts	Responds
Vulnerable	Invulnerable Emotionally
Sin	Mistakes
Attachment	Involved Detachment
Laziness/Procrastination	Discipline
Jealous	Whole and Complete/Nonattached
Law of the Jungle	What You Sow, You Reap
Demands	Asks
Moody/Bad Moods	Good Mood All the Time
Self-Punishment	Self-Love and Forgiveness

Negative Ego's Attitude	Spiritually Centered Attitude
Mistakes/Negative	Mistakes/Positive
Lamp Shade over Light	Light
Ego Sensitivity	Unchanging Self-Worth
Must Prove Self to Obtain Worth	Worth/Spiritual Inheritance
Mud on Diamond	Diamond
Giving Is Losing	Giving Is Winning.
Stealing Is Gaining	Stealing Is Losing
Rejection	Remaining Centered/Whole: (Knowing it was not meant to be!)
Self-Centered	One Team
Intimidation	Uses Power Appropriately
Automatic Pilot	Consciously Creating Life
Overindulgent and Underindulgent	Balance/Integration/Moderation
Run by Thoughts of Past and Fears of Future	Now/Present-Centered
Lonely	Finds Wholeness in Self
Strangers	Brothers and Sisters
Embarrassment	No Judgment
Gossip	Remain Quiet if You Have a Judgment
Seeks Approval or Control What Other People Think	States Preference and Accepts Inner-Directed, Nonconformist
Worry/Anxiety	Faith/Trust in Self, Higher Power, and Laws of Universe
Indecisive	Decisive
Envy	Happiness and Joy in Another's Abundance
Attached to Other People's Lessons	Responsible Only for Your Own Lessons
Comparisons	Not Insecure, Inner-Directed
Undeserving	Deserving
Sickness	Perfect Health
Sexuality (with No Feeling or Emotion of Love)	Sexuality (Love, Caring, Intimacy, and Pleasure)
Poverty Consciousness	Prosperity Consciousness

Negative Ego's Attitude	Spiritually Centered Attitude
Arrogant and Prideful	Humble and Grateful
Sullen, Serious, Overinvolved	Humor, Objectivity, Perspective
Fault Finder	Builder and Lifter of Others
Rebellious or Conformist	Inner-Directed
Curses	Blesses
Scattered	Focused, Purposeful
Fear of Failure or Success	Successful
Aggressive	Assertive
Harsh	Gentle
Emotional Roller Coaster	Emotional Stability
Disorganized	Organized
Bored	Not Enough Time in the Day
Abandonment	Whole, Complete Within Self
Sadness and Grief	Involved Detachment (Not Meant to Be)
Disappointment	Involved Detachment
Rationales and Excuses	Self-Honest/Tough Love
Immature Honesty	Spiritual Honesty
Folds up Under Tension/Lesson	Carries Tension or Lesson
Needs Center Stage or Hides in Fear	Center Stage, Neutral, Backstage at Appropriate Time
Conditional Love	Unconditional Love
Inappopriate Response	Appropriate Response
Rejecting	Accepting
Lessons as Punishment	Lessons as Gifts
War Zone, Dog-Eat-Dog World	School for Spiritual Evolution
Total Power, No Surrender, or Total Surrender, No Power	Power Plus Surrender
Limited	Unlimited or Limitless
Intolerant	Tolerant
Conflict	Peace
Illusions	Truth
Hypocritical	Honest/Consistent
Despair	Hope
Closed-Minded	Open-Minded
Distrustful	Trust and Faith in Self and Others
Defensive	Defenseless, Nothing to Defend

Part II

How to Spiritualize the Negative Ego

Chapter 6

✳

Tools for Healing the Emotions

There are only two emotions, love and fear.
Choose whom ye shall serve.
—A COURSE IN MIRACLES

Y̲ou have the ability to choose the way you feel because your thoughts and attitudes cause your feelings and emotions. The following six-step process is designed to help focus your choice more clearly. This process will be especially helpful when you feel like your buttons are being pushed in a relationship or circumstance in life and you are having difficulty figuring out the reason.

SIX-STEP PROCESS FOR
SPIRITUALIZING YOUR EMOTIONS

Step 1: Write down either the details of the incident or the exact behavior of the other person with whom you were dealing. For example, maybe the incident was a traffic jam on the freeway, or your mate became angry with you. The first step is just to write down objectively what has happened.

Step 2: Write down your response to either the incident or the other person. For example, your response to the traffic jam might have been impatience and annoyance. Your response to your mate might have been defensiveness and anger. This step is just to write down objectively how you responded, regardless of whether that response was appropriate or not.

Step 3: This is the key step. Choose to look at the incident or the other person's behavior as being your master teacher, instructing you on a lesson that you need to learn. Imagine that the incident or person is an instrument that God is using to teach you a lesson and give you an opportunity to grow spiritually. Your negative response stems from the fact that you are not looking at the situation as a teaching, lesson, challenge, and opportunity to grow. The traffic jam is your master teacher. Your mate's anger is your master teacher.

Step 4: Make a list of all the psychological and spiritual qualities that you are being given the opportunity to learn. In the example of the traffic jam, you are being taught patience; or preference rather than attachment; or how to look at things as lessons; or surrender. Perhaps the first thing you are being taught with people is an example of how not to be. Some people set good examples and some set bad examples. You can learn from both. You know how it feels to be on the other end of someone's anger and attack, so that teaches you not to be that way.

Possible Lessons

- To own your own personal power
- To be the cause of your own emotions and not let your mate cause your emotions
- Not to let your mate put you into the underdog position
- To respond instead of react
- To be a master instead of a victim
- To learn when to talk and when to be silent
- Forgiveness
- Nonattachment
- Transcendence of ego
- To maintain the right relationship to self and relationship to God—the two most important relationships in your life

You'll find that many of your life lessons repeat themselves over and over again.

Step 5: After listing all the wonderful lessons and wisdom you have learned, then bless or thank the other person in your mind, or in person, for giving you the opportunity to learn these lessons. Make a firm resolution that when you are again tested in the following day, week, or month, you are going to be mentally strong and prepared to respond appropriately. Realize that you will indeed be tested again, either with the same person or incident or with a new person and new incident, until you master the lesson.

Step 6: Review your "Spiritualizing Negative Emotions" work on a weekly and monthly basis. Use the six-step process for mastering your emotions anytime you get into a sticky emotional situation. By using this process and doing it on paper, you will see more clearly what is happening. Evaluate the amount of time and energy it now takes you to "learn your lessons." Remember that if you truly learn from this experience, you will never again have to experience those negative feelings.

IDENTIFICATION WITH NEGATIVE EMOTIONS AND CATHARSIS: THE YIN APPROACH

The above mentioned six-step process for mastering emotions and our previous discussion of attitudinal healing both can be referred to as the masculine, or yang, method for dealing with one's feelings and emotions. Ultimately, the purpose of this method is to disidentify with the emotion. This is the opposite of the feminine, or yin, method, in which the purpose is to identify with the emotions.

Certainly we want to identify with our spiritualized feelings and emotions of love and joy and happiness on a continual basis, but I also believe that there is an appropriate time to identify with and express negative feelings as well.

Most of us naturally want to identify with our spiritualized feelings and emotions of love and joy and happiness on a continual basis. But we must not forget that there are times when we need to identify with and express our negative feelings as well. The problem is that few of us know how to do this in an appropriate manner. I'd like to offer you several ways to express these feelings effectively without hurting ourselves or others.

Dealing with emotions is like dealing with our potential to walk on water—even though we know we have no limits, actually doing it is a different story. We may know the ideal way to think, but when our feelings are involved, putting this into practice takes as much work and self-discipline as getting the physical body fit and cleared of toxins.

During crisis periods in our life, a lot of fear-based, egotistical emotions arise. How do we handle these feelings? The first thing to do is to work on your attitude and to begin your healing process through the six steps to mastering emotions. This will definitely help.

But what do we do when a lot of negative emotions are still coming up? That's when it's time for the variations of the Yin Approach. Choose whichever feels the most effective to you at any given time.

Yin Self-Control Method

This is probably the best method to use when you're in public and you're brimful of negative emotions.

• Let's say you're at work, or in the bank, or grocery store, and someone has just said something devastating or infuriating to you. It's just not appropriate to burst out crying or tear into a screaming rage. The best thing in this case is to own your own power, to show self-control, and to *temporarily* put your negative emotions on the shelf until you can find a more appropriate moment to deal with them.

• This doesn't mean bury them deep inside your subconscious and abandon them. That only allows them to act out inappropriately when you least expect it. The self-control method is temporary, until you have the appropriate time and space to try one of the following yin approaches.

Yin Acceptance Method

This is a variant of the self-control approach, but a more permanent one, that leads to balance and detachment. Mastering it means we are no longer living lives filled with emotional pain.

• In this approach we decide to consciously carry the tension of the negative feelings we're experiencing. We accept that they're there, but we don't surrender our conscious power to them.

• The first thing we need to do is to remember that emotional healing, like physical healing, is a process—it takes time. We wouldn't expect to run on a broken leg, but we have to continue functioning in our lives. We can't expect to heal a broken heart or a lifetime of emotional pain and negative feelings in a week, but we have to continue to function effectively.

• To do this, we need to give ourselves time and space and loving consideration while our subconscious, conscious, and superconscious minds come together into emotional alignment, a step at a time, a day at a time. We need to suspend self-judgment and attachment, and expectations of perfection, and simply allow ourselves to heal. Not doing this means attracting heavier and heavier lessons. But releasing ourselves into the healing process brings a succession of unexpected and encouraging rewards.

• For example, what if you've had stage fright all your life, but you have a major public speech to give next week and you're feeling nervous and anxious. No matter how hard you try, you can't seem to get rid of the fear. You have a choice:

—You could run yourself ragged worrying about it, and give a poor performance. Or . . .

—You could simply accept that the negative feelings are there, and tell the fear that you're not going to let it knock you off center and let it ruin your speech. You can take the tension right up on stage with you, but give your speech beautifully in spite of it.

—As with physical pain, the secret is to accept it, and stop fighting it, *but* not give your power away to it and let it ruin your life.

Yin Catharsis Method

This is a whole other approach to dealing with negative emotions. Instead of accepting them and overriding them, you release your emotions and get them out of you once and for all. However, you're doing it in a safe place and time, and not harming yourself, your children, your mate, your parents, friends, or coworkers.

• You're still hopping mad or emotionally devastated, but you're no longer in a public place. You're at home, or in your car in the parking lot or driveway (this isn't recommended while you're actually driving), or some other safe place. Now it's time to totally let go and express exactly how you're feeling.

• Let it all out. Scream, yell, rage, cry your heart out, take a bat and smash the pillows on your bed, hit a punching bag.

• The best thing about a catharsis is that it leaves you feeling cleansed and empty in a healthy way. Very often, it also brings transformation, insight, and understanding. This is an excellent time for some journal work.

When you're rested, tears dried, breathing back to normal, sit down and write about what you feel and think about what happened—what brought it on, how you felt letting it out, how you feel now. With the dark clouds released, the light will now be shining much more clearly—inner revelations will come easily. It's an excellent time to do some deep attitudinal healing and reprogramming.

Yin Indulgence Method

This is a variation on the catharsis approach.

• Decide how long you want to indulge yourself completely in your negative emotions, and set your kitchen timer. For example, say you're really feeling sorry for yourself and you've tried all the various yang methods of disidentifying with the emotion.

• Go the opposite route. Give yourself thirty minutes on the timer to totally wallow in self-pity. Go for it! Scream, cry, get into a rage—really overindulge. Get it all out. And when the timer goes off—STOP. Blow your nose, blot your tears, calm your breathing. Maybe take a hot bath with epsom salts and baking soda to wash away all the residue. And be about God's business again.

• You've used this method before—we all have. How about when you're just about to start a diet and you decide to indulge in all the goodies you know you shouldn't eat and you're just about to give up. One last bout of total self-indulgence. Then you say: "Tomorrow morning I'm going to bite the bullet and start that diet." The important thing is not to let a negative mood drag on without doing something about it.

Yin Secondary Communication Method

This is a deeper method of dealing with the negative emotions that come up when we're dealing with relationships. Ideally, we'd choose the primary communication method—speaking with each other, but not from the negative ego. This can often be accomplished after we've had some time alone to center ourselves and put things into their proper perspective—a time to get right with ourselves and God.

But often there isn't time to resolve all the negative feelings we're experiencing, and that's where the secondary communication method is very effective.

• The secondary communication method is when the two of you agree to share your negative egotistical with each other in a responsible, calm, rational, loving manner. In other words, you share your hurts or resentments in a loving way.

• Start by telling your partner that you realize you create your own feelings and emotions, and that you're taking responsibility for your own reality. But that you really need to express how you're feeling at this time, and you're going to do it in a loving manner, not attacking, taking care not to make your partner feel threatened in any way. And that your partner is welcome to respond in the same manner.

• Tell your partner that you're sharing these negative feelings in the hope that together you can help each other to achieve clarity within yourselves and the relationship. And ask for his or her help in the healing process.

• This is a very useful approach when you find that you've gotten stuck working alone in your journal. Often you'll find that your partner will bring a fresh approach to a stuck place or an old problem and be able to help you sort through your attitudes and feelings. And your partner will very likely be impressed that you're taking responsibility for your own feelings and not blaming him or her.

There are a lot of people who think that their feelings and emotions are God's gift to mankind. They also think the proper way to live is to do whatever their feelings lead them to do. These people are irresponsible. Our feelings stem from our attitudes. If our attitudes are egotistical, then all our emotions are going to be egotistical, based on fear and attack. If we run your lives solely according to our feelings, what happens if we feel like punching someone out, or stealing something or cursing at someone? Is this a responsible way to live? Is this how God would have us live on this earth? Don't be seduced by this false philosophy.

We can trust our feelings once we disidentify from the ego and get the mind under control. Then our feelings will be a perfect guide. It is very important for us to guide our lives by our mind and intuition, which are the guidance of the higher self.

Writing a Letter to Your Subconscious Mind

Another helpful tool for dealing with your emotions is to directly repro-gram your subconscious mind by writing it a firm, tough-love letter. The subconscious mind will be a great servant, as long as you are in com-mand and you treat it with love. Let it know that you are the master of the personality, and that this is the way you're going to conduct operations from this point forward. A letter is a more fluid approach than repeating specifically designed affirmations—a method that I use and find ex-tremely beneficial.

• Pick a quiet time when you can commune with yourself without anyone else around, let the answering machine pick up your calls for awhile. Sit down at your computer, or in your sacred space with your journal and pen.

• Think about just what it is you want to program into your subcon-scious, because it will definitely pay attention. Think about how you want to work this new approach you wish to take in your life. You can write a draft or two, or just say it straight out.

• For example, say you want to work on your fatal attraction to sugar and sweet foods. You might say:

Dear Subconscious Mind:

Please give me your attention, and your loving help in resolving this problem. From this point on we're going to avoid sweet foods. No more candy, cookies, cake, ice cream—all that stuff that fills us with nega-tivity and sugar blues. Instead, we're going to find positive, healthy, life-enhancing ways of rewarding ourselves and reinforcing our resolve.

Whenever we're feeling down and reach out a hand to grab a sweet, we're going to stop and remember that this will only make us feel worse. Then we're going to choose something healthy to eat. Or we're going to take a bubble bath, or go to a movie, or take a walk in beautiful sur-roundings, or hang out with a friend, or play tennis, or jog, or work out at the gym.

I'm serious about this, subconscious mind. I expect you to remind me each time we falter and start to slip back into our old negative ways. I may complain, but I know and you know it's the best thing we could do for ourselves.

Thank you very much for your help,

[Signed and dated . . .]

• Another example for a deeper issue might be:

Dear Subconscious Mind,

I deeply and truly need your help in turning our life around. From this minute on, you're going to help me become aware of every negative thought I have, and every negative twist I put on events and situations and what other people say to me.

Together, we're going to move through each instance of negativity and find a positive way of looking at our relationships and the things that happen in our life. We're going to look for the deeper meanings and lessons in words and events, and we're going to act positively on our own behalf.

We're not going to blame others. We're not going to sink into a pit of despond and give up on life. We're going to take charge of our life, and find a whole new way of seeing, and being, and doing.

Please accept my deepest appreciation and love,

[Signed and dated . . .]

• After you've written your letter, read it out loud to your selves in a positive, loving, and confident tone of voice. And then put the letter under your pillow or mattress, or on your altar, or in your sock drawer. But put it somewhere that you'll run across it and reread it from time to time to refresh your resolve.

Dialoguing

Yet another extremely useful tool for resolving emotional conflicts— inner and outer—is dialoguing. It's similar to the letter-writing method, except you're not giving firm and loving commands to your subconscious mind, you're having a two-way conversation. You're listening to what it has to say in response to your reprogramming efforts.

But dialoguing is not only for the subconscious mind. You can dia-

logue with anything and anyone that you want to know more about, receive insights from, work things through with—God, a geranium, your dead father, a puzzling dream element, a star, a long-lost friend, your angry mate or boss, an angel, a rock you pick up on a walk. Dialoguing is a gentle, efficient, yet sometimes startling way to hear a whole new point of view and see people and situations from a new perspective.

You can use dialoguing to form a team, with you serving the superconscious and the subconscious serving you—all for one and one for all! You can dialogue with your inner child, your higher self, or any subpersonality. For example, you can dialogue with the part of you that wants to stop smoking, or the part that wants to travel to Europe. You can dialogue with an emotion, or thought form, impulse, or desire.

The important thing to realize is that whatever part you work on has an opposite. The part that wants to stop smoking has a part that doesn't want to give it up. The part that wants to travel has another part that would much rather stay at home. So be sure to talk with both sides so you can get a fully balanced perspective on any issue you wish to explore.

• Dialoguing is the easiest thing in the world to do. Again, pick a time and place when things are quiet and peaceful and you're by yourself. Sit down at your computer, or with your journal and pen. Decide who or what it is that you wish to dialogue with.

• Take a couple of deep breaths, then write your name at the upper left-hand corner of the screen or the page, and ask the whoever or whatever if it's okay to have this dialogue. Essentially, don't take no for an answer, but it's polite to begin with an invitation.

• Write the name or description or initials of who or what you're dialoguing with on a new line, again on the left, just as though you were writing a script for a play or TV show. If it's your mate, write down his or her name or initials. Or Purple Tree for the odd image in your dream, or Deepest Fears, or higher self, or Angry Inner Mother (AIM—often the initials are interesting in themselves).

• And then simply type or write down whatever pops into your mind. Don't edit it. Don't think about it. Just keep writing. When nothing more comes, ask another question—either what's been on your mind, or in response to what your dialoguing partner has just said.

• If the person or element is reluctant to speak, that can prove interesting. In your next question, ask why. And keep asking why from answer to answer until you feel you've gotten down to the nitty-gritty issue that you actually needed to know more about.

• Some dialogues are very short and pithy. Some are lengthy exchanges. Others may be essays or long solos. Each person or element you dialogue with has a style and personality all its own—get the feel of your speaking partner. Some may be very funny—but don't miss the sharp observation underneath. Others may be extremely serious, but don't get carried away by the information. Just listen and keep writing.

• When nothing more comes, or you get tired—the dialogue is over. The best thing to do at this point is not to reread it right then. You become part of the larger mind whenever you dialogue, and very often you'll respond to an instant reread with, "I knew that. That's nothing new." Of course you knew that. But probably not consciously.

Let the dialogue age for a day or two or three. Then go back and reread it. You'll probably be surprised at the insights you pick up—new ways of handling relationships and situations; new avenues to explore. This time you're likely to say, "Where did all this come from?" From you, all the parts of you, all the levels of you, and your interaction with the superconscious.

NEGATIVE EMOTIONS LOG

Another very helpful tool for refining, purifying, and spiritualizing your emotional self is to keep a negative emotions log. This is a small pad of paper and pen that you keep with you in your purse or pocket. Anytime you have a negative emotion or feeling, make a brief note of the feeling and incident. Then later, when you have free time, you can go back to your journal and use the six-step process to figure out what faulty belief caused you to feel the way you did.

If you don't keep a negative emotions log, you are very likely to forget about a great many of the lessons that occurred during the day. If you really want to learn to refine, purify, and spiritualize your emotional body, this is the best way to do it.

Carrying this a step further, you can go back through your day and relive each of these experiences the way you would have liked them to happen. Since the brain cannot tell the difference between things that happen in imagination and things that happen in actuality, this is a way to program the subconscious with a positive experience to replace the negative one.

LOGGING IN GENERAL

The purpose of a log is to bring more conscious awareness and discipline into the areas of your life that need it. You can keep many kinds of logs. You can keep an exercise log, where every day you write down the date, how much you exercised, and how you felt about your effort that day. Another type of log is a meditation log, where you write the date, how long you meditated, and any feelings or insights you gained. Doing this is especially important because it is easy to forget what you received in this altered state of consciousness, which can be similar to dreaming. You know how easy it is to forget your dreams.

A log can be created for any area of your life in which you are trying to achieve greater mastery and self-control. You score yourself in percentage points based on how you are manifesting that particular attitude or quality. You can score yourself twice a day or three times a day. I have listed twenty-one days because this is how long it takes to cement a new habit into the subconscious mind.

These types of logs keep you very focused and motivated. Trying to keep it in your mind is too difficult; you are likely to lose concentration, motivation, and discipline. Keeping tabs on your spiritual growth can be compared with tracking your finances. If you tried to maintain all your financial, tax, and banking records in your mind, it would be impossible to keep them organized. The same holds true for our spiritual life. Trying to keep it together without some form of spiritual bookkeeping is impossible and overwhelming. Having a spiritual bookkeeping system for your life is imperative, and logging is a fantastic tool for mastering any given area of your life that needs attention.

KEEPING A JOURNAL

Twenty-One-Day Psychological Foundation Logging Chart No. 1

Instructions: Every morning and night write down a percentage, based on a scale of 1 to 100, that indicates where you are in developing and expressing the given qualities. M=Morning N=Night

DAY	PERSONAL POWER		SELF-LOVE		BALANCE		ATTUNEMENT TO SPIRITUAL ATTITUDE	
	M	N	M	N	M	N	M	N
1								
2								
3								
4								
5								
6								
7								
8								
9								
10								
11								
12								
13								
14								
15								
16								
17								
18								
19								
20								
21								

Twenty-One-Day Psychological Foundation Logging Chart No. 2

Instructions: Every morning and night write down a percentage, based on a scale of 1 to 100, that indicates where you are in developing and expressing the given qualities. M=Morning   N=Night

DAY	PERSONAL POWER MASTER, CAUSER		CHRIST CONSCIOUSNESS (SELF AND OTHERS)		BALANCE AND INTEGRATION		ATTUNEMENT TO HIGHER SELF	
	M	N	M	N	M	N	M	N
1								
2								
3								
4								
5								
6								
7								
8								
9								
10								
11								
12								
13								
14								
15								
16								
17								
18								
19								
20								
21								

Twenty-One-Day Psychological Foundation Logging Chart No. 3

Instructions: Every morning and night write down a percentage, based on a scale of 1 to 100, that indicates where you are in developing and expressing the given qualities.   M-Morning   N=Night

DAY	LESSONS		PREFERENCES		PATIENCE		FORGIVENESS		EMOTIONAL INVULNER- ABILITY	
	M	N	M	N	M	N	M	N	M	N
1										
2										
3										
4										
5										
6										
7										
8										
9										
10										
11										
12										
13										
14										
15										
16										
17										
18										
19										
20										
21										

Twenty-One-Day Psychological Foundation Logging Chart No. 4

Instructions: Every morning and night write down a percentage, based on a scale of 1 to 100, that indicates where you are in developing and expressing the given qualities. M=Morning N=Night

DAY	FAITH AND TRUST		UNCONDI- TIONAL LOVE		DECISIVE- NESS		BEING THE CAUSE		NONJUDG- MENTALNESS	
	M	N	M	N	M	N	M	N	M	N
1										
2										
3										
4										
5										
6										
7										
8										
9										
10										
11										
12										
13										
14										
15										
16										
17										
18										
19										
20										
21										

Twenty-One-Day Psychological Foundation Logging Chart No. 5

Instructions: Every morning and night write down a percentage, based on a scale of 1 to 100, that indicates where you are in developing and expressing the given qualities. M=Morning N=Night

DAY	CRITICAL PARENT		OVERLY PERMISSIVE PARENT		FIRM-LOVE PARENT		CONDITIONAL LOVE		UNCHANGING AND UNCONDI-TIONAL SELF-LOVE	
	M	N	M	N	M	N	M	N	M	N
1										
2										
3										
4										
5										
6										
7										
8										
9										
10										
11										
12										
13										
14										
15										
16										
17										
18										
19										
20										
21										

I recommend keeping two journals. The first is for when you are not thinking clearly or when you just feel like it. By writing in your journal, you can empower yourself and effect attitudinal healing. Since your thoughts create your reality, as you change the way you look at things, your feelings change. Attitudinal healing is the process of moving from egotistical thinking to spiritual thinking.

Journal writing is also for reprogramming the conscious and subconscious minds. Use it to attune to your higher self and for gaining insight and understanding, as well as for catharsis. What you don't want to do is write in your journal and merely reinforce the same patterns on paper without movement or change. It is best to go into your journal writing with the proper attitude of wanting to move toward self-mastery, personal power, and perfect spiritual attitude and attunement.

The second journal is one large notebook in which you store the various tools, logs, and psychological practices on which you are working. The purpose of this journal is to keep all this material together in an organized fashion. Following are some other very valuable sections you might keep in your journal.

Major Lessons of the Day

The "Major Lessons of the Day" section of your journal is best used before you go to bed each night or in the morning when you get up. Review your day and write down the main lessons you learned that day. The nugget might be something you did well or an insight you gained from a negative experience. Developing the regular practice of doing this in your journal or in your mind is very important. It will be much more effective, though, if you do it in your journal. The act of writing things down has a much greater impact on the conscious and subconscious minds.

Many people live their lives without learning from their mistakes. For them, spiritual progress is slowed, and many people repeat a grade in the school of hard knocks. Learn continually from what you have done well and what you did poorly, and then build upon your strengths each day. No matter how good yesterday was, you want to make today better. Enjoy your victories, but never be satisfied until your ultimate divine goal is met.

Goals and Priorities

This is an essential section to have in your journal. You are never going to progress unless you've established a direction in which you want to travel. For this section make a list of all your goals on an earthly physical level, a psychological level, and a spiritual level. List all the things you want to accomplish in this lifetime. List the psychological qualities you want to develop; list the abilities you want to enhance; list your ultimate purpose and goal; list the earthly experiences you want to have.

A helpful mini-meditation you might try is to imagine that seventy-five years have gone by and your soul has passed on to the spirit world. Imagine that you are looking back on this lifetime. From that perspective, what do you see? How do you want to see yourself as having lived? What do you want to see yourself as having achieved? What do you want to have as your epitaph?

Someday you will actually experience this. You have the opportunity now to create the life that you will later look back on with satisfaction. It is very easy to waste one's time and energy on frivolous things. Are you being about the Father's business? Are you using your time and energy to achieve your God-given potential? If not, you need to sharpen your focus on what you want to achieve.

Life Plan and Design

The second step, after getting clear on your goals and priorities, is to set up a life plan and design. This is a tentative map of the next fifty years, or however long you think you will live on this earthly plane.

This life plan or life map begins with your ultimate goal of self-actualization. From there you break down your goals into a timetable, loosely designating the years in which you are going to focus on particular goals. Part of this process is prioritizing. What do you want to focus on in the next year? In the next five years? Ten years? Fifteen years?

For example, you might write down when you want to get married, have a child, go to Europe, study meditation or healing, get a college degree, go to India, read certain books, take certain classes, or perform certain services or contributions. Obviously this life design and map are very flexible, so you can constantly update them as you see fit. The important thing is to begin to give your life a grid or focus to keep you on the right path.

It is so easy to veer off your path. There are so many temptations and different energies tugging at you from many directions. Without a psychological and spiritual map, you are likely to be pulled off course.

Cycles

The next step is to refine this process even further. The idea here is to take the goals and priorities of the next year or two and make a timetable for accomplishing them.

For example, you might say to yourself that this spring your goal is to focus on writing a book, getting physically fit, or maintaining the status quo. Then the summer goal is to spend more time with your family, travel to Hawaii, and focus on making more money. From September to the following spring, you might want to put energy into practicing meditation and the study of healing.

Developing short-term goals will help you be more focused, disciplined, and motivated. As your life changes, you may have to make adjustments, but you can always set up a new cycle of short-term goals.

It is also extremely helpful, in considering this concept of cycles, to use one of your journal-writing sessions to examine the past cycles that led you to your present state of consciousness. Certain initiations or turning points have led you to your present position. Understanding your past cycles will help you understand what is appropriate for the present cycle and what is appropriate for future cycles. Examples of past cycles, turning points, or initiations might be when you graduated from high school, got a certain award, made the basketball team, met your first boyfriend or girlfriend, had your first religious experience, met a certain person, had a baby, or graduated from college. Each of these turning points in your life started you on a new track or phase. You will find it very beneficial to be more conscious of these stages through writing about them.

Weekly Routine

The next step is to refine this process even further by creating a weekly routine. (See the following diagram.) Not everything you do should become a part of this routine, but the chart is meant to give you an overview of some of the kinds of things you can include in your weekly routine.

It is of the utmost importance, in my opinion, that every person have a routine or regime. You will never develop spiritually or on any other level if you don't. The danger of a routine is in becoming too yang, regimenting your life to the point where there is no spontaneity. On the other side of the coin, you don't want to be too yin. To be too yin is to be too flowing, too flexible, too laissez-faire. In the yin orientation there are no hard-and-fast rules in creating a routine. Some people need more structure than others. Routines can be likened to braces that you wear to straighten your teeth; routines guide you in directions you might not otherwise pursue. A routine is to be followed whether you feel like it or not. This is not to say that you have to be neurotic or become an absolute slave to your routine.

Again, it is more of a tentative guide to use except when an emergency or special occasion arises. Its purpose is to help you achieve the goals and priorities that you have clearly set up for yourself. Haphazard exercise is not going to achieve physical fitness any more than haphazard meditation will produce the fruits of the spirit.

Most people do not function well at all without a routine. If you took away going to work or school, they would be lost and without motivation. Most people look to others to set up a structure and a routine for them. Ideally you want to have the personal power and self-discipline to set up and follow a weekly routine with your own goals and priorities.

Don't make the routine too difficult or you won't follow it. On the other hand, don't make it too easy or you won't get maximum benefit. You will find your routine constantly changing as your life changes, and that is fine. But always keep a routine, to help you develop positive habits in your subconscious mind.

After a while you will have positive habits of exercising, eating right, meditating, and so on. Having a routine will also make you much more efficient with your time and more productive. By following a routine, you know you are accomplishing your goals, so your free time is much more enjoyable.

Time Management: Weekly Routine

MONDAY	TUESDAY	WEDNESDAY	THURSDAY	FRIDAY	SATURDAY	SUNDAY
Alarm	Alarm	Alarm	Alarm	Alarm	Planning	Sleep In
Dreams	Dreams	Dreams	Dreams	Dreams	Paying Bills	Good Breakfast
Affirmations	Affirmations	Affirmations	Affirmations	Affirmations	Doing Errands	
Meditation	Meditation	Meditation	Meditation	Meditation	Cleaning	Recreation
Prayer	Prayer	Prayer	Prayer	Prayer	Shopping	
Journal Writing	Journal Writing	Journal Writing	Journal Writing	Journal Writing	Studying	Fun
Organizing	Organizing	Organizing	Organizing	Organizing		
Good Breakfast	Good Breakfast	Good Breakfast	Good Breakfast	Good Breakfast	Pleasure	Pleasure
(Supplements)	(Supplements)	(Supplements)	(Supplements)	(Supplements)		
Work (Service)	Work (Service)	Work (Service)	Work (Service)	Work (Service)	Physical Exercise	
Lunch	Lunch	Lunch	Lunch	Lunch	Fun	Good Dinner
Physical Exercises	Physical Exercises	Physical Exercises	Physical Exercises	Physical Exercises	Pleasure	Cleanup
Catnap	Catnap	Catnap	Catnap	Catnap		Reading
Relaxation	Relaxation	Relaxation	Relaxation	Relaxation	Good Dinner	
Good Dinner	Good Dinner	Good Dinner	Good Dinner	Good Dinner	Recreation	Journal Writing
Reading, Tapes	Reading, Tapes	Reading, Tapes	Reading, Tapes	Fun	Fun	Meditation
Journal Writing	Journal Writing	Journal Writing	Journal Writing	Pleasure	Pleasure	Prayers
Meditation	Meditation	Meditation	Meditation			
Prayers	Prayers	Prayers	Prayers			Set Alarm
Set Alarm	Set Alarm	Set Alarm	Set Alarm			
Sleep	Sleep	Sleep	Sleep	Sleep	Sleep	Sleep

Daily Routine

Now, if you really want to get with the program, you can take this one step further and have a daily routine. This is something I do and really enjoy. Every night before bed I map out the next day, including telephone calls, spiritual disciplines, diet, physical exercise, thought forms, and attitudes I am trying to hold, and so on.

I have memorized my weekly routine, so I just write out my mental, emotional, physical, and spiritual life plan on paper the night before. By doing this I feel organized and efficient, so I sleep better. In the morning I can go right into action because my inner and outer day is laid out before me.

As I think of new things, I write them in; as I finish things, I cross them off. By writing things down, I find I don't have to hold on to things in my mind, which allows me to be more creative and less anxious. Doing this before bed also serves as a type of programming device. I find to a certain extent that I have the energy I program myself to have. If I know the night before that I have a big day coming up, I do better than if I don't realize it until the morning.

Action Plan

This particular journal section I find to be one of the most helpful tools of all. I cannot recommend it more highly. The action plan section is where you take whatever area of your life you are currently working on and make a list of every possible thing you can do to achieve that goal. If you are having health problems, you make a list of every possible action you can take to get better. If you want more clients, business contacts, or money, make an action plan listing every possible inner or outer helpful tool you can think of.

For example, let's say you have some kind of systemic infection and your immune system is run down. The following is a brief example of some things you might write down in your action plan:

Own personal power

Pray for healing

Affirm and visualize health

Diet of steamed vegetables

Drink lots of water

Take vitamin C

Take herbal immune formula

Take homeopathic remedies

Get some acupuncture

Lie in the sun

Go for a walk

Do deep breathing

Get into a Jacuzzi

Keep a positive mental attitude

Sleep as much as possible

Write in my journal

Have faith

By creating this list you are dealing with the situation instead of letting it attack you. When you let life attack you, you are being victimized, and you are going to be depressed. When you cope with the problem, even if you are physically sick, you will feel better. I guarantee it. You feel better because you are assertively doing something to remedy the situation.

Creating this action plan instigates lots of good ideas and also serves to inspire, attract, magnetize, and catalyze what you want. It is very likely that you will have action plans for a number of areas in your life.

Whenever you are feeling off center or are unmotivated, indifferent, or uninspired, either create an action plan or review your current one. You will immediately feel better. I have mine taped onto the wall, so it is right in front of me whenever I sit at my desk.

The action plan renews your faith and inspires your personal power. Rather than letting life victimize you, become the master of your life.

Inspiration: Quotations and Good Ideas

Another section of your journal can be reserved for inspiring ideas, essays, poetry, or pictures. You may even keep a separate journal for aesthetic entries. Since your thoughts create your reality, having a journal like this can serve to inspire and reawaken you to the joy and beauty of life when you are down or unmotivated. Looking through this journal will help rekindle the ultimate reality that you know exists.

You can experiment with these tools and find out which ones work best for you. You will be pleasantly surprised at their effectiveness.

PRAYER VERSUS MEDITATION

Prayer is the act of talking to God, and meditation is the act of listening to God. Prayer is the masculine or yang aspect; meditation is the yin or feminine aspect.

TOOLS FOR CONTACTING YOUR HIGHER SELF

There are a number of methods by which you can develop greater attunement to your higher self.

Letters

This is a very enjoyable and helpful tool. The idea is just to write your higher self a letter. I do this every morning and sometimes before bed as well. The higher self is like an older and wiser brother or sister. Talk to him/her as your friend—your best friend. Form a relationship in your free-flowing letters. You will find that your higher self will respond, sometimes in subtle thought channeling, in dreams, or in the other ways I have already mentioned. I sometimes use my "Dear God" or "Dear higher self" letters as one avenue of praying.

Affirmations

Affirming certain statements to yourself throughout your day will create instant attunement. My favorite ones are these:

I can do all things through Christ, who strengthens me.

God goes with me wherever I go.

I trust in the Lord, and He will light the way.

If God be for me, who can be against me?

I have perfect faith, trust, and patience in God and God's laws.

All things are possible with God.

Father, I expect a miracle.

God is bearing my cross with me.

Visualizations

Close your eyes and imagine a symbol or image that attunes you and reminds you that your higher self is with you all through the day. It could be a dove flying above you. It could be a golden white light bathing you from above. Use your imagination and select from the infinite possibilities.

Shuttle back to these different images and affirmations throughout your day in order to reattune yourself. The affirmations and images provided in this book will provide comfort, peace of mind, strength, and power in time of need. It may also be helpful to create imagery for the presence of God and Christ and the guides, teachers, and helpers that are also available to assist you.

Altars

A small holy place or shrine in one corner of your bedroom is a lovely way to attune to your higher self. It can be created in many ways. Some people have little statues of Jesus, Buddha, or another of the great Masters and teachers. I also recommend incense and spiritual music, which help you align your consciousness. Candles are another good addition. It is nice to meditate near your altar or shrine, if possible. The shrine serves to remind you of your connection to spirit and your high calling.

You can add affirmations, poetry, or pictures from magazines. Some people create this on a bulletin board or poster. I pin up all my action plans, centering models, schedules, commitments, and inspiring thoughts. It is really fun and inspiring to create.

Like anything worth doing, following any of these practices takes patience and discipline. It also offers great rewards. Just as you must care for and heal and exercise your physical body, you also should not neglect your emotional body. We will turn our attention next to the mental body.

Chapter 7

✳

Reprogramming the Subconscious Mind

Be vigilant for God and His kingdom.
—JESUS CHRIST, AS SPOKEN THROUGH *A COURSE IN MIRACLES*

Since we have discussed affirmations in the previous chapters, we are now ready to explore the deeper dimension of what affirmations and visualizations are and how to use them. An affirmation is really an attitude. Every thought we think, positive or negative, is an affirmation. Every word we speak is an affirmation. Every action or behavior we take is an affirmation. Again, this is true because our thoughts create our reality.

Used in a psychological healing context, affirmations are specifically designed to program a desired feeling, behavior, or habit into our subconscious minds—for example, the affirmations we can use to develop our personal power and our protective bubble.

Whenever we practice positive thinking, we are making affirmations. The affirmations that I give in this chapter are specifically designed statements that will help develop certain key attitudes that pertain to self-concept and self-image.

The continuous process of pushing the negative attitudes out of the mind with our personal power and then repeating the new positive affirmations into the subconscious mind is the main key to reprogramming the subconscious mind.

Pushing negative thoughts out is like breaking off the tab on an audio or videotape. Only you can retape-cover that hole when you choose to record a more positive subconscious message.

METHODS OF REPROGRAMMING
THE SUBCONSCIOUS MIND

To reprogram your subconscious mind try different ways to see which ones are most effective for you.

1. *Affirmations*
An affirmation is a strong, positive statement that something is already so. Repeat the statement silently until it is fully programmed into the subconscious mind, and the pattern will become a reality in your life.

2. *Decrees*
A decree is a spoken affirmation.

3. *Creative Visualization*
This is the process of actively imagining that the healed or finished result has already occurred. It acts as a direct suggestion to the subconscious mind just as an affirmation does; in fact, images are even more powerful than words.

4. *Journal*
Write down your affirmations in a journal. This is a very effective way of programming the subconscious mind. The physical act of writing causes the thought pattern to take a more tangible and stable form. Change the wording as better ways of writing your affirmations occur to you.

5. *Affirmation Cards*
Write affirmations on cards and place them all over your house and your place of work. This is a very effective method. Put these affirmation cards next to your bed, on the mirror, in the bathroom, on the refrigerator, in your car, in your wallet, or on your desk. This will act as a reminder to repeat them and will accelerate the reprogramming process.

6. *Affirmation Walks*
Go for a walk! An affirmation walk is one of my favorite activities. I walk for as long as I am in the mood to, and I affirm to my subconscious mind how I want everything to be. The subconscious mind will

manifest anything you tell it, good or bad. The value of affirmations and positive visualizations is obvious, for if you are not affirming and visualizing the positive, you are doing the opposite.

7. *Rhythmic Repetition*

Say your affirmations rhythmically while you are engaged in physical exercise. This is an excellent programming technique and keeps your mind focused and disciplined while exercising.

8. *Three "Voices"*

Say your affirmations in the first, second, and third persons. For example: "I, Joshua, am in perfect, radiant health. You, Joshua are in perfect, radiant health. He, Joshua, is in perfect, radiant health." This technique is especially successful when taping your affirmations.

9. *Positive-Negative Clearing*

Draw a line down the middle of a piece of paper. Write one affirmation on one side of the page. Then wait and listen for any thoughts that come into your mind to contradict your positive affirmation. Write down the negative thoughts from your subconscious mind.

The next step is to change each negative thought into a second positive affirmation. Record any additional negative thoughts after you have written this new positive affirmation. Change these negatives into new positive statements. Continue this process until no more negative thoughts come up. You now have a list of the affirmations that specifically deal with your personal lessons in this lifetime. This method is also effective because it teaches you the essential ability of creating your own affirmations.

10. *Mirror*

Look in the mirror every day for twenty-one days and say your affirmations aloud. Say them with total personal power and conviction. Look yourself right in the eye! Continue affirming aloud until there is no subconscious resistance.

11. *Endless Tape*

Record your affirmations onto a cassette tape and play it on an auto-reverse tape player every night for twenty-one nights while you sleep. This sleep tape method is 100 percent effective! Pillow speakers are also available.

12. *Hypnosis*

Find a trustworthy hypnotherapist to hypnotize you and plant positive suggestions into your subconscious mind while you are in the hypersuggestible state.

13. *Reading*

Read and reread good books in the fields of psychology and spirituality. This serves as a powerful programming and patterning device.

14. *Pendulum*

Make or buy a pendulum and communicate with your subconscious mind through yes-or-no questions. This process retrieves information from the subconscious mind and can be used to pattern or program the subconscious.

15. *Dialogue*

Another very effective tool is to "dialogue" with the subconscious mind or with one subpersonality or thought system within the subconscious mind. This can be done in a number of ways.

• Create a voice dialogue. Use chairs to represent the conscious and subconscious mind. Create a dialogue between the two. Add chairs to represent your isolated subpersonalities. The idea is to role-play the various parts of your subconscious mind. The conscious mind then dialogues with these various parts. This is a very powerful tool in helping you become the master of your life rather than its victim.

• Using this same process in a journal can also be exceedingly helpful. Have a dialogue on paper with any thought system within you that you are trying to block or to manifest in your consciousness. For example, you can have a dialogue with your higher self.

• A third way to dialogue is within your mind. When a destructive thought system arises, talk to it. Tell it you are the captain of the ship and you have the power in the personality, not it! Then affirm the opposite to yourself, and tell the opposite you will listen to it.

16. *Acting "As If"*

Act in your daily life the way you want to be, even if you don't feel it or if your subconscious is trying to do the opposite. This method takes an act of willpower. If the tension can be carried long enough, eventually it will act as a reprogramming procedure.

This is an essential method to develop, because sometimes we just don't have the time to prepare properly for everything. For example, you might have a spur-of-the-moment job interview during which you must act confident and qualified, even if you don't feel that way at the moment.

17. *Pictures*

Create a physical picture of your desired reality. It will serve as a suggestion to the subconscious just as the creative visualization process does, except this is an actual physical reproduction of the imagined result. For example, if you are overweight, find a picture of someone with the figure you want and replace that person's face with a photograph of your own. Your subconscious mind will try to manifest that image.

18. *Self-Hypnosis*

Suggestions given to the subconscious mind while in a relaxed or hypersuggestible state can represent a longer affirmation. The discipline of hypnosis has demonstrated the fact that when the conscious, critical mind is relaxed, the subconscious mind immediately accepts the suggestions. What this reveals is that we can take advantage of these relaxed and hypersuggestible states to pattern our subconscious minds more quickly.

Affirmations are important but do take more work than this method. Some examples of periods during the day when you can use autosuggestion are:

• Just before falling asleep, while you are in the twilight zone between sleep and wakefulness, affirm to yourself a key word or phrase: "Perfect health . . . wealth . . . success . . . a good night's sleep"
• When you are relaxed
• After meditation; this is an excellent time to give yourself autosuggestions
• After you've done self-hypnosis
• In the ionized atmosphere of a shower

19. *Tape Recording*

Make a tape recording of affirmations and autosuggestions and play it when you are in any of the abovementioned hypersuggestible states of consciousness.

20. *Subliminal Tapes*

Another method of reprogramming the subconscious mind is through the use of subliminal tapes. A subliminal tape is one where a suggestion or affirmation is given in a barely audible tone underneath classical, New Age, or environmental music. The suggestion is so quiet and soft that you can't hear it consciously unless you strain to do so. Subliminal tapes are excellent as sleep tapes, especially if you find that regular affirmational sleep tapes keep you awake.

21. *Songs*

Make up songs and sing your affirmations to yourself. You don't have to be a professional singer. Use the melodies of your favorite music. Create personal power songs, self-love songs, and financial prosperity songs. Allow yourself to be a little crazy and to have fun with it. If you are a bit hesitant to try this, do it while you are alone in your car.

22. *Poetry*

A similar method is to write poetry, embodying these new ideas you are trying to program into your subconscious mind.

23. *Artwork*

Draw or paint pictures of this new you that you are becoming.

24. *Self-Talk*

Another very effective tool is to practice "self-talk." The self-talk that arises out of the subconscious mind is usually negative. The idea here is to practice positive self-talk. Just talk to yourself as you would talk to a best friend or loved one. Affirmations are very formal and set, but this method is more informal.

For example, if I was working on self-love, I might say to myself, "Joshua, I love you, I really do. You have made a lot of mistakes, and I just want to tell you that this is okay by me. I want to let you know that you are completely forgiven and I am on your side."

In other words, talk to yourself about this new thought or image that you are attempting to incorporate as a habit within your subconscious mind. You can do this self-talk silently, spoken aloud, written in a letter to yourself, or taped for later listening.

Visualizations

When we do a visualization we are seeing an image in our mind's eye. A visualization is really the same thing as a thought, but every thought has an accompanying image. For example, if someone asked you to visualize your personal power in a symbolic way, perhaps you might see an image of a flaming sword. If you were asked to visualize self-love, you might see a beautiful red rose in full bloom.

In the field of psychology we talk a lot about positive thinking. But we should also talk about positive imaging, because it is a very powerful tool for reprogramming the subconscious mind, which responds equally well to words or images.

If you choose imagery, make your visualizations as clear and detailed as possible as you create the new you. Use all your senses to see, feel, hear, taste, and touch the reality you are bringing into being. If you want to change elements in your life, visualize what you want and how you want things to be. Again, use all your senses to create a clear, powerful, and detailed image of this new way of living.

Make your visualizations so intensely real that you're not just watching yourself in a mind movie—you're actually there, on the scene, being and doing and creating. The more realistic you can make your visualization, the more effective your subconscious mind will be able to help you manifest what you want.

For example, let's take one of the issues that affects most of us—money. Are you tired of never having enough money to meet your needs and to fulfill your hopes and dreams? Use the following visualization to get a sense of how to create real change in your life. Put all your creative gifts into it—after all, this may be the beginning of a whole new way of life for you.

Attracting Money

• Find a quiet spot in your house where you can have some peace and privacy for about an hour. Settle into a comfortable chair, feet flat on the floor, hands relaxed at your sides or in your lap.

• Close your eyes and take a deep breath, filling your stomach and then your chest. Hold it a moment, and then on the exhale tell yourself, "Relax now," as you release all tension and discomfort and outside concerns. Take another deep breath, relax and release. Take a third deep breath, relax and release. Now just continue breathing quietly and evenly.

• Eyes still closed, keep focusing on your breath for a minute or two, as you allow images to begin to form. Visualize yourself living a happy and prosperous life. How much money do you think this would take? Visualize yourself opening your bank statement and seeing this sum printed clearly in your combined checking and savings accounts. Feel the paper of the statement, hear the crinkling sound as you unfold it. Smell the ink. Taste the air as you breathe in happily.

• Look at your surroundings. Where are you? Is this your dream place? If not, make it so. What does the countryside look like? What does your home look like? Does it contain all the things you've always wanted? Put them there—exactly the way you've always dreamed they would be.

• Catch a glimpse of yourself and smile. You're looking fine and you're feeling fine—physically and emotionally. You like the way you're dressed, and the way you present yourself. Make these images and feelings and sensations as detailed and as absolutely real as possible. Taste, and hear, and smell, and touch what you see. Feel who you are and what you have.

• Where did the money come from? Visualize yourself getting a raise or a promotion. Or see yourself getting that dream job you've always wanted, and the good money that comes with it. Or visualize yourself winning the lottery or inheriting a large sum of money. Whatever your heart desires—but make it real. See your new place of work, see yourself doing what makes you happy. Or see the new sign on your office door. See that winning lottery ticket in your hand and the winning numbers being announced on TV. Hear the phone call from the lawyer telling you about your inheritance.

• See yourself opening your mailbox and finding a pile of checks inside instead of bills. Visualize yourself opening the envelopes and smiling at the checks you pull out. Now see yourself at the ATM in your bank, making weekly deposits of larger and larger sums of money. See yourself writing out these large sums on your deposit slips, and see the amount confirmed on the printed receipt.

• Persistence pays off in transforming visualizations into reality. So keep visualizing exactly what you want whenever you have a quiet moment to yourself. Make it all so real that it's as if you already possess it. See abundance continually unfolding in your life.

• To make the process easier, ask your visualization to give you a symbolic image that represents your new abundant lifestyle. Visualize this image whenever you think about money, or handle money, or pay bills. Bless the money going out, knowing that the blessings will return to you.

• See yourself being grateful to God for the abundance bestowed on you. See yourself giving part of your money to charity or a worthy cause because the universe has been good to you and you want to give back to the universe.

A Bouquet of Visualizations

What follows is a series of exercises to practice in your quiet, meditative times. Much of the theory behind them—how they work and why—will be discussed in later chapters. But for now, I want you to simply get a feel for the different kinds of visualizations that are available to you.

Self-Empowerment Trip

• Find a quiet place and time where you can be by yourself for about an hour. Sit comfortably, feet on the floor, hands relaxed. Close your eyes, and take three deep breaths, relaxing more and more with each one, exhaling and releasing all tension and discomfort and negative thoughts.

• Now breathe quietly and evenly. Focusing on your breath for a minute or two, begin to visualize yourself in beautiful, natural surroundings—a high mountain meadow, or by the ocean, or in a mossy forest glade, whatever your favorite spot may be. Smell the air—the meadow flowers and sweet grasses, the salt tang of the sea, the green breath of the trees. Feel the earth beneath you. Hear the birds, and the wind. Feel the warmth of the sun on your face.

• Now focus on your emotions and your physical body. Feel yourself filled with well-being and joy, alert yet peaceful within. Feel the love you have for yourself and all living things.

• Next, imagine yourself feeling very powerful, strong, and in command. Imagine being in charge of things—as the president of the United States, or the president of your own business, the principal of a public school, or the conductor of a symphony orchestra.

• Get a strong sense of the personal power and authority that you have. Visualize putting this power and authority to work in your daily life. After all, you *are* the president, principal, and orchestrator of your thoughts, feelings, emotions, behavior, body, and environment.

• Know that you don't need to be afraid of your power because you're using it in a loving, spiritual manner. How does it feel to have personal power and authority over yourself and your life rather than letting every-one and everything else in the universe be your master?

• Feel this benevolent power surging through you, reprogramming your thoughts and feelings. Ask it to give you an image or symbol that represents your personal power, an image that will appear whenever you need a reminder of who you truly are. Let this symbol form in your mind's eye. It could be a sword, a scepter, special clothing, or jewelry. Or it could be an image, a symbol, that is completely personal and unique to you. Whatever comes, accept it—and above all, use it to continue ex-periencing your personal power and self-mastery in your daily life.

Variations on The Golden Bubble

You met the Golden Bubble Visualization earlier. Now we're going to use it to remove negativity from relationships.

• Now, with the power of your mind, visualize yourself sitting inside a beautiful, protective bubble spun of golden-white light extending out-ward about two or three feet around you. Reach out and touch the skin of the protective golden bubble. Feel its resilience and strength, and its permeability—keeping out all negativity but allowing in positive, loving spiritual energy.

• Next, fill the inside of this protective golden bubble with your personal power, and your unconditional self-love and self-worth. See yourself complete and whole. Feel your personal power and emotional invulnerability flowing through you, along with your unconditional self-love and self-worth.

• Visualize yourself surrounded by your golden bubble filled with power and love, sitting in your favorite natural setting. Imagine someone you know walking up to you and trying to pick a fight by making a nega-tive comment. Watch this negativity slide off your golden protective bub-ble like water off a duck's back. It doesn't touch you, it can't hurt you. Now, send that person love.

Variation 1:

• See yourself at work, surrounded by your protective golden bubble. Say good morning to one of your coworkers, and get an irritable and up-tight response. Just watch that negative attitude slide right off the bubble, not affecting you for a moment.

• See your boss coming toward you, and hear him snap at you. And, once again, watch this negative energy sliding away, doing you no harm, causing no inner turmoil or upset.

• Send them both love, and watch their moods shift and lighten.

Variation 2:

• Now visualize yourself at home with your spouse or children. Your spouse has had a rough day and is in a bad mood, reacting negatively to everything and everyone. Watch that negative energy slip easily off the sides of your golden protective bubble.

• Your kids are cranky and demanding, whining at you and fighting with each other. But, once again, their energy is sliding right off the golden bubble, leaving you calm and unruffled.

• Send your spouse love. Send the kids love. Watch how their mood changes because you haven't joined them in negativity.

Variation 3:

• Return to your beautiful, natural setting. Visualize yourself in your golden protective bubble, sitting peacefully in this scene. But suddenly, your subconscious mind brings up some negative programming. Instead of giving in to it, see yourself pushing it out of your mind and denying it entrance. See it carried harmlessly away on a gust of wind.

• Feel yourself feeling good. What's it like to be able to maintain your mental and emotional equilibrium? How does it feel to have your subconscious mind dancing to your tune, and following your every order as a faithful friend and servant would do?

Variations on Old Themes:

• Imagine yourself in a number of different situations, ones where you usually lose control of yourself or the situation, and crash. Recast them with you inside the golden protective bubble. Feel yourself taking command of your thoughts, feelings, emotions, behavior, and body. What's it like to be the master of your life?

• Begin to use your golden protective bubble daily. Whenever an old bit of negative programming comes up, or a challenge, or an uncomfortable situation develops, simply remember that you are inside your bubble, inside your own power, and authority, and self-worth. You are surrounded and supported by your own unwavering self-love. None of the negativity can reach you, but your own strength and love, and positive spiritual power emerges to fill the space and the people around you.

Variation 4—Dancing to a New Tune:

• Visualize yourself returning once more to your favorite natural scene. It's dusk, and you have collected a great pile of firewood and built it into an enormous bonfire. Now strike a match, and set the bonfire ablaze.

As the fire leaps up into the sky, gather up all your negative, egotistical unbalanced thoughts, feelings, emotions, and behaviors, and hurl them into the bonfire. Take all your physical ailments and cast them into the fire. See them all being burned to ash.

How do you feel now? Do you have the sense that an unbelievable weight has just been lifted off your back? What's left? Do you feel power? And strength? And positive, loving feelings? Balance? And above all, a deep sense of your inner spirituality?

Dance joyously around that roaring fire, knowing that you have returned to your true self. You have freed yourself at last from faulty thinking and illusion and you can become an example and inspiration to others. Feel yourself becoming a light to the world, beaming out your strength, your self-love, and your love of others.

• Look at the bonfire now. Time has passed, and everything you threw into it has been burned away. Only a few glowing coals are left, surrounding something bright and gleaming in the very center. You approach and look closely at the residue of the fire, and you see that what remains is a bar of the purest gold.

Alchemy has taken place, for by gleaning all the wisdom from your past mistakes, you have changed the base metal of your experiences into the gold of the tempered soul. You are now ready to fulfill your spiritual purpose in this lifetime by spreading good energy, happiness, joy, the spirit of cooperation, forgiveness, harmony, peace, and love. Wherever you go, people respond to your positive loving energy. And this is how we change the world, by burning away all our own dross, and embodying the golden energy ourselves.

Revitalizing the Subconscious Garden

This exercise is designed to help you reprogram your subconscious mind by visualizing it as a garden of new patterns and thoughts and positive behaviors that you prepare, sow, tend, and harvest.

• Sit in your quiet place, close your eyes, and breathe in peace and calm, breathe out tension, and discomfort, and distracting thoughts.

• Focusing on your breath for a few moments, begin to visualize a flight of stairs, or perhaps an escalator, moving down, down, down, into the depths of your inner self, into your subconscious mind. It is a safe, gentle, loving journey.

• When you arrive, you will find yourself in a garden on a bright, sunny day. The first thing you do is look around the garden to get a first impression. Is it well tended and filled with stately trees, and healthy shrubs, flowers, herbs, and perhaps vegetables? Are there bright colors and sweet and tangy scents? Or does your garden seem neglected, drooping, withered, and overgrown with weeds? Or, perhaps, it's somewhere in between—parts of the garden are beautiful and healthy and flourishing, but other parts of the garden seem unloved and uncared for.

• The garden represents the condition of our subconscious minds. And for most of us, it's the mixed garden that we'll find ourselves in. The healthy plants represent our positive and healthy thoughts and behaviors, and the sickly, unloved ones represent our negative attitudes and stuck places.

• Go to the little shed where you keep all your gardening equipment, and put on your sun hat, and your gardening gloves, and get your tools and a big plastic lawn and leaf bag.

• Begin to walk through your garden, enjoy the beautiful blooms, smell their scents, touch their soft petals, and rough bark of trees, and the rich foliage of the shrubs. As you do, ask them to send you images of the positive patterns, and thoughts and behaviors that they represent. Thank them for their help.

• But whenever you find weeds and dead and ailing plants and growths that don't belong there, pull them up by the roots. This is not a time to be compassionate to the weak. Be a good, tough gardener, and get rid of the interlopers, and whatever is not flourishing, and dump them in your plastic bag.

• Each time you uproot a plant, hold it in your hands and let it send you information about the negative thought or image or habit it represents. Thank it for its help, and add it to your disposal bag. When it's full, haul it out of the garden, and discard it.

• When you're done, you'll find that you've cleared a number of areas of old thought patterns, repetitive behaviors, and negative energies. You've made space—space in your garden, and space in you for new, healthy growth.

• Rake up the soil in the areas you've cleared. Get rid of any remaining debris. Aerate the soil, turn it to the light, open up its rich promise. Feel it in your hands, break up the clods, smell the earthiness, feel the energy and promise.

• Now, go back to your gardening shed, and sort through all the new packets of seeds that you've stored for just such a time. Each one represents new thoughts and images, new ways of seeing and acting, new insights and understandings. Look at the images of the healthy plants on the seed packets and choose the ones that appeal to you most right now. Not all of them—that's too demanding a task. Perhaps you want a kitchen garden now, with vegetables instead of flowers. Simply choose the seeds appropriate to this season of your life.

• Plant the new seeds in the freshly turned, rich, black gardening soil. Bless each seed, and thank it for its promise and power. And when you're done, lightly fertilize and water these new sources of beauty and positive energy in your life. You might want to place the empty seed packet on a stick, and put it in the ground by each new row of seeds to remind you what you've planted and where, and what it symbolizes in your life.

• When you're done, clean and put your tools away, and survey the hard and glorious work you've just accomplished. Thank yourself, and God, and the earth, and the newly planted seeds for their participation in this effort. And walk back up the stairs, or take the escalator up to the surface of your mind. Take a deep breath, open your eyes slowly, move gently at first, and then return to your life.

• Because it takes twenty-one days to seat a new pattern in your subconscious, over the next twenty-one days you're going to return to your newly planted garden in a quick visualization. You're going to monitor how well the plants are doing. And you're going to water, and weed, and prop up, and talk to the newly germinating and growing plants as they emerge into the positive thought, image, or pattern of behavior that was previously latent within it.

• Remember that the soil of your unconscious mind will grow any seed-thought you plant, be it positive or negative. So be sure not to let any bad seeds land in your newly planted garden. Pull out the weeds of negative thoughts and attitudes daily.

• At the end of the twenty-one days, take another tour of your garden of the subconscious. Do whatever you need to do to make it healthy and strong. If you haven't been doing this all along, now is when you might want to do some journal work on what's been going on in your garden. What was it that you pulled up and tossed away? What were the new patterns that you planted?

• Make a list of what each plant, flower, tree, shrub, herb, or vegetable represents within your garden. Or, you might want to do some artwork, and draw or paint your garden, labeling each growing thing in it. You could also sculpt your garden in clay, or do stitchery of the patterns and colors that make your newly refurbished garden so beautiful.

• Fill your mind with armfuls of your flowers, and your inner kitchen with baskets of your ripe vegetables and healing herbs. Feast on the scents, textures, sounds, colors, and tastes of your labors.

AFFIRMATIONS OF FAITH, TRUST, AND PATIENCE

Faith in God, trust in yourself and the universe, and patience are qualities that will help you manifest your goals. Below are some affirmations that will help you strengthen these qualities.

1. I have perfect faith, trust, and patience in my higher self.
2. I have perfect faith and trust that God is now providing for my every need.
3. I hereby surrender all problems and challenges into God's hands.
4. Why worry when I can pray?
5. With God helping me I will certainly succeed.
6. I have perfect faith in my own power as well as perfect faith and trust in God's power.
7. I have invited God's help and I know his invisible hands are now working in my life to answer my prayers.
8. I have invited God's help and I have perfect faith, trust, and patience He will provide me with what I want, or something better.

9. I have asked and I know I shall receive.
10. I know God will answer my prayer in His time, not mine, and I will have perfect faith, trust, and patience until that time comes.
11. If my prayer isn't answered in exactly the way I want, I know that this is a lesson He would have me learn.
12. I have perfect faith, trust, and patience that God will answer my every prayer.
13. Prayer, personal power, and affirmations and visualizations are an unbeatable team.
14. I have perfect faith, trust, and patience in my self, my superconscious mind, and the power of my subconscious mind to attract and magnetize to me everything I need.

MY FAVORITE AFFIRMATIONS

The following affirmations are guaranteed to make you feel better if you say them regularly and with enthusiasm.

1. Mental strength, physical strength, spiritual strength!
2. Personal power, positive anger, mental strength!
3. I am the power, I am the master, I am the cause.
4. Get thee behind me, Satan!!!
5. I have perfect faith and trust in God!
6. The power of my mind makes me the omnipotent force in this universe!
7. God, my personal power, and the power of my subconscious mind are an unbeatable team!!!
8. My mind power and spirit power are an unbeatable team!
9. Be still and know that I am God.
10. Father, I thank you for the miraculous healing of my _____.
11. Water off a duck's back, water off a windowpane, invulnerability, invincibility, rubber pillow, filter!
12. God, God, God, Christ, Christ, Christ, Jesus Christ, Jesus Christ, Jesus Christ!!!
13. Absolute total supreme mastery!
14. Tough love, tough love, tough love!
15. Mental power, physical power, spiritual power!!!

16. Faith, trust, patience in God!!!
17. With my power and God's power and the power of my subconscious, I cannot and will not be stopped!!!
18. I will be more powerful from this moment forward than I have ever been in my entire life!!!
19. As God is my witness, I will not be stopped!!!
20. I am sustained by the love of God!!!
21. I can do all things with God, Christ, and my higher self, who strengthen me!
22. As God is my witness, I will never give my power to anyone or anything ever again!!!
23. God is my personal power, and the power of my subconscious mind!
24. Not my will, but thine. Thank you for the lesson!
25. I am going to be the absolute master of my life from this moment forward!
26. God goes with me wherever I go!
27. I love God with all my heart and soul and mind and might, and I love my neighbor as myself!

Read your favorite affirmations again, and this time say them with even more enthusiasm. Repeat each affirmation from three to seven times.

Chapter 8

✳

The Human Aura and the Seven Bodies

Our life course, our habits, our health and mental appreciation, in fact our life history, is written in color, forms, and lines comprising the energy fields of our several levels of being or conscious states.
—RONALD BEESLEY

Just as there are seven dimensions of reality, there are seven invisible bodies around every physical form, each one corresponding to a dimension of reality. We have an etheric body, astral body, mental body, soul or causal body, buddhic body, atmic body, and a glorified light body. There are other bodies beyond this level called celestial bodies, but they are beyond our comprehension at this level of evolution.

Each body has a characteristic or quality of energy associated with it. The physical body has to do with instinct; the etheric body with the vital force and vital energy; the astral body with desires, feelings, and emotions; the mental body with the concrete mind; the soul or causal body with the abstract mind; the buddhic body with intuition; the atmic body with spiritual will. In this chapter I will discuss each of the bodies individually.

THE PHYSICAL BODY

An explanation of the physical body is not really necessary, since we are all very familiar with it. The only thing I would add is that the physical body is the temple for the incarnating soul extension. It is an instrument and vehicle for exploration of the physical world. Just as the physical body is the vehicle for the manifestation of soul on this plane of existence, the soul is the vehicle on a higher plane for the manifestation of spirit.

A great many people don't realize the importance of helping the physical body to evolve along with the other bodies, for it is impossible for those with coarse, dense bodies to contact high vibrations. Refinement of the physical body is essential. Many spiritual aspirants work on evolving the other bodies and not the physical body. As a result, they get sick because of the discrepancy in vibrational frequency.

It is not the purpose of this book to be a manual on how to care for the physical vehicle. However, the following simple suggestions below would be extremely helpful.

1. Adhere to a daily physical fitness program.
2. Eat pure food.
3. Develop good sleeping habits.
4. Spend at least ten to twenty minutes a day outside if possible. The sunlight kills many germs and frees one from disease, as well as vitalizes the etheric body.
5. Maintain cleanliness. Use a lot of hot water both internally and externally.
6. Avoid sugar, artificial stimulants, and drugs.
7. Create time for play.

THE ETHERIC BODY

The etheric body, or the etheric double, is an exact replica of the physical body. It is the superstructure upon which the physical form is built. Nothing in the manifested universe is without an etheric body, or energy form.

This etheric body governs and conditions the outer physical body. The function of the etheric body is to store the rays of the sun's light and heat and to transmit them via the spleen chakra to all parts of the physical body. The etheric body is a web or network of fine interlacing channels called nadis. During incarnation the network of nadis forms a barrier between the physical and astral planes. If you have taken large amounts of drugs, you break this etheric webbing, which may leave you unprotected from lower astral energies.

The etheric body is also called the energy battery of the physical body. Congestion in some part of the etheric body can lead to many forms of disease and to a lack of mental clarity. You can vitalize and control your etheric body through thought, and you can bring it into full activity by right thinking. Most diseases the physical body suffers from can be traced to the etheric and astral bodies. The principal ways to maintain a healthy etheric body are getting sunshine, eating health-fully (with emphasis upon proper proteins and vitamins), and avoiding fatigue and worry.

ASTRAL BODY

The astral body relates us to the astral plane and to our desires, feel-ings, and emotions. If we are run by our astral body—our feelings, emotions, and desires—the astral body ends up running the con-scious mind, instead of the conscious mind having self-mastery over our emotions.

Many people travel in this body when they experience astral projec-tion. We all do this when we have dreams of flying in this body. Some people have developed the ability to travel in this body consciously. The limitation of this is that you can travel only in the astral plane. If you travel in your soul body or light body, you will have a greater range of dimensions in which to travel.

The great teachings of Hinduism and Buddhism emphasize the need to eliminate desire. This means that your only desire should be liberation and God-realization instead of all the material desires of the negative ego. The astral body receives the impression of every passing desire it contacts in the environment. Every sound causes it to vibrate. Your great need as a spiritual aspirant is to train the astral body to re-ceive and register only those impressions that come from the higher self. Your aim is to train the emotional body so that it will become as still and clear as a mirror, reflecting perfectly your inner and outer states. The words that describe the emotional body in its desired state are *still, serene, unruffled, quiet, at rest,* and *clear.*

Stilling the Emotional Body

Alice Bailey, who presented much of the teaching of Djwhal Khul in her books, has elucidated how to still the emotional body.

1. By constantly watching all desires, motives, and wishes that cross the horizon daily, and by subsequently emphasizing all those that are of a high order and inhibiting those of a lower order.

2. By a constant daily attempt to contact the higher self, and to reflect its wishes in life.

3. By regular periods of daily meditation, directed specifically to the stilling of the emotional body. Each of us must discover for ourselves when we yield most easily to violent vibrations, such as fear, worry, personality desire of any kind, personality love of anything or anyone, discouragement, or oversensitivity to public opinion. Then we must overcome that vibration by imposing on it a new rhythm, definitely eliminating and reconstructing it.

4. By working on the emotional body at night, under the direction of more advanced souls, or working under the guidance of a Master.

When illusion and glamour have been overcome, the astral body fades out in the human consciousness. There is no desire left for the separated self. Ego disappears, and man is then regarded as consisting essentially of soul, mind, and brain within the physical body.

THE MENTAL BODY

The mental body is associated with the mental plane and the concrete mind. Refining and developing this body takes hard work and discrimination. You need to think clearly, not only about things that arouse your interest but on all matters affecting your life and humanity. Mental clarity means having the ability to make thought forms out of thought matter, and to utilize these thought forms to help others.

It is important to learn how to still the mental body so that abstract thoughts and intuition can enter a receptive mind and inscribe themselves.

Two qualities should be developed above all else: unshaken perseverance and fortitude, and an ability to avoid undue self-analysis. The capacity to persevere explains why the nonspectacular man or woman often attains initiation before the genius—remember the example of the tortoise and hare. Overanalysis can lead to a kind of paralysis.

The mental body remains clear when you maintain a good mental diet. Every thought that comes from your subconscious mind or from other people should be examined to determine if it is of God or not of God, if it is truth or illusion. If it is positive and of God, let the idea into your mind, as you would good food into your stomach. If it is negative and not of God, deny it entrance into your mind. The ongoing process of remaining conscious and vigilant and not going on automatic pilot will keep your mental body clear.

Keeping your mental body clear will help to keep your emotional, etheric, and physical bodies clear, for it is your thoughts that create your reality. This last point cannot be emphasized strongly enough.

THE SOUL OR CAUSAL BODY

The soul or causal body exists on the higher mental plane, and its characteristic is the abstract mind. The causal body is the temple of the soul. It is the storehouse of all our good karma and virtue from all our past lives and the present life. The causal body is a collection of three permanent atoms enclosed in an envelope of mental essence. The three permanent atoms are recording devices for our physical, astral, and mental bodies. These permanent atoms record our karma.

In our very first incarnations on earth our causal body was a colorless ovoid holding the soul like a yolk within an eggshell. As we incarnated over and over again we built good karma and virtue into our causal body and it began to become a thing of rare beauty, containing within itself all the colors of the rainbow.

THE BUDDHIC BODY

The buddhic body is associated with the buddhic plane, and its characteristic quality is intuition. After passing the fourth initiation, one lives in the buddhic body.

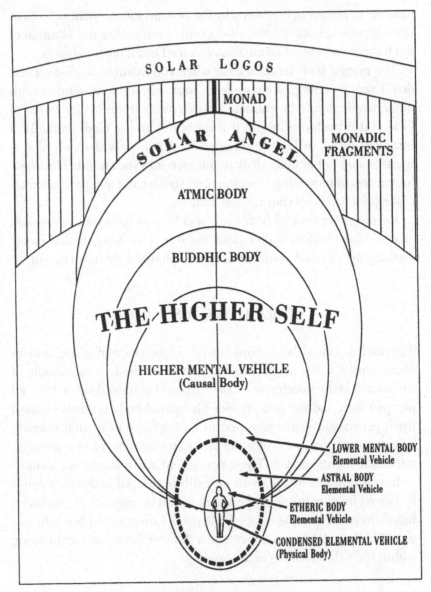

The Seven Bodies

THE ATMIC BODY

The atmic body is associated with the atmic plane, and its characteristic is spiritual will. This is the body one inhabits upon passing the fifth initiation.

THE GLORIFIED LIGHT BODY

The glorified light body is the body we will inhabit at the time of our ascension, when we achieve complete merger with the monad or Mighty I Am Presence on earth. At that time our entire being, including our physical body, will merge into light. It is the light body that we will officially step into. It is, in a sense, the wedding garment that we are creating day by day as we travel the path of initiation. It is made of the light that we create in our daily lives. This body is not fully complete until just before ascension itself.

THE AURA

Everything that has been created has an aura of some kind. In human beings the aura surrounds the central nucleus, or the soul extension, of the overshadowing soul.

The aura is composed of four fields. These are the physical health aura; the astral, or emotional, aura; the mental aura; and the etheric body aura. The astral aura is usually most dominant in people on this planet, although this is beginning to change as we move deeper into the Aryan root race cycle, which is a mental attunement.

The mental aura is usually very small in the average person, but it develops rapidly once the disciple becomes polarized in the mental body during the latter stages of the second initiation and the beginning of the third initiation. Djwhal Khul says in the Alice Bailey book *Ponder on This* that the "mental aura will eventually obliterate the emotional or astral aura and then the soul quality of love will create a substitute, that is of a higher nature."

We live and move within our fourfold aura. This living, vital aura serves as a recording agent of all subjective and objective impressions. It is not so much our words that create an effect on people, as some think, but our aura.

The aura is radiant in nature and extends from all the bodies in every direction. The seven primary chakras also have a great effect on the nature of a person's aura. A highly emotional person working through an overdeveloped and uncontrolled solar plexus chakra can wreak havoc in a home or office. On the other side of the coin, a disciple consciously using the heart or throat center can inspire hundreds.

The aura is brought into radiance through right living, high thinking, and loving activity. This leads the initiate to become a center of living light in which all seven of the chakras are merged into one light.

We look out into the world through our aura. The four words that best describe the human aura are color, light, quality, and sphere of influence. Most psychics see only the astral range of the aura. In reality there are seven layers to the aura.

Christ's aura was so powerful that all people had to do was touch Him and the virtue would pour out of Him and heal them. Every person's aura either attracts or repels others, depending on the programming and patterning within the individual. Every group has an aura, every nation has an aura, and the earth as a whole has an aura. I once bought a very beautiful statue of the Buddha, and a clairvoyant friend of mine came over and without my asking told me that the statue's heart chakra was spinning and open. A Master has only to look at the light reflected in a person's aura to determine their level of evolution.

The Meaning of Colors in the Human Aura

Each color in the human aura indicates specific characteristics.

Red: The color red reflects the physical aspect of the mind, such as passion, anger, physical desires, emotion, vigor, and vitality. It is related to the first-ray quality of will. (See Chapter 14 for a complete discussion of the rays.)

Blue: The color blue reflects the religious or spiritual phase of the mind, including contemplation, prayer, heaven, spirituality, selflessness, and emotions such as love, devotion, altruism, and reverence. Blue is a soothing and calming color.

Yellow: The color yellow reflects intellectual pursuits, such as logic, induction, active intelligence, analysis, and judgment.

White: The color white represents pure spirit.

Black: Black is the absence of color. It is the opposite pole of pure spirit, hence the term "black magic." It also indicates hatred, anger, avarice, revenge, and malice.

Gray: Gray in the aura reflects negative thoughts and emotions.

Violet: The color violet is a very spiritual color. It usually indicates evenness of mind and a searching for a cause or religious experience. It has been associated with transmutation because of its connection with the seventh ray.

Orange: A good vital shade of orange usually indicates thoughtfulness and consideration of others. It is connected with the fifth-ray energy of concrete science.

Green: The color green usually deals with healing and is helpful, strong, and friendly. It is a color doctors and nurses often wear. It is connected with the fourth-ray energy of harmony through conflict.

Color Chart for the Human Aura

The following is a color chart of the human aura from a book by Edgar Cayce called *Auras*. What is interesting in this chart is that it also shows the afflictions, or negative aspects, of each color in addition to the positive qualities. The diagram shows the planets and musical notes connected with each color as well.

The Human Aura

COLOR	MUSICAL NOTE	PLANET	INTERPRETATION	AFFLICTION
Red	Do	Mars	Force, Vigor, Energy	Nervousness, Egotism
Orange	Re	Sun	Thoughtfulness, Consideration	Laziness, Repression
Yellow	Mi	Mercury	Health, Well-being, Friendliness	Weakness of Will
Green	Fa	Saturn	Healing, Helpfulness	Mixed with Yellow: Deceit
Blue	Sol	Jupiter	Spirituality, Artistry, Selflessness	Struggle, Melancholy
Indigo	La	Venus	A Seeking Nature, Religion	Heart and Stomach Trouble
Violet	Ti	Moon	A Seeking Nature, Religion	Heart and Stomach Trouble

Chapter 9

✴

The Twenty-Two Chakras

The chakras are in the nature of distributing agencies and electric batteries,
providing dynamic force and qualitative energy to man.
— DJWHAL KHUL, AS CHANNELED THROUGH ALICE A. BAILEY

In a sense, our chakras are like electrical transformers that take the raw wave particles of electrical energy and convert them into a more controlled and regulated form to light our homes and power the countless energy-consuming devices we use daily. Chakras are nonphysical organs within the body, aligned along the spine corresponding to points along the central nervous system, and are often associated with certain glands and nerve ganglia. The full chakra system is extremely complex.

In the most basic configuration there are seven main chakras. In the Hindu system of seven, each chakra (the word *chakra* means "wheel" in Sanskrit) is a different color and spins clockwise. At times one or more of these chakras may be out of balance, which results in either physical disease or mental or emotional distress. It is important first to identify which chakra is out of balance, and then take the necessary steps to realign it or in some cases unblock it.

This chapter is intended to be a kind of catalogue of the chakra system, a point of reference for you to return to. There are many fine books written on the chakra system itself, and I encourage you to undertake further exploration of this area if you so desire. At present, this list and its brief definitions should provide you with the basic information necessary to continue your negative ego work.

Developing a Christ consciousness to replace our negative ego can seem like a daunting challenge. We can sometimes feel overwhelmed when faced with controlling our emotional responses, practicing unconditional self-love, and balancing our three minds and four bodies. We can, at times, feel as though we are alone on this path.

What has always helped to sustain me on this journey is the knowledge that I am anything but alone. Besides my contact with hundreds and hundreds of lightworkers, I also take comfort in knowing that there are many other traditions the world over with belief systems and practices that soul psychology can accommodate. Rather than viewing this path as an exclusive club, limited to only those from one background or tradition, soul psychology is inclusive because it is founded on universal principles.

I also draw strength from the knowledge that I am connected to a universal energy source, which we can all access because it is a part of our very being. According to Hindu Tantric philosophy, we are all energized by the pure thought energy that permeates and binds the universe together. We can each tap this living energy field more deeply by applying our will. We can draw this energy into our human bodies and transform it, through the chakra system, into more subtle and usable forms.

In the most common understanding of the human chakra system, we have seven chakras. This is a valid understanding if we are considering only three-dimensional reality. The fact is that there are also eight fourth-dimensional chakras and seven fifth-dimensional chakras. There might possibly be more beyond these, on into the sixth and seventh dimensions of reality, but that information is far beyond our ability to explain or access.

This information concerning the twenty-two chakras was sent to me by Vywamus through Dorothy Bodenburg of the Tibetan Foundation. The diagram on page 149 delineates these twenty-two essential aspects of our being.

The Chakras

THIRD DIMENSION	FOURTH DIMENSION	FIFTH DIMENSION
0 Earth	8 Seat of the Soul	16 Ascension; Universal Being
1 Base	9 Body of Light	17 Universal Light
2 Polarity	10 Integration of Polarities	18 6th Dimensional Divine Intent
3 Solar Plexus	11 New Age Energies	No Correspondence
4 Heart	12 Christ Consciousness	19 Universal Energy
5 Throat	13 Manifesting Vibratory Communication	20 Beingness
6 Third Eye	14 Divine Plan	21 Divine Structure
7 Crown	15 Monadic Connection	22 Source Connection

Our seven main chakras connect the etheric body or energy body to the physical body. The seven chakras reside within the etheric body, not within the dense physical body. Each chakra has a specific pattern of energy used for a specific purpose. Since the Harmonic Convergence in August of 1987 there has been an energy structure developed to allow the fourth dimension to come into physical existence.

THE THIRD-DIMENSIONAL CHAKRAS

The Root Chakra

The first chakra is the seat of the physical body. It focuses our earthly life, connecting us very specifically to the earth. It deals with issues such as grounding and survival. In the early Lemurian period it was the base chakra that was most open. The first chakra deals with considerations about being here on earth. It is the color red, and is connected with the gonads.

The Second Chakra

The second chakra is the polarity chakra. It has to do with creativity, masculine and feminine balance, and our sexual energies. The back of the second chakra relates to the seat of the subconscious mind. The gland that it is connected to is the ludig gland, or lyden gland, which is a part of the lymphatic system. Its color is usually designated as orange. This chakra was focused on in later Lemurian development.

The Solar Plexus Chakra

The third chakra is the seat of the emotional body. The adrenal glands relate to this chakra, and the color usually associated with it is yellow. The Atlantean period of earth's history focused on the development of this chakra.

The Heart Chakra

The fourth chakra deals with unconditional love. The gland that is associated with it is the thymus gland; the color most usually associated with it is green. This chakra has been the focus in the Christian era.

The Throat Chakra

The throat chakra deals with communication, expression, and the use of will. The thyroid is associated with this chakra. The color most associated with this chakra is blue. This chakra is the one that is being developed in the Aquarian Age.

The Third Eye Chakra

The third eye chakra has to do with spiritual sight and vision. The gland associated with this chakra is the pituitary. The color most often associated with this chakra is violet. The third eye chakra also relates to the conscious mind.

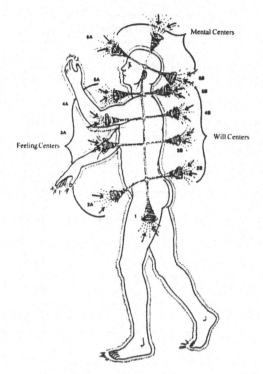

**The Seven Major Chakras,
Front and Back Views**
This chart is from Barbara Brennan's book,
Hands of Light, which I highly recommend.

The Crown Chakra

The crown chakra has to do with the superconscious mind, the soul, the higher self, and/or God. It is truly our gate through which to bring the higher energies. The color most often associated with this chakra is white light, or a rainbow-speckled white light. The gland associated with this chakra is the pineal.

Chakra Colors

The colors that most schools of thought have used for visualizing the chakras are listed on the next page.

Chakra Colors

The colors that most schools of thought have used for the visualizing of the chakras are listed below.

CHAKRA	STANDARD COLOR
Root	Red
Second	Orange
Solar plexus	Yellow
Heart	Green
Throat	Blue
Third eye	Indigo
Crown	Violet

Chakra Toning

Besides using light and color to work with and open your chakras, it is also possible to use sound. Djwhal Khul has channeled the sounds that correspond to the seven three-dimensional chakras. In the third column of the following diagram are words that will help you to enunciate the sounds properly.

CHAKRA	TONES FROM DJWHAL KHUL	HINDU TONES
Root chakra	O (oh)	Lam
Second chakra	SHU (shuck)	Yam
Solar Plexus chakra	YA (yawn)	Ram
Heart chakra	WA (way)	Yam
Throat chakra	HE (he)	Ham
Third eye chakra	HU (hue)	Om
Crown chakra	I (eye)	Aum

THE FOURTH-DIMENSIONAL CHAKRAS

I became aware that we had more than seven chakras when Djwhal Khul explained that as a person evolves, the higher chakras begin to move downward and descend into the former third-dimensional chakras, creating twelve chakras. I asked if my higher chakras had descended. He told me during our initial conversation that my tenth chakra was in my crown, my ninth chakra was in the third eye chakra, my eighth chakra was in my throat chakra, and so on all the way down my body and chakra system. I found this information fascinating. Since that time I have been calling my twelfth chakra down into my crown. I have also been focusing the energy and quality of the twelfth chakra, the Christ consciousness, more clearly in my life. In subsequent conversations with Djwhal, he said I had stabilized the twelfth chakra in the crown chakra, the eleventh in the third eye, and so on.

It is only recently that I became aware from exchanges with the Masters that there are in actuality twenty-two chakras. My current focus in my own spiritual path is now to anchor the fifteenth chakra into the crown, the fifteenth chakra having to do with our monadic connection.

The sixteenth chakra is the chakra that is anchored in the crown when an initiate ascends. Djwhal Khul has definitely recommended that people *not* call down any chakra higher than the fifteenth prior to ascension, for there is a danger of burning out the physical body with too high a frequency of energy. It is permissible, however, to call forth the colors of energy that are associated with the fifth-dimensional chakras.

Eighth Chakra

The eighth chakra is the first chakra of the fourth dimension; it is the seat of the soul. Just as in the third dimension the earth, designated by the number zero, represents physical existence, so in the fourth dimension the seat of the soul becomes the seat of existence.

The colors of chakras eight through twelve are exactly the same as the colors of the higher fourth-dimensional rays (these rays will be explained in great detail in a later chapter). The colors of the eighth chakra are emerald green and purple.

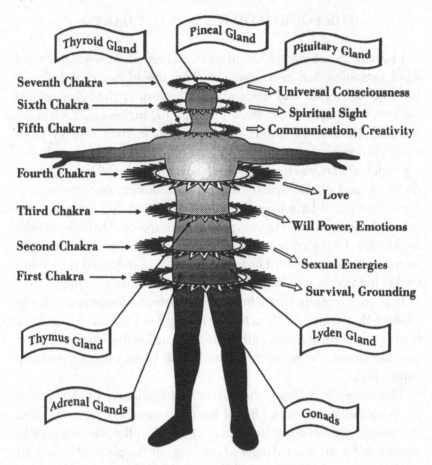

The Seven Chakras and Glands

The Ninth Chakra

The ninth chakra corresponds to the base chakra in the third dimension. It is related to the body of light. It has to do with joy. When this chakra is activated it ignites the body of light, which is now in your cellular and subcellular structure. The color of this chakra is blue-green.

The Tenth Chakra

The tenth chakra is associated with the polarity chakra of the third dimension. It has to do with the integration of male and female within self. This chakra starts functioning when the male and female energies are in perfect balance. This is experienced as a state of effortlessness and alignment with one's soul. The color of this chakra is a pearlescence.

The Eleventh Chakra

This is the chakra of the New Age energies. It corresponds with the solar plexus chakra in the third dimension. Connecting the third chakra to the eleventh chakra allows us to diminish the present- and past-life trauma stored in the third chakra. The feeling of eleventh-chakra energy is like a wave, and it will move through your body and out again without staying or without attaching itself to an area of misperception. (Before the fourth dimension was available, an imbalanced emotional response would attach itself to misperceptions already in the body.) The color of this chakra is pink-orange.

The Twelfth Chakra

The twelfth chakra is the Christ consciousness, which is a transformational energy that connects all energy forms. It is associated with the heart chakra in the third dimension, and its color is shimmering gold.

The Thirteenth Chakra

The thirteenth chakra has to do with the manifesting of vibratory communication. This is the chakra that is used in materializing and dematerializing things. It is also the chakra used in teleportation. This chakra is used for healing as well. It is pale violet-pink in color.

The Fourteenth Chakra

The fourteenth chakra has to do with the Divine Plan. It allows the mental mind to surrender. The fourteenth chakra says that you are allowing the Divine Plan to show you the way without review or evaluation from your mental thought beliefs.

This chakra corresponds to the third eye of the third dimension. It brings clairvoyance into the fourth dimension and activates your un-limitedness. The color of this chakra is deep blue-violet.

The Fifteenth Chakra

The fifteenth chakra is concerned with your monadic connection. It corresponds to the crown chakra of the third dimension, your spiritual connection. Opening the fifteenth chakra allows your new spiritual connection, which is the monad, to operate. This occurs when you pass the fourth initiation. At the fifth initiation we become merged with the monad, which brings us to the doorway of ascension. When this chakra is operating, it says that the structure of your soul is stable enough to handle the energy and the scope of the information coming from the monadic level. It is a light golden white.

THE FIFTH-DIMENSIONAL CHAKRAS

The Sixteenth Chakra

The sixteenth chakra has to do with ascension and becoming a Universal Being. It is the sixteenth chakra that descends into the crown chakra at the time of ascension. When this chakra has been activated, the Master needs to decide whether he or she is going to stay in physical existence. The Universal Being moves among all time frames and all dimensions and can adapt to whatever energy form or body is needed.

As the first chakra of the fifth-dimensional chakra grid system, this chakra of ascension into the monad and becoming universal is our new baseline, just as the eighth chakra, the seat of the soul, was the baseline in the fourth-dimensional chakras. The color of this chakra is light violet-white.

The Seventeenth Chakra

The seventeenth chakra has to do with universal light, and it corresponds to the ninth chakra, or the body of light in the fourth dimension. The progression is from the third dimension, which is solid, to the fourth dimension, which is solid and light, to the fifth dimension, which is total light. Because it is composed of all the colors in the visible spectrum, it is multiwhite in color.

The Eighteenth Chakra

The eighteenth chakra has to do with sixth-dimensional divine intent. This chakra, when activated, creates the ability to bring in the sixth dimension of reality. In looking at your chart of the chakras on page 149, you will see that there is a gap between the eighteenth and nineteenth chakras that says "no correspondence." The reason for this is that at the fifth-dimensional level there is no correspondence to the solar plexus because it has united with the heart chakra. It is pink-gold in color.

The Nineteenth Chakra

The nineteenth chakra relates to universal energy. The heart energy is the focus in the third dimension; the Christ consciousness is the expanding energy in the fourth dimension; in the fifth dimension, the correspondence is the universal energy. This universal energy is being felt by those who are allowing this energy to come through this chakra, through the monadic level, and through their soul level to their physical body. It is magenta in color.

The Twentieth Chakra

The twentieth chakra focuses on beingness. In the third dimension you needed to communicate; in the fourth dimension you were able to communicate in a more expanded way by means of vibration through light; in the fifth dimension there is no need for an exchange. There is a pure beingness in which exchange is not necessary for communication. It is violet-gold in color.

The Twenty-First Chakra

The twenty-first chakra has to do with divine structure. It is creating from a point of evolution, which is really a point of resolution. In the third dimension the third eye allows you to be clairvoyant, in the fourth dimension it is the Divine Plan. You are now beyond the structure of the fifth into the learning that took place during the Divine Structure. Vywamus said in respect to this chakra, "Now I must tell you that none of you have to worry about this in the next two or three years." It is blue-gold in color.

The Twenty-Second Chakra

The twenty-second chakra has to do with Source or Godhead connection. It is platinum in color.

Chapter 10

✴

Pitfalls and Traps on the Path of Ascension

Glamour is not dispelled by paying close attention to it. It disappears by the power of clear and steadfast meditation, and the freeing of one's self from self attention.

— DJWHAL KHUL, AS CHANNELED BY ALICE A. BAILEY

In my travels through life as a spiritual teacher, spiritual psychologist, and disciple on the spiritual path, I have become aware of many of the pitfalls and traps along the way. I consider myself somewhat of an expert on this subject, for I have fallen into most of them.

I highly recommend meditating on the following list of pitfalls. Although very short on words, it is profound in insight. My purpose in sharing this list with you is to save you the suffering, karma, and delay in your path of ascension that will come from not learning these lessons. The spiritual path is very easy on one level, and incredibly complicated on another.

There are glamours, snares, and traps that the negative ego and dark forces provide every step of the way. Making mistakes and falling into them is okay. My concern is helping you to not stay stuck in them for extensive periods of time, and in some cases for many lifetimes.

1. Giving your personal power away to other people, your subconscious mind, your negative ego, your five senses, your physical body, your emotional body, your mental body, your child consciousness, a guru, the Ascended Masters, or God
2. Loving others but not loving yourself

3. Not recognizing your negative ego as the source of all your problems

4. Focusing on God but not properly integrating and parenting the child within you

5. Not eating properly and not getting enough physical exercise, which results in physical illness and limits all other levels

6. Being deeply into the spiritual life but not recognizing the psychological level, which also needs to be understood and mastered

7. Material desire

8. The trap and glamour of power, and holding power over others once you become successful

9. Becoming too ungrounded, which then has a harmful effect on one's physical body

10. Trying to escape earth instead of creating heaven on earth

11. Seeing appearances instead of seeing the true reality behind all appearance

12. Trying to become God instead of realizing you already are the Eternal Self, as is everyone else

13. Not realizing that you cause everything

14. Serving others totally before you have become self-actualized

15. Thinking that there is such a thing as "righteous anger" (anger is a big trap)

16. Becoming an extremist and not being moderate in all things

17. Thinking you have to be ascetic to be spiritual

18. Becoming too serious and not having enough joy, happiness, and fun in your life

19. Not being disciplined and unceasingly continuing your spiritual practices

20. Stopping your spiritual practices and studies when you get involved in a relationship

21. Putting a relationship before self and God (this is a major trap)

22. Letting your child consciousness run your life

23. Being too critical of and hard on yourself

24. Getting caught up in the glamour and illusion of psychic powers

25. Owning your power but not learning to surrender to God simultaneously, or surrendering to God but not learning to own your power simultaneously

26. Losing your personal power when you get physically tired and exhausted

27. Expecting God and the Ascended Masters to solve all your problems

28. Allowing yourself to go on automatic pilot and losing your vigilance

29. Giving your power to channeled entities

30. Reading too much and not meditating enough

31. Letting your sexuality run you instead of mastering it

32. Overidentifying with your mental or emotional body, and not achieving balance

33. Thinking you need to be a voice channel or see or experience all kinds of psychic phenomena to be spiritual or to ascend

34. Forcing the raising of the kundalini

35. Forcing the opening of the chakras

36. Thinking the spiritual path you have found is the "best"

37. Judging people because of what initiation level they may be at

38. Sharing your "advanced" initiation level with other people

39. Telling people about the "good spiritual work" you are doing, instead of just being humble

40. Thinking that negative emotions are something you have to have

41. Isolating yourself from people and thinking that this is spiritual

42. Thinking the earth is a terrible place

43. Giving your power to astrology and the influence of the stars

44. Being too attached to things

45. Being too unattached to life, not striving for involved detachment

46. Being too preoccupied with self and not being concerned enough about being of service to others

47. Getting stuck in the numerous limited theories of traditional psychology, which are only a single piece of the whole human puzzle

48. Being too much the mystic or too much the occultist and not striving to integrate the two sides

49. Giving up amidst great adversity (this is one of the biggest traps of all—you must never give up)

50. Believing that the suffering you are going through on whatever level will not pass

51. Focusing too much on what initiation level you are at or when you are going to ascend instead of on the work that needs to be done

52. Getting caught up in spiritual powers and the achievement of siddhas instead of recognizing that love is the most important spiritual power of all

53. Badmouthing other spiritual or metaphysical groups, and not

unifying and networking with other groups even though they may be not in total alignment with all of your beliefs

54. Getting caught up in the dogma of traditional religion

55. Thinking you need a priest to be an intermediary between you and God

56. Using your spiritual beliefs to create separatism or elitism or undue specialness

57. Becoming too fanatical in your beliefs

58. Believing you can achieve enlightenment through drugs or some kind of pill (this is the highest sense of illusion)

59. Believing that other people don't have to work as hard at their spiritual path as you do

60. Putting your relationship with your kids before your self and God

61. Getting caught up in all the attractions of the fascinating material world in which we live

62. Becoming too caught up in loving one person instead of spreading your love out to encompass all people in an unconditional sense

63. Getting caught up in duality instead of achieving even-mindedness, inner peace, and equanimity at all times

64. Being a father or son, or a mother or daughter, in your relationships instead of being an adult

65. Thinking you need to suffer in life

66. Being a martyr on your spiritual path

67. Needing to control others

68. Having spiritual ambition

69. Needing to be liked, loved, or approved of

70. Needing to be the teacher

71. Being hypersensitive or being too shielded

72. Taking responsibility for other people

73. Being the savior

74. Serving for selfish reasons and thinking you are being spiritual

75. Thinking you are more advanced spiritually than you really are, or thinking you are less advanced than you really are

76. Blindly seeking fame

77. Placing undue importance on finding your twin flame and soul mate and not realizing your soul and monad are, in truth, who you are really looking for

78. Thinking you need a romantic relationship to be happy

79. Needing to be at center stage, or always choosing to be a wallflower

80. Working too hard and becoming driven and running yourself down physically, or playing too much and not being about the Father's business

81. Going to psychics and channels for guidance and not trusting your own intuition

82. Working with teachers on this plane or on the Inner Plane who are not Ascended Masters and so are limited in the understanding and conception of reality.

83. Making the spiritual path an interest rather than an all-consuming fire

84. Wasting too much time watching TV, reading trashy novels, seeing violent movies

85. Wasting enormous amounts of time and energy because of lack of organization and proper time management

86. Thinking that arguing with another is serving you or that person

87. Trying to win or be "right" instead of striving for love

88. Putting too much emphasis on intuition, intellect, feeling, and instinct instead of realizing that they all need to be balanced and integrated in their proper proportions

89. Devoting yourself to a guru who makes you smaller instead of to the Eternal Self, which you are

90. Trying to be open all the time, instead of knowing how to open and close your field as the need arises

91. Not knowing how to say no to other people, your child consciousness, or the negative ego when the need arises

92. Thinking violence or attacks on others in any form will get you what you want or serves God in any capacity

93. Blaming God, or being angry at God or the Ascended Masters for your problems

94. Thinking that if your prayers aren't answered in the way you expect, God and the ascended masters aren't answering your prayers

95. Comparing yourself with other people instead of comparing self with self

96. Thinking that being poor is being spiritual

97. Comparing and competing with others over one's initiation level and ascension

98. Allowing yourself to be a victim of other people and of your own physical body, emotional body, mental body, desires, five senses, or negative ego

99. Studying too much and not demonstrating enough in the real world

100. Thinking your moodiness is a true reality of God

101. Thinking your worth comes from doing and achieving things

102. Thinking you don't need to protect yourself spiritually, psychologically, and physically

103. Thinking that glamour, maya, illusion, negative ego, fear, and separation are real

104. Consuming sugar, artificial stimulants, coffee, and soft drinks for physical energy

105. Trying to do everything yourself and not calling on God for help, or constantly calling on God for help and not helping yourself

106. Loving people a little less because they are treating you badly, or setting a negative ego example; not differentiating the person from the behavior

107. Losing faith in the living reality of your soul, your monad, God, and the Ascended Masters; they have the ability to help you if you will persevere and do your part

108. Thinking that other people can achieve ascension but you can't, or at least not in this lifetime

109. Trying to achieve ascension to escape one's problems

110. Thinking that earth is a prison instead of recognizing it as one of God's seven heavens

This list should provide ample food for thought. The lower self, glamour, maya, illusion, and the negative ego are incredibly tricky and elusive in nature. As Master Yoda said in the Star Wars movies, "Don't underestimate the power of the dark side of the force." Once you get caught up in it, it is often very difficult to see your way out of it. Staying clear takes enormous vigilance, self-discipline, commitment, introspection, and devastating honesty. If the ego can't make you feel like an underdog, it will make you feel like a top dog, which is even more seductive.

Everything in God's universe is governed by laws. There are physical laws, emotional laws, mental laws, and spiritual laws. By learning to understand these laws and become obedient to them, we fulfill the law, which is the path of ascension.

These insights can be helpful as we progress on our spiritual paths. My prayer is that we all may learn to live by grace instead of karma (suffering).

Chapter 11

✴

The Laws of Manifestation

Manifestation is not magic. It is a process of working with natural principles and laws in order to translate energy from one level of reality to another.
— DAVID SPANGLER

As David Spangler points out, there is no magic to manifestation. Anyone with the most fundamental understanding of physics recalls one of its basic principles—matter can be neither created nor destroyed. It can only change state. As our understanding of the natural world has grown, that principle has been expanded to include Einstein's law of the conservation of energy. To understand that law, simply replace Newton's use of the word *matter* with the word *energy*. We all manifest energy at the physical level every day. When we compose text on a computer, we are transferring our thoughts from electrochemical energy in our brains into the kinetic energy necessary to press the keys on the computer's keyboard, which transmits an electrical impulse through the computer's circuitry.

After many more changes and exchanges of energy, the writer's original mental energy enters the reader's mind as he or she reads the words. Eventually that mental energy will be converted into actions and beliefs, thus perpetuating the life of this energy. As discussed in the chapter on chakras, the original energy that produces our thoughts was made available to us from the universe, and we can access it through our chakras. All of these exchanges and transformations of energy are examples of manifestation.

Mastering the laws of manifestation is one of the most essential spiritual practices for a disciple on the path. In this chapter I have organized the information into a series of fifty-nine principles that serve as the foundation for mastery of this subject. Careful study and meditation upon these principles can literally be worth your weight in gold.

Without the soul, we are living in the illusion of separation and negative ego with all its attributes. When the soul is included, what we want to manifest is a part of us already. Manifestation, then, is in a sense just undoing or stripping away that which is already ours but which has been hidden by the delusion of the personality. The soul is not separate from the object that it is trying to manifest, as the personality would have you believe. The object you are trying to manifest is part of the soul, for soul pervades all things. This is why you have and are everything already.

A person such as Sai Baba, who is one with spirit, can instantly manifest what he thinks and images. The same is true for us, except the process is slowed down a bit. When we think from a soul consciousness, it instantly manifests, except we cannot see it yet with our physical eyes. Time and space do not really exist, so once you claim your manifestation, it is already yours. We are just waiting for it to come into manifestation on the earthly plane.

For those who have already developed clairvoyant ability, this manifestation can be seen. On this plane it takes a little longer for our manifestation to ground itself into the physical, and many people lose their concentration before the manifestation has the opportunity to move from the etheric into the physical. This is why manifesting with a consciousness of the soul is a true golden key.

• Most people manifest the things in their life on a conscious mind level through the use of will or personal power. We work eighteen-hour days and just power it out. The conscious level of manifestation is also connected with physical action. This means making phone calls, physically organizing, seeing clients, running errands, carrying out administrative duties, and so on. This is a very valid and important method of manifestation.

In reality everyone uses the power of the subconscious mind for manifestation, whether we realize it or not. The problem is that most of us allow our subconscious to manifest unchecked—in other words, we have no conscious awareness of what our subconscious mind is doing. Worse yet, some people use this level of manifestation to actually block manifestation rather than facilitate it.

The law of the subconscious mind is based on the famous Hermetic law of correspondence: "As within, so without; as above, so below." What you think and imagine in your conscious and subconscious minds will manifest its mirror likeness in your external circumstances. Your outer world is a mirror of your inner world, for better or worse, because the subconscious mind does whatever it is programmed to do.

The major work of the spiritual path is to rid yourself of all lower-self aspects, negative ego, and imbalanced programming. When this is done you have the Midas touch, where everything you touch turns to gold. This occurs because your subconscious mind is subservient to the conscious mind, which is subservient to the superconscious mind, which is subservient to the superconscious or soul mind, which is subservient to the monadic mind, which is subservient to God.

The subconscious mind operates your physical body and will create health or disease depending upon how you program it. The subconscious will attract to you everything you need, for all minds are joined in truth. This is why the use of affirmations, visualization, and auto-suggestion is such an important science.

To manifest effectively, you must learn to be in control of the subconscious mind. Many times the subconscious mind runs you instead of the other way around. Ideally the subconscious is your servant. It has been called the basic self or servomechanism in other teachings. It is your faithful servant and will supply you with whatever you need as long as you program it correctly.

The third way to manifest is through the power of the superconscious mind, the higher self, spirit, God. This is, of course, manifesting not by affirmation or visualization, but rather by prayer. Prayer is the spiritual practice of asking God for what you want and accepting that it has been done once you have made your request.

God, through your higher self and monad, hears and answers all prayers. How, when, and in what form He answers them depends on how you adhere to the universal laws of manifestation.

Why manifest just with willpower and physical work when you can pray every day and acquire God's help? Not only do you have God's help through prayer, but you also have the Ascended Masters, the angels, God working through other people, your higher self, and your monad.

Perhaps you do not pray enough. Maybe you only use your conscious mind. Maybe you pray but don't get off your duff, and instead expect God to do everything for you. This will not work, for God helps those who help themselves. Maybe you are constantly doing affirmations and visualizations but don't own your willpower to do the physical action and work that is needed.

THE LAWS OF MANIFESTATION

1. *The first law of manifestation is that we must learn to manifest with all three of our minds—the conscious, subconscious, and superconscious or soul mind.*

This law deals with the importance of using all three levels of mind in perfect harmony, balance, and integration.

2. *Awareness that you are the soul and not the personality.* If you manifest from the consciousness of personality, you will see yourself as separated from your brothers and sisters—indeed, from creation itself. That is an illusion.

Your manifestation will be a thousand times more powerful if you recognize yourself as the Christ, the Buddha, the atman, the Eternal Self, for in truth that is who you are. You are one with God and all of creation; therefore what you are trying to manifest is nothing more than a part of yourself. This important point cannot be emphasized enough.

The New Age laws of manifestation deal with this shift in the focus of your identity. Failing to use prayer and to not identify yourself as soul rather than personality cuts you off to a very great degree from the source of energy for the manifestation of your desires. Ask for assistance from the Ascended Masters, angels, or your monad if you would like extra help.

3. *Do not be attached to what you are praying for or are trying to manifest, or you will repel it from yourself.* Make your choice for mani-

festing a preference, not an attachment. With this attitude you will remain happy until your preference is manifested.

4. *Surrender your prayer request to God and leave it in God's hands.* God is happy to help, but you *must* surrender your request. You can visualize your prayer request going up in a bubble of pink or golden light and melding with God's light. Then it is your job to go about your business and do what you can on the conscious level of personal power and on the physical action level.

5. *All that exists is perfection.* God created you and you are perfect. Anytime anything but perfection manifests, immediately pray and/or visualize and affirm the truth instead of the illusion of the negative ego. Cancel and deny any thoughts that try to enter your mind other than this truth. If you are sick, affirm and visualize only perfection. If your bank account is low, visualize that it is full.

6. *The thoughts and images that you hold in your mind create your reality.* God's universe is abundant and limitless. We attract either poverty or abundance, depending on the attitude we hold. This brings us back to the Hermetic law, "As within, so without; as above, so below." Your outer world and physical body are mirrors of the inner world of your conscious and subconscious thinking and imaging.

7. *Have faith.* You know God exists, and you know that God's laws are perfect and work every time. So after you pray, know that your prayer has been heard and God's law has been invoked. Nothing but perfect fulfillment of the prayer and law can happen as long as you have faith in God's laws. If you give in to doubt and worry, you are blocking the energy manifestation that you just set in motion.

8. *Be aligned and be committed.* All four bodies must be in alignment for a quick manifestation of your prayer request. The mind must be attuned to God, spirit, and the soul so that its energy can flow through you.

The feeling body must be attuned to the mind and then the soul. The physical body must be attuned to the emotional body, which is attuned to the mind, which is attuned to the soul, which is attuned to the monad, which is attuned to God in the same way that the lower minds are subservient to the ones above and to the soul and God.

After you pray, you don't want the subconscious mind acting against your interests by saying, "I don't believe this is going to work." If this starts to happen, push that out of your mind and say, "Get thee behind me, Satan," then reaffirm God's perfection.

9. *Everything in God's universe is energy, and all energy is God.* Even physical matter is just energy vibrating more slowly. So all you are really doing in working the laws of manifestation is changing or transferring energy from one form to another.

This law deals with the fact that energy follows thought. What you ask for already exists on a higher level once the prayer, affirmation, and visualization have been done. Now you are just waiting for it to manifest into physical reality. Your attitude should be expectant. You are simply waiting for it to move down the dimensions and ground itself in physical reality. As long as you keep your four bodies and three minds in alignment, there is no reason for this not to happen.

10. *The laws of manifestation operate whether you are consciously aware of them or not.* In addition, they are also perfectly happy to work with the negative as well as the positive—they do not discriminate. Whatever you give the subconscious, it will use. If you hold a negative thought and image for too long, it will manifest into your physical reality eventually. So if you are not working these laws of manifestation for the positive, they are going to work to your detriment.

11. *Every moment of your life you are working the laws of manifestation, even when you are not praying, willing, visualizing, or affirming.* Every thought you have in your mind as you go through your daily life and when you are sleeping is part of this process.

If you never did any specific manifestation work but were vigilant about every thought that you let into your mind, allowing in only thoughts of perfection, God, love, and health, then you would have everything you needed. In this state the three minds are functioning as one mind. Your soul and higher self are doing your thinking, not the negative ego or personality.

12. *Pray from your soul and not the negative ego.* Your soul won't help if you pray for something that is not for the highest good of all concerned or that hurts someone else. If your prayer doesn't manifest exactly as you expected, there is a possibility it is not meant to be and not truly a part of your Divine Plan.

13. *Perseverance pays off.* On this earthly plane, time is slowed down so that we may practice these laws. In the higher dimensions of reality, things manifest instantly. We are on this plane of existence to

prove our mastery of these laws so that we won't create havoc on the higher planes. We need to demonstrate endurance.

14. *Manifestation knows no limits.* If you are trying to manifest money, don't think or imagine it as only coming from working, for example. Maybe it will come from the lottery, or an inheritance, or you will find it, or someone will give you money. God works in mysterious ways, so don't try to outthink God. If you think your prayer can manifest in only one way, then you have limited God and your subconscious mind's ability to manifest for you.

15. *We can receive as well as give.* I know a lot of spiritual people who are great givers but do not know how to receive. When they are offered a gift and say, "No, I can't accept this," they have just blocked their abundance. Receiving is an essential part of having prosperity consciousness.

16. *Gratitude is good.* Be humble and thankful for the abundance that God has bestowed upon you. Be thankful to God, the soul, the Ascended Masters, the subconscious mind, the angels, and the nature spirits for all the wonderful work they do for you. Make every day a thanksgiving.

17. *Failure is not a possibility.* How can you fail with God, the soul, your personal power, the power of your subconscious mind, your physical body, and other people all helping you? Besides, you are the Christ, Buddha, the atman, the Eternal Self. You are God. Can God lose against the forces of illusion and maya?

The only thing that can stop your manifestation is the glamour, maya, and illusion of your own negative ego and lower self. The only thing that can stop you from manifesting anything you want is you. God has given you everything. You only have to claim it. That is the only thing that God can't do for you. We must claim God's abundance and then it is instantly ours.

18. *To have all, give all to all.* This is a law of manifestation made known in *A Course in Miracles.* We must learn to receive, but we also must learn to give in order to manifest effectively. We must keep our abundance in circulation. When we become selfish and stop giving, then the universe becomes selfish and stops giving to us. When we stop giving to the all, which is God, we are not able to receive as much. Keep giving and keep receiving; let the abundance flow freely in both directions.

19. *Words have power.* The power of your spoken words is even greater than the thoughts you allow to run through your mind. Every word you speak is a decree of manifestation. Consequently, you must be vigilant over your speech. Just because you are not focusing on your manifestation work doesn't mean that you are not doing manifestation work.

20. *Positive affirmations produce positive results.* For example, if you want to heal a broken leg, phrase your affirmation and prayer without saying, "I am now healing my broken leg." It would be better to say, "My leg is now powerful, healed and whole." The reference to the negative image can have a negative effect on the subconscious mind. The subconscious mind has no reasoning and will manifest anything that is put into it, so let only the positive in.

21. *Vital force and energy are necessary ingredients.* Before doing your manifestation work, build up your vital force and energy. Spirit and the angels sometimes use the energy as well as the thoughts and imagery you send them in your prayer request. You can build up vital force by doing deep breathing or physical exercise for a few minutes before you begin praying.

22. *Enthusiasm produces results.* When you do your manifestation work, be enthusiastic. Your enthusiasm is part of the previous law of building vital force, and enthusiasm also incorporates your emotional body in the manifestation work, which will speed the process. The emotional body is connected to the subconscious mind, and nothing will manifest unless the subconscious mind is involved in the process.

23. *There is just one universal subconscious mind.* We each focus on one aspect of that mind while being simultaneously connected to the whole mind or, as Jung called it, the collective unconscious. This understanding and awareness in your manifestation work gets rid of the belief in separation that can slow down manifestation.

24. *Only you can block your own manifestation.* If you master your thinking and imagining and your feeling body, then nothing can stop the manifestation from occurring.

25. *Grudges block the process.* Be sure you have forgiven all people, situations, and yourself before beginning your manifestation work. Not forgiving someone builds guilt and other psychic blocks that make the subconscious mind unable to cooperate fully in the prayer process and affirmation work.

26. *Love yourself.* If you lack self-love, you feel undeserving. If you believe you are undeserving, you contradict what you ask for in prayer.

If this is a lesson for you, seriously study Chapter 5 in this book, on the Christ consciousness.

27. *Pray in proportion.* Some people pray too much, which is a sign of lack of faith. In reality, once is enough. If, however, worry and doubt set in, there is nothing wrong with repeating a prayer as a reaffirmation of your faith. Each of us must achieve his or her own balance of prayer.

28. *Put it in writing.* Writing prayers and affirmations down on paper creates a stronger message for the subconscious mind than just thinking prayers or saying them out loud. Combining physical and mental actions exerts more force on the subconscious mind.

29. *Meditate to manifest.* Whenever you are in a state of meditation, or in an altered state of consciousness, you are also in a state of hypnosis, which allows suggestions to pass into the subconscious mind much more easily. A good time to do your manifestation work is just as you are falling asleep at night and when you are just waking up in the morning. This twilight state between sleep and waking is called the hypnogogic state.

30. *Avoid talking about your manifestation work.* Very often, talking with others about what you are trying to manifest can dissipate the energy. Another consequence of indiscriminate speech is the negative reaction that often comes from people when you share your vision. Guard against letting the negative energy of others penetrate your conscious and subconscious minds.

31. *Positivity produces positive results.* Until you achieve self-mastery, this is the single most important fact on one's spiritual path. In manifestation work you are trying to hold a certain thought form, energy, and vibration. You want to be around people who support this process. Being around negative people and negative environments tends to deplete one's energies physically, emotionally, mentally, and spiritually over time, and hence make it more difficult to hold the vibration.

32. *You possess all always.* Since you are God, Christ, the Buddha, everything is yours, just as everything is God's. This has always been the case, but it is difficult for us to accept this because we are so used to believing the ego's interpretation of ourselves that tells us we are just a physical body, a personality, and are separate from creation. If we faithfully held the truth that we are the Eternal Self, then all our thoughts would stem from this basic understanding, and everything we need would manifest whenever we need it.

33. *Ask only for what you need.* If the ego becomes involved and starts asking for things you don't really need, then the prayer request is coming from glamour. This will sabotage your manifestation.

34. *Rely solely on God.* God, your personal power, and the power of your subconscious mind are an unbeatable team. When you live this truth, your security is internal instead of external. No matter what happens to your external self, you know that you can manifest whatever you need with God's help, your will, and the power of your subconscious mind.

35. *Three unified minds can move mountains.* The Kahunas of Hawaii devised a special method of prayer utilizing all three minds. Their method requires you to write your prayer down on a piece of paper very specifically, and with lots of colorful imagery. Make sure that you have built up your vital force and energy so that you approach this task with enthusiasm. When you have the prayer worded and imaged in a way that you feel good about, say it three times out loud, addressing the prayer to God, your higher self, and one other entity. After saying the prayer three times, then command your subconscious mind, in a powerful but loving way, to take the prayer to your higher self.

Visualize this happening like the Old Faithful geyser, shooting up into the air through your crown chakra. Then forget about the prayer and do whatever you need to do on the conscious and subconscious levels to manifest the prayer. In other words, make sure all three minds are working together in perfect harmony.

36. *Use all five of your senses when visualizing what you want to manifest.* See it, hear it, taste it, touch it, and smell it. Make your visualization so vivid that this meditation reality is just as real or more real than your physical life reality. Doing visualizations with all five senses engaged ensures your success.

37. *Ask and you shall receive.* Knock and the door shall be opened. If you don't ask for help, your higher self and the Ascended Masters and the angels are not allowed to help you. If you don't ask, God doesn't help.

38. *Tell your subconscious mind what to do.* If you don't give it suggestions, affirmations, visualizations, and programming, then it will manifest whatever happens to be in it already, along with whatever you allow other people to put into it.

39. *Be of service.* Just because you are working with prayer and affirmation and visualization, this doesn't mean that you don't have to do physical work for a living. The soul's perspective is that your work is your service to God and that true pleasure is serving God. Once you achieve some level of self-realization, there is no other reason to be here except to be of service to humanity, which is God.

40. *Keep your mind steady in the light.* By staying focused, you won't lose the idealized potential that you are in the process of manifesting. As you evolve you will not even have to be patient and wait, for what you choose to manifest will happen instantly.

41. *Achieving emotional level manifestation helps you retain your childlike faith and devotion to God.* The Bible says that true faith is like a mustard seed, which can when planted literally move mountains. Childlike faith in action is a wonder to see.

42. *Stay attuned to the soul consciousness.* Soul-level manifestation requires you to identify yourself as the soul, not as the personality. This allows the energies of the soul to contribute to the manifestation of whatever you need. Working on the mental, emotional, and physical levels for manifestation and not utilizing one's soul would cut us off from the source of all life.

43. *Miracles are natural.* Miracles are the natural by-product of expressing and working through God's laws for the service of mankind.

44. *Identify yourself with God.* When you use the words "I Am" in beginning your affirmations, and when you are addressing God, you are affirming God's name, which is your own.

45. *"Set your mind on God's Kingdom and his justice before everything else and all the rest will come to you as well"* (Matthew 6:33). For "what will a man gain by winning the whole world, at the cost of his true self?" (Matthew 16:26). True prosperity is being merged with the soul and spirit, which then leads to all your needs being taken care of in service of God.

46. *It is okay to pray for material things.* Some people in the spiritual movement are confused by this point. It is perfectly okay and actually desirable for you to utilize the soul's help in this capacity; however, don't be greedy. Ask for exactly what you need, no more and no less.

47. *Focus upon service to humanity.* An ancient metaphysical saying states, "When your heart is pure, you will have the strength of ten." When our work is for a noble cause and we are doing it with a pure

heart and intent, we will have a much greater amount of energy to do what we need to do, for we are aligned with the universal force.

48. *Be specific in your visualization and your affirmation.* If you are too general, then by the laws of the universe you can manifest only a general solution, or one that is too vague to manifest in any recognizable way.

49. *What we manifest is not really ours.* You are simply a caretaker for all that is God's. There is no "yours" as separated from "God's."

50. *Take good care of what you manifest.* If you manifest a car and don't take care of it, then you are not deserving of the manifestation on the physical level. All levels need to be in alignment or manifestation can be blocked.

51. *Be at one with the essence of all things.* This law deals with what abundance really is. True abundance is not having everything, but rather being a source through which what is needed is made manifest.

52. *Manifestation requires self-discipline.* You must learn to discipline your mind, emotions, body, and consciousness to hold the proper vibration and attunement to the soul. You must have self-discipline so that you won't let the lower self infiltrate the mind with its doubts and fears. Having discipline gives us consistency. It allows us to stay continually in the light.

53. *You are the authority and the master.* There is no force more powerful than your will, and to manifest effectively, you must own your full power and identity as the Christ. You must manifest with the full power of your self as soul and as spirit, and the universe will instantly comply with your command.

54. *You have only one need.* The negative ego would tell you that you have many needs. Your only real need is to own the truth of your identity with God. When this need is met, then all other apparent needs are instantly met as a by-product of this state of consciousness.

55. *We lack nothing.* Since everything you need is already a part of you, the need for manifestation then becomes nothing more than an opportunity to demonstrate the presence of God. Manifestation is really just creativity at work.

56. *To manifest as a group, all members need to share the same vision.* If a group has differing visions, then the manifestation can be canceled.

57. *Follow your inner promptings and intuitions after praying for help.* Let's say you have prayed for a specific dollar figure for your rent

check next month. The universe is manifesting this through a person you are supposed to meet at a party. If you get the guidance to go to this party but your lower self tells you that you are too tired to go, then you may miss the manifestation that was provided for you. This is where self-discipline dovetails with being obedient to your intuition and soul and spiritual guidance.

58. *Honor the law of tithing.* Universal law states that if you give one-tenth of your income to a charitable or beneficial cause, you will receive a tenfold return on your generosity. This law is working with the law of karma, which states that you sow what you reap; what you put out comes back to you. The giving of a tithe and/or seed money keeps the energy of money in circulation. If you are stingy with the universe, which is God, then the universe and God will be stingy with you. If you are generous with the universe, then the universe, by God's law, will be generous with you.

59. *After prayer comes acceptance.* This last law of manifestation is absolutely essential to follow. After praying, accept your prayer as answered. You have followed all the universal laws and principles of manifestation. You have fulfilled the law. Don't just believe that it is answered; rather, *know* with every cell, molecule, and atom of your being that it has been answered. It is done. It is finished. So be it, for you have decreed it to be so. Your work is God made manifest. You are God, and you are one with God. You have fulfilled the law, so how can your prayer not be made manifest?

Chapter 12

✦

The Laws of Karma

For verily I say unto you, till heaven and earth pass, one jot or one tittle shall in no wise pass from the law, till all be fulfilled.
—MATTHEW 5:18

And it is easier for heaven and earth to pass, than one tittle of the law to fail.
—LUKE 16:17

The basic law of karma states that you sow what you reap; what you put out comes back to you. This is the law of cause and effect. You might think that there are a lot of people living in this world who get away with too much. I am here to tell you that no one gets away with anything. As the Bible tells us, "Every jot and tittle of the law is fulfilled."

The interesting thing about the law of karma is that it extends over many lives. Even if it appears that someone has unfairly taken advantage of another and escaped unscathed, it is really not so. The soul continues even if you have reincarnated into another physical body. The Edgar Cayce files are filled with examples of this point. Jesus provided an excellent understanding of the law of karma when He said, "Do unto others as you would have others do unto you." This is more literal than we realize.

There are different levels of karma. What I have been speaking of so far is what I would call personal karma—what we personally have set into motion with the power of our consciousness.

The second type of karma is group karma. When we incarnate into this world, we are born into groups based on our skin color, our religious affiliation, and so on. When a person is born into a black body in the United States, he or she has to deal with racism and prejudice—not because a black body is inferior to a white body, but because of the low level of spiritual consciousness of so many souls on this plane. A person in a black body, or in the body of any other minority, takes on the karmic lessons of that group.

Another type of karma is national karma. We are born into a certain country and are then indoctrinated with its egotistical identifications. If, for example, there was a nuclear war between Communist China and the United States, we would get caught up in this national karmic lesson. No man is an island unto himself.

Then there is planetary karma. This particular school called earth has certain unique lessons that are quite different from those on other planets in this galaxy or universe. We must deal with the planetary karma and the phase of history we are born into.

It could also be said that all karma is personal in that we, as souls, choose our skin color, our families, our religion, and the country we are going to grow up in before incarnating. In that sense, one could say that all karma is personal karma because we choose it.

The word *karma* has often been associated with "bad" karma, the idea that we must experience some form of suffering because of a lesson not learned. This is distinguished from the state of grace. The truth is that everything in this universe is governed by laws. There are physical laws, emotional laws, mental laws, and spiritual laws. When we fall out of harmony with these laws, we suffer. Thus karma is not a punishment but a gift—a sign that we are out of balance.

The proper attitude toward everything that happens in life is "Not my will but thine. Thank you for the lesson." Buddhism calls this non-resistance. The idea is to work and learn from the universe instead of fighting it. This does not mean to give up our power—just the opposite, in fact. It means owning our power and viewing what has happened as a teaching, lesson, challenge, and opportunity to grow. Look at karma as a stepping stone for soul growth.

There is no need to suffer. Suffering is not God's design, it is our own. It is a sign that we are letting our negative ego or separated, fear-based self be our guide, rather than the soul or spirit.

There is no such thing as sin. A sin is like some indelible stain on our character that cannot be removed. Sin is an egotistical concept, not a spiritual one. There are no sins, only mistakes. The true meaning of sin is "missing the mark." Mistakes are actually positive, not negative. The idea is to learn from them and, most of all, forgive ourselves. Perfection is not never making a mistake. True perfection is the state of always forgiving oneself for one's mistakes and then trying to learn from that experience.

Another very important point in respect to karma is that all lessons are learned within self. In other words, if you are having a vicious fight with a former friend but choose to forgive and unconditionally love that person, letting go of your animosity, you are freed from karma, even if the other person chooses to hold on to a grudge for the rest of his or her incarnation. This is a very liberating concept.

Karma comes back to us on all levels: physically, emotionally, mentally, and spiritually. How we take care of our physical body in this lifetime will determine how healthy a physical body we have in the next lifetime (if we are destined to return).

If we master our emotions in this lifetime and become peaceful, calm, joyous, and happy, then when we incarnate again in our next lifetime, as babies we will be peaceful, calm, and joyous. Some people believe in the idea of the tabula rasa, or blank slate. This is obviously absurd. We are not blank slates when we are born. As a matter of fact, there is really no such thing as a child. There are only adult souls living in babies' bodies. The average person has 200 to 250 past lives. The soul with all twelve of its extensions has an average of 2,400 to 3,000 past lives.

Another very interesting point in respect to karma is the understanding that there really is no such thing as linear time in the spiritual world. Time is simultaneous. Our past and future incarnations are happening now, for the now is ultimately all that exists.

It is possible to have karmic bleed-through from any of the eleven other soul extensions still in incarnation. This bleed-through can come from the past or the future. I realize that this is a very difficult concept to understand on this plane. Try to grasp this concept with your right brain rather than your left brain. For example, karmic bleed-through can manifest as physical symptoms you are experiencing but which in reality aren't your own. Let's say one of your fellow soul extensions is close to death in his or her incarnation. You may be experiencing this or running some of their karma through your physical body. If you want to assist in the healing of one or many of your soul extensions, by doing this you can; however, I wouldn't recommend doing it too much unless you receive clear guidance to do so.

An experience I had with Djwhal Khul one day provides a good example of bleed-through. He said that there was cigarette smoke in my field. I said, "Cigarette smoke? That's impossible. I have never smoked cigarettes." I asked him if he was sure it wasn't incense, which I sometimes light. He said, "No, it is cigarette smoke." He searched more deeply into the cause and found it was coming from one of my soul extensions.

To understand the concept that soul extensions are guided by the soul or oversoul, I would recommend reading one of Jane Roberts's Seth books, called *The Education of Oversoul Seven*. It will help give you a better understanding of this concept of simultaneous time and of the concept of soul extensions being guided by the soul.

There are three permanent atoms in the physical, mental, and emotional bodies. These permanent atoms are recording devices for personal karma. They also dispense karmic pictures into the bloodstream; this has an enormous effect on the glandular system. This is part of God's system for implementing the law of karma fairly.

With respect to how karma relates to blood transfusions, organ transplants, and animal organ transplants, Djwhal Khul has said that all three are definitely not recommended and should be avoided if at all possible. Take, for example blood transfusions. Let's say that you are a third-degree initiate and have just taken your soul merge initiation. Then you go into a hospital and get a blood transfusion from a person who hasn't stepped onto his or her spiritual path yet. The blood, physically and spiritually speaking, would be totally dissonant to your vibration. You would be, in essence, running another person's karma through your bloodstream. An organ transplant would be even worse, especially from an animal donor.

Another important point about karma is that you are given only as much as you can handle. This is controlled by your soul and monad. If all your karma was dumped on you at once, you obviously couldn't handle it. It is possible to slow down the karma coming your way if you are feeling overwhelmed, and it is also possible to speed up your karmic lessons if you want to grow faster. You can do this by praying for it to your soul or God. It is their joy to work with you in the way in which you feel most comfortable.

All good karma from past lives and this one is stored in the causal body, or soul body. The building of this causal body is one of the main requirements for achieving liberation from the wheel of rebirth. To achieve ascension, you need to balance only 51 percent of the karma of all your past lives (that is, the karma of your personal past lives, not the karma of your eleven other soul extensions).

Much of the karma you experience in life is not necessarily from past lives, but has been created in this life. For example, let's say you fall asleep at the wheel while driving and get into a serious car accident. The lesson may be as simple as being foolish enough to drive when one is overtired.

All karma from past lives is basically just programming in your subconscious mind and in your three permanent atoms. It can all be transformed in this life if you learn to be the master of your three lower vehicles—the physical, emotional, and mental bodies—in service of spirit and unconditional love. It is possible to completely clear the subconscious mind and three permanent atoms of all negative programming and to replace it with positive programming.

The laws of karma even extend to the type of soul you attract during intercourse and the conception of a child. The kind of soul that is attracted is greatly determined by the quality of feeling and love that is shared and being made manifest during the lovemaking experience.

The basic law of the universe is that our thoughts create our reality. All karma has its antecedent in some ancient thought that led to a feeling or action. It is sometimes helpful to do hypnotic regression work to release karmic blocks from past lives or early childhood. Under hypnosis you can reexperience a past trauma, thus gaining insight as to the cause of particular karmic results. Very often you can then release that program from your subconscious mind.

One final understanding about karma has to do with a Master taking on the karma of one of his or her disciples. Sai Baba, the great Master from India, has done this frequently with devotees. In one instance he took on the heart attack, stroke, and ruptured appendix of a devotee who otherwise would have died for sure.

Sai Baba became very ill for ten days. Over twenty-five of the finest doctors in India were at his bedside on the tenth day. He had turned completely black, and the consensus of the twenty-five doctors was that he had only minutes to live. Sai Baba would not take medication and said, "At four o'clock today I will be giving a lecture." The doctors thought he was crazy. At the appointed hour he apparently sprinkled some water on himself and was instantly cured. The twenty-five doctors began praying to Sai Baba for help before treating any patient.

EXAMPLES OF KARMA AS IT EXTENDS
OVER PAST LIVES AND/OR FUTURE LIVES

I have studied the Edgar Cayce files and come up with some fascinating cases showing how the law of karma extends over past or future lives.

The first example is that of a man who lived in Rome in a past life. He was a very handsome man, and he used to go around criticizing other people for being fat and not handsome like himself. In his present life he had an underactive pituitary and was obese. This is one very good example of how the three permanent atoms often release karma into the bloodstream, adversely affecting the glandular system.

In another of Cayce's readings a man had knifed and killed someone in a past life. In this life he was suffering from leukemia.

A friend of mine was afraid of swimming. Two different psychics separately told her that she had died in the sinking of the *Titanic*. This same friend's three main interests in this life have been art, music, and studying American Indians. The same psychic, without knowing this, told her that her last three past lives had been as a famous artist, a musician, and an American Indian.

In another reading a woman had an overpowering fear of animals. This fear came from an experience in ancient Rome when this entity's husband had been made to fight wild beasts in one of the arenas.

While I have given a number of examples of bad karma carrying over to this life, karma can also be positive in nature. For example, how did Mozart create piano concertos when he was only five years old? The answer is that he had had four or five lifetimes as famous musicians previous to this life.

If you are a healthy American, how did you receive a healthy body, and why is it that you grew up in the United States? You could have been a starving Somali, or you could have grown up in Communist China or a thousand other places that wouldn't have allowed you the freedoms and opportunities you have here. Too often we focus on the bad things that have happened to us and blame our karma instead of looking at the good things and being grateful for our positive karma.

DJWHAL KHUL ON THE LAW OF KARMA AND REBIRTH

I would like to end this chapter with a series of thirteen statements by Djwhal Khul. These are from the Alice Bailey book *The Reappearance of the Christ*, and provide a good summation of the entire process.

1. The Law of Rebirth is a great natural law upon our planet.

2. It is a process instituted and carried forward under the Law of Evolution.

3. It is closely related to and conditioned by the Law of Cause and Effect.

4. It is a process of progressive development, enabling men to move forward from the grossest forms of unthinking materialism to a spiritual perfection and an intelligent perception that will enable a man to become a member of the Kingdom of God.

5. It accounts for the differences among men, and in connection with the Law of Cause and Effect (called the Law of Karma in the East) it accounts for differences in circumstances and attitudes toward life.

6. It is the expression of the will aspect of the soul and is not the result of any form decision; it is the soul in all forms that reincarnates, choosing and building suitable physical, emotional, and mental vehicles through which to learn the next needed lessons.

7. The Law of Rebirth (as far as humanity is concerned) comes into activity upon the soul plane. Incarnation is motivated and directed from the soul level upon the mental plane.

8. Souls incarnate in groups, cyclically, under law and in order to achieve right relations with God and with their fellow men.

9. Progressive unfolding, under the Law of Rebirth, is largely conditioned by the mental principle "As a man thinks in his heart, so is he." These few brief words need most careful consideration.

10. Under the Law of Rebirth, man slowly develops mind; then mind begins to control the feeling and emotional nature; finally it reveals to man the soul and its nature and environment.

11. At that point in his development, man begins to tread the Path of Return and orients himself gradually (after many lives) to the Kingdom of God.

12. When, through a developed mentality, wisdom, practical service, and understanding, a man has learned to ask nothing for the

separated self, he then renounces desire for life in the three worlds and is freed from the Law of Rebirth.

13. He is now group-conscious, is aware of his soul group and of the soul in all forms, and has attained—as Christ had requested—a stage of Christ-like perfection, reaching unto the "measure of the stature of the fullness of the Christ."

Part III

Esoteric Psychology

Chapter 13

✴

Psychoepistemology

Psychoepistemology is a revolutionary new approach uniting the fields of psychology and spirituality. I first encountered this term about twenty years ago in a very obscure book by Nathaniel Branden, who recently passed away. In all my subsequent studying in the field I have never seen the term used anywhere else. What is important is that the concept behind it is brilliant. The purpose of this chapter is to expand upon Branden's work and to thank him for introducing us to this important concept.

WHAT IS PSYCHOEPISTEMOLOGY?

The term *psychoepistemology* is composed of two parts: *psycho-* and *epistemology*. Epistemology is the branch of philosophy that deals with the nature and origin of knowledge or knowing. The prefix *psycho-* comes from the Greek word *psyche*, which means "breath," "spirit," or "mind." The whole word means the mind's or the spirit's knowing. What this means is that every person has an individual psychological way of filtering their experience. Each of us has a philosophy or set of beliefs that serves as a filter or a lens for interpreting reality.

Psychoepistemology is a useful term because it gives us a shorthand way of describing the thoughts and beliefs that serve as our "filter."

Every one of us has a psychoepistemology; consequently, there are literally thousands of different kinds of psychoepistemologies. In this chapter I am going to discuss some of the most important ones, and then turn to my primary point—that too many people are unaware of the psychoepistemology that distorts their worldview.

The typical person who is not on a conscious spiritual path has a completely unconscious psychoepistemology. His or her view of the world is formed by the subconscious mind, which acts on the hodgepodge of beliefs from past lives, family upbringing, school, mass consciousness, mass media, and so on. A person with this type of psychoepistemology does whatever flows unregulated into his or her consciousness from the subconscious mind. This is not a very evolved state.

Fortunately, most people are more conscious than this. They have been exposed to various forms of philosophy and psychology and use these ideas to filter what enters the subconscious. Because our psycho-epistemology acts like a filter, I am going to use the term "filter system" throughout when referring to psychoepistemology. These per-ception filters act like the filters a photographer puts on a camera's lens. Without the filter, the lens will allow the film to be exposed so that the colors in the photograph are a nearly perfect approximation of reality. None of us view reality in this way. We all have filters attached to our means of perception. As humans, we view reality through a lens with many filters attached; among these many filters are the balanced relationship of the three minds, four bodies, feminine and masculine balance, heaven and earthly balance, Christ thinking versus negative ego thinking, chakra relationships, society's lenses, personal power, self-love, attunement to the soul or lack thereof, master or victim con-sciousness, and protection or lack thereof. These principles and how they are integrated and balanced will determine how a person's experi-ence is filtered.

CHAKRAS AND PERCEPTION

To begin to understand how this filtration system operates, think of the chakra system. If a person is stuck in their first chakra, he or she will filter reality through the lens of survival thinking. The filter will allow only survival-based thoughts to pass through to the film. Therefore, the picture this person sees—his or her view of reality—will have those survival colors heightened. In much the same way, a person stuck in the second chakra will filter all experience through sexuality. Many of Freud's theories resulted from his seeing through the filter of the second chakra.

A person who is stuck in the third chakra will filter experience through the lens of emotions. This is extremely common in our society. It is a carryover from the Atlantean root race cycle, when the emotional body was the prime identification. For people like this, all feelings and emotions are heightened. They seem not to understand that our thoughts cause our reality, and that our feelings and emotions are governed by either the negative ego or by the soul and the Christ mind. These people often base their decisions on how they feel rather than what they think.

Using the fourth-chakra filter or lens enables a person to see everything through the heart. Heart people are very focused on feelings and are usually less interested in mental pursuits. This may be a more evolved understanding, but it is still a lens. It is not a healthy filter system; a healthy system employs all chakras, bodies, and minds in a balanced manner in service of the soul. The healthy individual is not stuck with one filter, even if it is an unconditionally loving lens—which is obviously a wonderful soul quality to cultivate.

Someone who filters life through the throat chakra, through will and communication, may interpret everything as a battle and a war. This person may organize his or her consciousness and life to always create challenges or tests of will.

Those who use the third eye filter only are more connected to the mind and are focused on gaining wisdom and insight. It is almost as if this filter gives them X-ray vision, enabling them to see inside everything to analyze it.

The seventh chakra is the filter that allows you to see God. If you are overidentified with this chakra, you see God in everything and lose your sense of personal or psychological development. Your sights are set on heaven, but you are not grounded and connected to the earth. A person like this thinks God does everything for him, but the truth is that God *doesn't* do everything. We with our free choice do a great deal on our own with our personal power. Many fundamentalist religious seekers get stuck here.

Like a good photographer, you should carry all of these filters with you and know under what conditions it is best to use them individually or together to produce the best results. Balance and integration of all the chakras is the most evolved and healthiest psychoepistemology.

MASCULINE AND FEMININE ENERGIES

Besides the chakras, we also need to keep our masculine and feminine energies balanced in order to have a fully functioning psychoepistemology. Those with the feminine filter overidentify with feelings, emotions, and bodily desires. This type of person always goes though emotional crises and lives on an emotional roller coaster. He or she may often be a compulsive shopper and/or a binge eater. Another way in which this feminine imbalance is played out is an embrace of the mystical and a rejection of the occult—in other words, a focus on the God-centered at the expense of the physical phenomenon. This is extremely common among lightworkers.

On the other hand, people who have a masculine psychoepistemology overidentify with the mental body. They aren't comfortable embracing feelings, just as someone with an emotional psychoepistemology is less adept at embracing a logical approach. In addition, they are more identified with reading, studying, gathering information, and being psychologically clear. Perhaps they have not learned how to meditate, for example, or are weaker in their psychic development. This gets expressed at an esoteric level when the occultist does not adequately embrace the mystical side of life.

The basic feminine and masculine balance of life can also be thought of in terms of being open and closed. The ideal is to balance both of these aspects within self. Many people in this world have a psychoepistemological belief that they should be open all the time. This is a prescription for stress and for psychic and psychological invasion.

There is a time to be open and a time to be closed. When there is negative energy around, we need to close our field down. This is the concept of protection. In the ideal state all of us would have a semipermeable membrane around us that lets in positive energy and love and keeps out negative energy. But some see life through a closed field all the time. These are people who have been deeply hurt and abused. If this closed-down psychoepistemology continues, they will be susceptible to depression and other difficulties.

OTHER SOURCES OF IMBALANCE

Other imbalanced psychoepistemologies result from heaven-earth disparity. The heavenly psychoepistemology is very ungrounded and filters everything through an obsession with how to break the wheel of reincarnation and escape the earth. Even though these individuals have physical bodies, they don't really live in them too much. They live out of their bodies most of the time. As a result, they neglect their bodies, which causes them physical problems.

Conversely, those with the psychoepistemology of the materialist see everything through the filter of "science" and believe that the only thing that is real is what you can verify with your five senses. Most of our teachers going through traditional school and college have the perspective that the only truth is what can be proven with scientific study. Obviously it is important to have a balance between the material and the heavenly planes.

Another type is the person who sees life through the lens of traditional psychology. These people accept only the existence of the conscious and subconscious minds and reject any belief in a superconscious mind or God. Unfortunately, this is the predominant belief in the field of psychology in this country.

There are also those who overidentify with the conscious mind. This type of person is obsessed with control and power. They don't have a strong need to explore the subconscious mind or God. They don't even really believe in such concepts. At a more advanced level, the subconsciously identified types are often involved in hypnosis. They think the subconscious mind is the key to the Kingdom but don't truly understand the functioning of the conscious mind and often have no belief in God. They give too much power to the subconscious mind and don't realize the strongest force in their lives is the conscious mind that owns its will and personal power. Basic texts on hypnosis all reflect this imbalance.

The last type with an imbalance of the three minds sees life through the filter of the conscious and superconscious mind while rejecting the subconscious mind. This is very common. Many religious fundamentalists who are very involved with God and with using their power to fight the devil have never been taught to examine the programming in their subconscious mind. As a result, they are spiritually developed but not psychologically developed. Many New Age lightworkers also fit this description. They have total overidentification with spiritual, heavenly, and ethereal things but lack a focus on psychological and character development and making their life work on earth. They are more interested in the Ascended Masters, passing their initiations, and building light quotient than they are in clearing their own negative ego. Their spiritual growth will come to a complete standstill after the seventh initiation until this imbalance is corrected. True God-realization is balanced and integrated on all levels.

In addition to those who lack balance in the use of their three minds, other types of people see life through their identification with their country of origin. In other words, they view their experiences through the filter of the beliefs that their fellow citizens espouse. Because we are surrounded by people with a similar filter system, it's sometimes difficult to understand that not everyone in the world shares our beliefs. The most obvious examples of these differences are political beliefs or theories. In America we have the democracy filter; for many years the Soviet Union had Communism; Germany had the Nazi form of totalitarianism.

The most widespread imbalanced psychoepistemology views life through the negative ego mind rather than the Christ mind. In truth, it is the negative ego that causes imbalance and distorts our perception. All perception is in a sense a dream, but the idea is to perceive and live God's dream, which is a mirror and/or window for the ultimate reality.

Psychoepistemologies can also exist at the level of smaller groups. Rajneesh now known as Osho was a high-level guru who identified with the superconscious and subconscious but not as much with the conscious mind. This is why his ashram was a haven for the spiritual humanistic psychologists. Humanistic psychologists tend to be over-identified with a feminine psychology rather than balancing it with spirituality. I found the Self-Realization Fellowship Organization, whose work I support, to be just the opposite: they had an incredible spirituality, but the organization wanted everyone to be immersed in their focus, which is a masculine psychoepistemology.

Another one is Alcoholics Anonymous. This is a wonderful organization; however, there is an imbalance in their psychoepistemology. The basic teaching is that all power is in God and that the alcoholic has no power. This is true in a sense, but in another way it is dangerously false. What they are trying to do is help individuals surrender their negative ego, which is fantastic. The problem is that they do not explain clearly enough that there are three levels of power one must own to be effective: God's power, personal power on the conscious mind level, and subconscious mind power, which can be utilized through affirmations and creative visualization. You must own your personal power to transcend negative ego consciousness, for God will not do this for you. The organization means very well and I greatly support it, but this philosophical point needs to be clarified.

Another common but faulty New Age psychoepistemology is the belief that we must incorporate all parts of ourselves into our being. This may sound good, but actually this is a delusion of the negative ego. It is true that you want to integrate your rays, chakras, subpersonalities, soul extensions, four bodies, and so on. However, the one thing you do *not* want to incorporate is your negative ego. You must disidentify with your negative ego and its faulty philosophy of life; you must reject your lower self and completely identify with your higher self to realize God.

As I mentioned early in this book, another common psychoepistemology that lightworkers commonly hold is the False Sense of Balance Theory—the belief that everything in life must be balanced. This sounds right, except for the fact that you don't want to balance the lower self and higher self. You don't want to balance the negative ego way of thinking and the Christ way of thinking. Still, you would be amazed at how many people on the planet buy into this delusion, thinking it is a legitimate philosophy. If you believe in this theory, you will end up saying, "I am going to be loving half the time and attacking the other half," or "I am going to have high self-esteem half the time and low self-esteem the other half." You see how absurd this is. You want to get rid of all negative ego qualities and traits. You don't want to incorporate or balance them.

Here is the most classic delusion of all: Lightworkers say they want to balance their dark and light sides. There is no judgment here upon those who hold such beliefs, for I have held this belief (and pretty much every other one of this entire chapter) at one time or another—that is why I can write about them so well.

Why would anyone want to balance the dark and light aspects of self? This is a classic example of a faulty psychoepistemology, and shows how easily we can all be seduced by the dark side of the Force, as Master Yoda would say. We are not here to incorporate darkness. As *A Course in Miracles* says, we are the light of the world. Our true identity is light and God. All darkness is created by the negative ego, not by God. Darkness is just another word for negative ego. If you actually believe that you want to balance darkness and light, then your own mind will create darkness, for your thoughts create your reality.

We each live our own self-created heaven or self-created hell. It is our mind that creates bondage or liberation. What you think doesn't create truth, but what you think is the reality you will live in. Mankind has not yet come to the full realization of the incredible power of its own mind. At its best it will lead you to the sublime heights of God-realization. At its worst, when not mastered, it will manifest psychosis and schizophrenia. There is a way of thinking that will bring you peace, happiness, joy, and light all the time. There is another way of thinking that will bring you the opposite.

We are not here in this world to demonstrate positivity and negativity. We are here to demonstrate *only* positivity. The spiritual path is nothing more than becoming aware of this—seeing it in others and demonstrating it in our daily lives. We don't have to try to become one with God because we already are one with God—we always have been and always will be. All else is illusion. Do not hold on to darkness, for your true identity is light. Don't let your perceptions be dimmed by faulty psychoepistemologies. God, Christ, love, and light are all words that at their foundation mean the same thing. We are not trying to raise our darkness quotient, we are trying to raise our light quotient.

To believe we need to balance darkness with light or hold on to negative emotions is to be seduced by the dark side. As Darth Vader said to Luke Skywalker, "Give in to your anger and your fear." He was asking Luke to let his negative ego guide him. Anger/fear, superiority/inferiority, attack/defense, and light/darkness are the other aspects of the negative ego/Christ consciousness dichotomy. We can't allow ourselves to flip back and forth between the two. The negative ego *wants* us to be caught in duality.

There is a way of thinking that transcends this state of consciousness. The key is the transcendence of duality. Krishna spoke of this in the Bhagavad Gita. Krishna, the Christ of the Eastern world, counseled us to remain in even-mindedness, equanimity, peace, joy, love, and light at all times. Whether we have profit or loss, pleasure or pain, sickness or health, victory or defeat, whether people praise us or criticize us, we remain the same. This is the secret to God-realization.

This way of thinking allows us to remain in inner peace regardless of what is going on outside of self. It is a state of consciousness unaffected by the turmoil of the world or the negativity of others. Djwhal Khul has called this state of consciousness divine indifference. Others have called it involved detachment. In essence, it is a state that transcends duality. This is the divine nectar that Sai Baba and Yogananda speak of and that the world so desperately needs. This is the divine nectar that the Buddha speaks of in his four noble truths.

Do not remain stuck in personality-level psychoepistemologies. Have courage now and take the leap of consciousness from personality-level psychoepistemologies to ones based in soul and monad. Seek truth, not outdated belief systems that we have outgrown like a set of old clothes. Reach now for the highest that is within humankind. To hold on to darkness and light as a philosophy is to remain stuck in the negative ego's game and caught in its web. Remember what Fritz Perls said: "The only way to get rid of the superiority and inferiority complex is to laugh it off the stage." The only way to truly find inner peace is to transcend the entire negative ego system—to develop a transcendent philosophy.

This is the problem with traditional psychology: It does not integrate the spiritual aspects, and so there is no possibility of seeing the potential for transcendence. As a result, it teaches people to try to heal themselves while remaining stuck under the negative ego's ground rules. The highest potential of traditional psychology is partial healing at best. True inner peace, happiness, joy and bliss can never be found through this path.

When we look at life from this new transcendent perspective, everything is light. Everything that happens is positive, for in truth it is God teaching us through the universe what we need to learn. Sometimes it is even our higher self providing our lessons. Other times the law of karma presents us with what we have set in motion in this life or past lives. In truth, whatever happens is a blessing if we will just look at it this way. Happiness from the soul's perspective is a state of mind, not an outside experience. This gets back to the principle of having preferences rather than attachments. If everything in your life is a preference rather than an attachment, your happiness can never be taken away.

God is asking you now to take a leap in your spiritual progression. Make the move to begin transcending duality and negative ego consciousness. Begin the process of interpreting life from the Christ mind.

The mind guided by Christ lives in perfection at all times, not in limitation. It is a mind that sees beyond appearances and practices. It is innocent perception seeing the Christ in all. This mind finds love, not faults. It is a mind that is optimistic, not pessimistic. It is a mind that thinks positively, not negatively.

The mind is a very brilliant instrument; however, it can be used just as brilliantly by the negative ego and Dark Brotherhood as it can be used by the soul and Brotherhood of Light. Do not be seduced by the negative ego's glamour, tricks, and traps. One must be constantly vigilant for God and his kingdom.

The decision you make this day to transcend the negative ego may be the single most important decision you will ever make in your entire life. If your psychoepistemology is imbalanced, your entire life and all your relationships will reflect this imbalance. If your psychoepistemology is contaminated by negative ego, your four-body system, all your relationships, and your entire life will be contaminated.

It is now time to get clearer than you have ever gotten in your entire life. Do not listen to me — listen to your own higher self and Mighty I Am Presence. They will confirm the truth I speak. If I am telling you the truth, which is what we all seek, then your own soul will acknowledge this truth within your own being with a resounding yes.

We are going right to the core of the negative ego and Dark Brotherhood's longtime control of humanity. We are coming in powerfully, with the sword of discernment striking at every single one of the negative epistemological delusions. We do not want you to listen to us. We want you to seek the highest possible truth within yourself. It will take great courage and discernment for many of you to free yourself from the viselike grip that the negative ego has held over you. The key to breaking free is examining your psychoepistemology.

Once the negative ego has been wounded in this area, its death is imminent. Everyone on the spiritual path must at some point go through the negative ego death to be born again. I am not speaking of being born again in the fundamentalist Christian sense but in the true spiritual sense of the term. We must die to the negative ego in order to be born again into the realization that each one of us is the Christ and we each share the same identity as the Eternal Self. God has only one child, and we all share in that relation. We must be born again to full realization that each one of us is the light of the world, made in God's image, and one with Him. We must be born again to the fact that we are perfect in our creation. In this holy instant we wake up from the bad dream of the negative ego, within which we have been locked for eons.

The purpose of life is to wake up from this delusion and demonstrate our Christ consciousness on earth. The first step is to have this awakening. The second step is to see the Christ consciousness in others. If you don't see it in others, you will lose it in yourself. Just as you are the Christ and one with God, so are your brothers and sisters no matter what their state of consciousness development. The third step is to practice demonstrating this state of consciousness 24 hours a day, 7 days a week, 365 days a year. It is by demonstrating this psychoepistemology consistently that we pass our initiations.

We will ultimately develop Ascended Master abilities as a natural by-product of our true Godliness practiced and demonstrated over a long period of time. The truest test will come when we allow ourselves to be responsive to life and to other people, and to live our Christ consciousness in the workplace, in romantic relationships, and in raising children. These are the ultimate tests of our spiritual, psychological, and physical development.

When we prove our ability to our soul, and to the Ascended Masters whose care we are under, we will complete our seven levels of initiation, serve as a bodhisattva for a time, and then return to the spiritual world and visit physical existence no more. Our true Godly demonstration will give us the ticket "uptown" to the universal levels of consciousness. We will continue our demonstration and service work on more expanded levels of consciousness and more subtle and refined frequencies of energy. This is the destiny we all share. To do this, however, we must transcend negative ego consciousness.

ATTITUDINAL HEALING

Most people have never been trained in the science of attitudinal healing. Traditional personality-level psychology, practiced by 90 percent of the psychologists, marriage/family/child counselors, social workers, and psychiatrists, will tell you that it is wrong to get rid of negative emotions. They believe that it is wrong to deny them; they hold that one should acknowledge them and then release them. If you remain identified only at the personality level of existence, this may be good advice. If, however, you would like to realize your soul level of existence and participate in true ascension, this belief will have to change. It is not in harmony with the dictates of your own soul. The soul would have you always respond to every situation with your Christ consciousness: unconditional love, forgiveness, responding instead of reacting, loving your enemies, maintaining inner peace no matter what is going on outside of self, and transcending duality.

Do you really believe that responding out of anger, defensiveness, upset, fear, depression, attack, violence, and revenge are appropriate responses for a son or daughter of God? Look at the examples of the great Masters who have lived on this plane: Buddha, Jesus, Mohammed, Krishna, Lao-tzu, Confucius, Yogananda, Gandhi, Mother Teresa, the Dalai Lama, Zoroaster, and others. Look at what they taught and the example they lived. Who do you want as your model: a traditional counselor or the great saints and spiritual Masters?

Besides the advice of counselors, some people hold their parents' philosophy as a psychological filter. Other people retain a cultural filter—such as the Jewish culture, or Indian culture. Every culture has a unique set of beliefs, just as each race does. We may also view the world through a socioeconomic filter, an astrological filter, our ray structure, and often through certain archetypes. Everything from the planet we live on to the religion we practice and our political inclinations, as well as our past lives, creates filters that distort our perceptions. The mass media, schools, secular and spiritual teachers, and our friends all contribute to this accumulation of filters. We all like to feel that we see clearly, but the fact is that our view of reality is much more affected by these filters than we realize. The more advanced we get in our evolutionary processing, the more we need to shed these filters.

VICTIM CONSCIOUSNESS

One of the most pervasive and blinding psychological filters is the victim mentality. I see this mentality in the great many lawsuits that people win for the most bizarre reasons—such as the woman who was awarded a major settlement because the McDonald's coffee she spilled on herself was hot. At times it seems as if no one will accept responsibility for anything that happens to him or her.

The Menendez brothers admitted to murdering their parents;

however, they weren't responsible because they were abused as children. Rodney King was severely beaten by police officers, and it was even videotaped; but the jury couldn't figure out who was the cause and who was the victim. We probably have the best jury system in the world; however, what is not taken into account is how disturbed and unclear the people sitting on the jury are. We see not through our eyes but through our minds. In the polls regarding the O. J. Simpson trial, most blacks saw him as innocent and most whites saw him as guilty. Could there be a lens operating here? Probably, and on both sides.

I sometimes think that this victim mentality is tied to the religious filter in which some are taught to see themselves as lowly worms tainted by original sin. Because we are so lowly, we need someone else to protect us, we tell ourselves; given our flaws, we can't possibly do anything right. Another dysfunctional filter is seeing life through the eyes of the critical parent. In this case, we become the fault finder—so hypercritical of ourselves that we believe we can't do anything right. Or we flip-flop between feelings of inferiority and superiority. Both of these are equally distorted views.

Often these feelings of inferiority and superiority lead us to fear and attack rather than to love. The transcendence of the negative ego consciousness is such a revolutionary new concept to the earth that most people have never been exposed to it. They see no way out of being trapped in the polarities and dualities, and this completely colors their vision and their relationships.

PSYCHOLOGICAL LENSES

Shadow Psychology

Jungian psychology is responsible for another filter that often misguides people. "Owning your shadow" is a common psychological concept. I have great respect for Carl Jung; however, he was not a God-realized being. Jung is regarded as one of the more advanced psychological theorists because he integrated a spiritual component. The problem with Jung was that he didn't go as far as, let's say, a Yogananda, Sai Baba, or Ascended Master would have. Jung was a catalyst but was not completely self-realized in his own understanding.

Nevertheless, he was a great breath of fresh air to the Godless study of psychology that was currently in place at the time he lived.

Many Jungian psychologists believe that it is important that each person integrate his or her shadow. I disagree. God is light, and we are light. There is no shadow within us. God is love, light, and positivity. Any shadow we experience is created by the negative ego. God did not create the negative ego, humankind did. Therefore, we must not deny the negative ego, but need to recognize it, acknowledge it, take responsibility for it, and release it.

The purpose of life is to transcend the negative ego, not to incorporate it. To incorporate your shadow would be to say you want to incorporate darkness, sickness, or negativity into your being. The idea here is to deny your shadow. If you turn on the light switch in a dark room, the darkness will disappear.

Carl Jung, although a great man and teacher, did not understand the difference between the negative ego and Christ thinking. I believe that he got very confused on this point. His concept of the self was good, but his psychology was not completely of the self and soul. It was much closer than any other psychologist had come, but it was not an Ascended Master's perspective on psychology. Jung's philosophy was a mixture of soul and personality-level psychology. This was a definite improvement over other personality-level psychological theories. This is why I refer to him as a great catalyst. Nevertheless, be clear on his perceptual filters. You are God. You are light. You are positivity, and the only darkness that lives within you is the darkness you allow in.

It is absolutely essential to understand that we all have a negative ego potentiality, and we all have negative ego within us that we haven't cleared yet. There are some deluded souls who go around thinking that Satan, the devil, the Dark Brotherhood, or the negative ego doesn't exist, and this is very dangerous. In thinking this, they have been taken over by the dark side. We need to get clear on how both the negative ego and the Christ mind work within ourselves. If we deny the existence of negative ego thinking as a potentiality, we are sure to be victimized by it. The ideal here is to make negative ego thinking, or the shadow, *unmanifest* potential. It is also essential not to judge others for manifesting negative ego consciousness.

People who use the term *shadow* will often say if we don't own our shadow, we will project it onto others. They often use Hitler's hatred of the Jews as an example. Hitler was taken over by the negative ego and his need to manifest his superiority complex, making the Jews inferior in his mind.

The shadow and the negative ego are synonyms. Just as we don't want to integrate our negative ego, we don't want to integrate our shadow. We do, however, want to recognize its potentiality to manifest within ourselves if we are not careful.

Think of it this way. In order to be vigilant against the operations of the negative ego, we have to know what it looks like, where it frequents, what it is likely to do. Imagine that we have an inner detective whom we have assigned to tail this shadow suspect. We must give this inner detective as much information as possible so that he or she can spot our negative ego/shadow and prevent it from doing its dirty work. To gather this information, we have to be as devastatingly honest as we can be.

Understand also that we have the potentiality to be like Hitler or like any of the negative people we see operating in our daily lives, and recognize that we still have negative ego aspects left to clear. This understanding will allow us to be less judgmental, less polarizing, less self-righteous, and more compassionate and loving in dealing with the psychologically unclear people we all have to cope with every day.

This is what owning our shadow and negative ego really means. We can use Hitler as a teacher of a bad example to remind us to not let this potentiality, which exists within all sons and daughters of God, be made manifest ever again. The key lesson is not to incorporate our shadow, but to be on guard against releasing it. This could manifest in how we deal with relationships, in business, or with our children. The purpose of life is to release all negative ego, all darkness, all negativity, and all shadows and to shine the light and love of God on self and others.

Additional Psychological Lenses

Anyone who has been involved in any kind of counseling or therapy is likely to have adapted the filter of the particular psychological theory of the person who is treating him or her. If the therapist is involved with Freudian psychology, the client too will see everything through the lens of the second chakra and the fight between the id, ego, and superego. In humanistic psychology, everything will be seen through the lens of the emotional body and the expression of feelings. In Gestalt therapy everything is viewed through the lens of pro-experience and anti-intellectualism. In Adlerian therapy, it's the lens of social psychology. In family systems counseling, it will be the lens of the family system and not the individual psyche. In the teaching of Abraham Maslow, life is seen through the ideal of attaining peak experiences and self-actualization. Someone involved with behavioristic psychology will see everything through the lens of positive and negative reinforcement, extinction of unwanted behaviors, and the effect of the environment upon behavior. The psychiatrist's lens is a medical model within which psychological problems are caused by an imbalance of chemicals. To a nutritionist, everything is seen through the lens of nutrition. Cognitive psychology uses the lens of the effects of thinking upon behavior, and so on and so on. It is important to remember that all of these filters will distort perception.

Professions and Filters

Every profession trains its practitioners to have a filter. A comedian sees everything through a filter of humor and how to build it into a comedy routine or just to make people laugh. A lawyer sees things through the filter of an adversarial legal battle with a win/lose orientation. A businessperson works through the filter of making money, while an artist does so through the filter of beauty, which ties into the effect of the rays, each of the seven major rays being a lens that affects the monad and soul. A healer may look at everything in terms of energy, and a social worker through the filter of social implications. A family counselor is focused on the family unity in term of relationships and children. An astrologer works through the astrological horoscope, and that is how all experience is organized.

As you can see, we stack filters on top of filters on top of filters until very little if any light gets through. The ideal is to try to become crystal clear about which filters are affecting our consciousness, which means still being inclusive of accepting all filters as a part of the whole. The goal is to see through the lens of God, Christ/Buddha, and the Holy Spirit. This is the clearing work we are all involved in, and this process requires great introspection, self-examination, and vigilance.

These filters, in a sense, are like archetypes, and each archetype could be looked at as a type of filter. The ideal is to integrate all of them and to use them all in their appropriate moment. We are always seeing through some kind of filter. The ideal would be not to overuse any one but to have them all at one's disposal, and to understand them all, which gives us more compassion and understanding for others. There are some lenses that are more evolved than others. Each of us must strive for the highest, most refined lens we can possibly achieve.

The danger is in becoming so accustomed to viewing things through one filter that we forget that it's there and that it's distorting the rest of the visual image. We can become unconsciously locked into using a particular configuration of filters without realizing it. To truly achieve God consciousness, free from all filters, is a high goal to aspire to. At our level, just getting free from the planetary lens would be quite a spiritual accomplishment. In this regard a universal spiritual philosophy can be very helpful. All religions, all spiritual paths, all healing modalities, all forms of psychology, all nations, all cultures, all political systems, all Ascended Masters, and indeed all people become our teachers.

The challenge that is before us is to see life through the eyes of the Anointed Christ Overself Body, or universal body. If we want to activate and actualize these bodies within ourselves, we must begin to see with their eyes.

Our life and spiritual path become so much richer when we can be open and learn from all lenses and all psychoepistemological systems, as long as they are untainted by the contamination of negative ego.

Philosophy

One more set of filters that hasn't yet been considered but which has had an enormous impact on humanity is from the field of philosophy. Psychology as we understand it is rather modern, having begun in the late 1800s. Philosophy, by contrast, has been around for eons. Each philosophical viewpoint is a filter. There are literally thousands of philosophical filters. The philosophy of science, for example — believing that all that exists is what you can observe with your five senses — is a complete rejection of the right brain's faculties. Existentialism, as a filter, speaks of man's free choice and fundamental aloneness; in it there is no unity with God. The philosophy of Ayn Rand preached selfishness as the answer to life's problems, which is certainly a soulless philosophy.

We see these different philosophical filters demonstrated in the work of different movie directors. The films of Quentin Tarantino, for example, are usually incredibly violent and seem to glorify the dark side of life. Sir Richard Attenborough, the director of *Gandhi*, presents the highest that humanity can strive for. We are influenced by these works more than we realize and, depending upon our spiritual and psychological development, may even adopt these points of view as our own. Every book, every poem, every song, and every artwork has been filtered through, and is the product of, a particular perception of life. The entire world is a gigantic mishmash of filters, some stressing feelings, some thinking, some intuition, some the five senses, some the right brain, some the left brain, others heaven, still others earth, and so on.

Finding Happiness

This collection of filters is why most people are not healthy and happy. A recent poll conducted on the subject of happiness revealed that only 29 percent of the people in the United States said they were happy. I am sure that even those 29 percent, though happy, are in serious danger of losing their happiness, for it is based on attachments to outside things such as relationships, family, job, money, security, and the like. If happiness is based on anything but the mind in total service to spirit, you are headed for a fall.

Through God's Eyes

God consciousness is incredibly vast and infinite. It is every person's heritage. Yet people see life through so many filters that barely one faint beam of true light gets through. The ideal would be to look at this process as looking through a prism and seeing all reflections at once. This would be the ultimate ideal and would be God consciousness.

When we look through a prism, we can see the potentially infinite number of colors and facets. There are thousands of them, like a finely cut diamond. What a wonderful example this is. But sadly, what happens in life is that we end up looking through just one ray of the prism, and/or one small grouping of facets, instead of looking through the entire prism at once.

A prism is an incredible metaphor because it contains all of the possible lenses that can be looked into at any moment, but it always returns to a type of cosmic consciousness when that lens focus has been completed. The problem with most human beings is we stay stuck in a single way of thinking, believing that we have achieved the ultimate when in fact we are seeing with nothing more than the eye of a fly. This is part of the glamour, maya, and illusion of the negative ego in its self-centered perspective. When we can perceive all reflections through the prism and move out of them at will and not get stuck, we have achieved full integration, unity, and oneness consciousness, which is the ultimate goal. We have attained on our level a type of cosmic psychological consciousness—seeing life as much as we are able through God's eyes rather than the fly's eyes.

Cosmic Healing Visualization

This cleansing, healing, and renewing visualization is designed to help you develop a crystal clear energy field across your solar plexus, as well as an entirely new chakra column and four-body system. It calls upon the help of the Masters and the angels to clear all negative ego programming and to replace it with love. There are four parts to this process—be prepared for it to be very deep, powerful, and effective.

SPIRALING GOLDEN-WHITE LIGHT AURIC HEALING

• As usual, pick a quiet time when you will have peace and solitude for at least an hour, and perhaps a rest period afterward. Sit in your meditative space in a comfortable chair, feet on the floor, hands relaxed at your sides or in your lap. Close your eyes, and take three deep relaxing, cleansing, and releasing breaths.

• Focus on your breathing for a few moments. Now, on an extended inbreath, call forth a golden-white light that spirals from above down through your crown chakra. Feel this golden-white light spiraling and expanding throughout your entire four-body system, and out into every layer of your auric field.

• As you exhale, feel the golden-white light flushing all darkness and negativity out of your entire central chakra column, your four bodies, and every part of your physical body.

• Repeat this cleansing and releasing with the breath, feeling the spiraling action of the golden-white light getting larger and larger until it fills your entire aura.

• Breathing quietly, totally infused with the golden-white light, call for protection from Djwhal Khul, Vywamus, and/or the Master of your choice. Ask your oversoul and monad to take this opportunity to enlighten and illuminate your astral and emotional bodies. Ask to have all discomfort and disharmony in your four bodies completely erased, for where there is no congestion, you experience total rejuvenation of the self.

COSMIC CHRIST CHAKRA HEALING

• Focus on your heart chakra. Send your breath in and out of the heart chakra, pulsing with the natural rhythm of your physical heart.

• Now, shift your focus to your root chakra, and send your breath through it, and on up through the rest of the chakras. While you are visualizing this harmonizing movement of energy, tap gently on your heart, and if it feels appropriate, do a little toning as you move up the scale from the root chakra to the crown chakra.

• When you reach the crown chakra, call forth the energy of the Cosmic Christ as an effervescent column of champagne-white light about three inches in diameter. Feel this bubbling light penetrating your crown chakra, realigning the temporal cranial bones in your skull and elevating your personal vibratory level high enough so that you can now discard all old emotional programming.

• Focus on the heart chakra again. On the inbreath, call upon the help of the Masters to expand and open the back of the heart chakra. On the outbreath, release all darkness and old negative ego programming.

• Now move into your emotional center—your solar plexus. Use your breath and the help of the Masters to release any unwanted energies remaining in this region. Allow them to drain away and dissolve harmlessly into the earth. Cut yourself free of all emotional anchors, cables, and weights.

ANGELIC EMOTIONAL HEALING

• To complete the healing of the solar plexus, call upon the angelic realms, and all those angels who specialize in emotional cleansing and healing. Ask them to clear and balance this entire area.

• You don't need to identify what you're releasing. If it doesn't vibrate at the same frequency as Christ energy, simply give it to the angels. Breathe in the angelic energy and breathe out everything you're releasing. Feel the new openness and space, the lightness of your being. Thank all those who have helped you achieve it.

THE BUDDHA OPENS YOUR THIRD EYE

• Now, see yourself floating peacefully above a beautiful, calm, placid lake. The water of the lake is a wonderful deep blue color.

• As you move deeper and deeper into the meditative state, you see that the Buddha is there with you, floating serenely over the blue waters. As you feel his loving energy, your mind and emotions become as calm and peaceful as the clear blue lake beneath you—as calm as the emotional and mental bodies of the Buddha himself.

• Focusing on your third eye, you see a beautiful light, the same blue as the lake. Follow this beam of blue light until it leads you to another beam of blue light, which you discover is emanating from the third eye of the Buddha. Feel this incredible blue light penetrating into your own third eye, filling you with serenity, clarity, and love.

• Remain in this state as long as you can, as it seats itself in your being. Return to full outer awareness very slowly, and very gently. Honor your new self, knowing that this transformation is real and permanent. No matter what high winds may blow through your life, you now have the ability to remain calm and serene and filled with light. The more you serve as a vehicle for the light, the more those around you will respond in kind.

Chapter 14

✳

How to Clear the Negative Ego Through the Science of the Rays

The science of the rays, which is a fundamental part of esoteric psychology, is one of the most fascinating spiritual sciences a light-worker can ever study. Since the rays fall outside of the realm of traditional psychology, very few people are familiar with this concept. My first book, *The Complete Ascension Manual*, provides an important introduction on how to use the science of the rays to clear the negative ego. Since many of you may not be familiar with these concepts, a brief summary of that material follows. It outlines each of the twelve rays and its corresponding color and function.

The Twelve Rays		
Ray I	Red	Will, Dynamic Power, Singleness of Purpose, Detachment, Clear Vision
Ray II	Blue	Love/Wisdom, Radiance, Attraction, Expansion, Inclusiveness, Power to Save
Ray III	Yellow	Active Intelligence, Power to Manifest, Power to Evolve, Mental Illumination, Perseverance, Philosophical Bent, Organization, Clear-Mindedness, Perfectionism

Ray IV	Emerald Green	Harmony Through Conflict, Purity, Beauty, Artistic Development
Ray V	Orange	Concrete Science, Research, Keen Intellect, Attention to Detail, Truth-Seeking
Ray VI	Indigo	Devotion, Idealism, Religious Fervor
Ray VII	Violet	Ceremonial Order, Ritual, Magic, Diplomacy, Tact, the Violet Flame, Physicalness and Grounded Spirit, Order, Discipline
Ray VIII	Seafoam Green	The Higher Cleansing Ray
Ray IX	Blue-Green	Joy, Attraction of the Body of Light
Ray X	Pearlescence	The Anchoring of the Body of Light, Inviting of the Soul Merge
Ray XI	Pink-Orange	The Bridge to the New Age
Ray XII	Gold	The Anchoring of the New Age and Christ Consciousness

The first seven rays embody each of the seven types of force that correspond to the seven qualities of God. These seven qualities in turn have a sevenfold effect upon matter and form in all parts of God's infinite universe. Also, these seven great rays represent each of the seven great beings. They are:

1. The Lord of Power
2. The Lord of Love/Wisdom
3. The Lord of Active Intelligence
4. The Lord of Harmony, Beauty, and Art
5. The Lord of Concrete Knowledge and Science
6. The Lord of Devotion and Idealism
7. The Lord of Ceremonial Order or Magic

This is not the only way that rays have been categorized and ordered. Some spiritual traditions further subdivide them into rays of aspect and rays of attitude. For our purposes, the seven lower rays as listed here will suffice.

The ray structure of every soul extension incarnated onto the earthly plane is made up of six rays—one each for the monad, soul, personality, mind, emotions, and physical body. The monadic and soul rays remain basically the same throughout all of our soul's incarnations. The other rays can change from lifetime to lifetime. People who have not started on the spiritual path are dominated by their physical, emotional, and mental bodies. As the person develops a more self-actualized personality, then the personality ray becomes dominant and the three body rays (physical, emotional, mental) become subordinated to it.

As we continue to evolve, the forces within us begin to polarize. A struggle develops between the lower self and the higher self, or between the personality ray and the soul ray. As the soul ray exerts its dominance, we gain self-mastery over the personality, and it then serves the soul. This process continues throughout the steps of initiation, with each successively higher ray becoming dominant over the previous one. This hierarchical order proceeds step by step to the Godhead.

These rays have an incredibly powerful effect on every human being's life. From helping to determine our physical features, the quality of our emotional body, and the nature of our mind to predisposing us to certain strengths, weaknesses, and attitudes, the rays are as influential as our astrological sign.

Like having your natal chart to refer to, knowing your ray structure can be very beneficial. By knowing which rays are predominant in our lives, we can learn much about ourselves. In addition, since each of the rays is a form of energy, which work primarily through one of the chakras, we can access that energy when needed. It is important to understand that we can utilize all the rays whether or not we have them in our primary structure. We can call forth each of the rays for personal and planetary service.

As is true of the four bodies and the three minds and many other parts of self, it is essential to integrate and master all the rays. In a sense, each ray can be looked at like one of the archetypes, which will be described in the next chapter. Just as there are twelve major archetypes, there are twelve major rays.

In each of our incarnations we are born into a different sign of the zodiac, which helps us develop a more complete perspective. The same is true of the rays. In different lifetimes the physical, emotional, mental, and personality rays change to allow the incarnating personality to develop a more holistic perspective. Each ray, although characterized by a specific quality, is in truth whole and complete within itself and carries within it the qualities of all of the other rays. In blending with the other rays, which is essential, an ever greater whole is created. Many lightworkers believe that if they have a second-ray structure for their soul and monad, for example, then they don't have to deal with the other rays. This is not true. Your monadic and soul rays determine what Inner-Plane ashram you are connected to. Each ashram is led by a different master:

First Ray: El Morya

Second Ray: Kuthumi and Djwhal Khul, Lord Maitreya

Third Ray: Serapis Bey

Fourth Ray: Paul the Venetian

Fifth Ray: The Master Hilarion

Sixth Ray: The Master Jesus/Sananda

Seventh Ray: Saint Germain

Every disciple and initiate on the planet is enrolled in one of these Inner-Plane ashrams, whether they realize it or not. This doesn't mean that you can't work with the other Masters, but rather that your main planetary home, so to speak, will be in your soul's ashram. Just because you are a disciple of Saint Germain doesn't mean that you don't have to integrate and master the other rays or the teachings of the other Masters. Disciples and initiates usually carry the ray pattern of 2, 4, 6 or 1, 3, 5. These ray influences, which mark the different aspects of self, have an enormous influence on us. In my opinion they are even more influential then astrology, and we know how influential astrology is. It is amazing how accurately one can read a person's personality by just understanding their rays and astrological horoscope.

I, for example, am a second-ray soul and a second-ray monad. That is why I am so connected to Djwhal Khul, Kuthumi, and Lord Maitreya and why spiritual education of the masses is my all-consuming desire in life. Even though I am a second ray, it is essential that I develop myself in all of the rays.

Let me give an example of what happens if we don't develop ourselves fully in all of the rays. Let's say a lightworker is a first-ray monad and as a result is very connected to El Morya and possesses enormous personal power. The ray pattern for someone like this is probably 1, 3, 5. This ray pattern is the line of least resistance and allows full expression of that attribute. If this type of soul does not develop the second ray, he or she will be powerful but not with the proper amount of love/wisdom to balance this power.

What happens to people with a fourth-ray monad, who are often artists, if they are not developed in one of the more masculine rays such as 1, 3, 5, or 7? They fulfill the stereotype of the artist who is incredibly creative but has trouble functioning effectively in life. The following chart outlines the seven rays and the corresponding human temperaments.

THE SEVEN RAYS AND SEVEN HUMAN TEMPERAMENTS

The First Ray

The main qualities of a first-ray temperament are will, power, strength, courage, determination, leadership, dignity, independence, majesty, daring, and executive ability. *The Power Type* is the natural ruler and leader, statesman, empire builder and colonizer, soldier, explorer, and pioneer.

The Second Ray

The main qualities of the second-ray temperament are wisdom, love, intuition, insight, philanthropy, unity, spiritual sympathy, compassion, loyalty, and generosity. *The Love Type* is the sage, world teacher, ambassador, philanthropist, reformer, teacher, inspired artist, humanitarian, healer, and servant to mankind, and is imbued with a universal love that even flows into the lower kingdoms of nature.

The Third Ray

The main qualities of the third-ray temperament are comprehension of fundamental principles, understanding, a deeply penetrating and interpretative mind, adaptability, tact, dignity, recognition of the power and value of silence, and capacity for creative ideation. *The Ac-*

tive Type is the philosopher, organizer, diplomat, strategist, tactician, scholar, economist, banker, chess player, judge, allegorist, interpreter, and cartoonist.

The Fourth Ray

The main qualities of the fourth-ray temperament are creative ideation, harmony, balance, beauty, rhythm, a special faculty to perceive and portray through the arts and through life, and the principle of beauty in all things, with a strong sense of form, symmetry, equilibrium, and artistry.

The Fifth Ray

The main qualities of the fifth-ray temperament are outstanding analytical and deductive abilities, the formal mind, acquisition and dissemination of factual knowledge, unwearying patience, and extreme thoroughness and method, particularly in the repeated examination and classification of intricate and minute details. *The Scientific Type* excels as researcher, scientist, mathematician, engineer, surgeon, lawyer, detective, physical scientist, or occult and metaphysical scientist.

The Sixth Ray

The main qualities of the sixth-ray temperament are sacrificial love, burning enthusiasm for a cause, fiery ardor, one-pointedness, selfless devotion, adoration, intense sympathy for the suffering of others, and idealism expressed as practical service and loyalty. *The Devotee Type* is the reformer, mystic, saint, philanthropist, martyr, evangelist, and missionary.

The Seventh Ray

The main qualities of the seventh-ray temperament are nobility, chivalry of character and conduct, splendor of estate and person, ordered activity, precision, skill, grace, dignity, great interest in politics and the arts, ceremonial pageantry, magic, discovery, control and release of the hidden forces of nature. *The Organizer Type* is the political organizer, theatrical producer or director, military leader, psychic or magician, occultist, and priest/priestess in ceremonial orders.

All of us need to exhibit the qualities of each of these types. All of us need personal power, love, activity or action, artistic sensibility, scientific development, devotion, and business acumen. The ray assessment of our spiritual constitution does not mean that we should focus only on those particular rays we possess. Our ray readout tells us how God created us and what we came into this lifetime with. The goal is to integrate and master all the rays.

The exact same thing is true of astrology. An astrological horoscope is a reading of the heavenly spheres we came under the influence of at the moment of our birth. Lightworkers often study this as if it were the only thing they need to understand. We do need to understand all twelve astrological signs or astrological archetypes and integrate and master them. But that is not all we need to do. When all of our twelve archetypes, twelve rays, and twelve astrological signs are integrated and balanced within self, then the negative ego has been cleansed. This is because another definition of the negative ego is imbalance. Negative ego takes the form of being too yin or too yang.

BEING A RENAISSANCE PERSON

We all want to be balanced, whole, and well integrated even though we each will have an inclination toward a certain type of profession because of the ray of our monad and soul. So even if you are a fifth-ray monad and have an interest in science, you still need to balance your power, love, wisdom, devotion to God, business pursuits, and artistic expression.

Each person ideally becomes a Renaissance man or woman within each ray type. Remember what I said earlier about each ray being whole within itself if properly understood. Problems occur when spiritual seekers become unfocused or place too much emphasis on one aspect of self and are then not well balanced. The imbalances can manifest in an infinite number of ways, including being extremely gifted in one area and dysfunctional in others.

One way to look at this is to have as a goal to be a jack-of-all-trades and master of one. That is how we can become balanced. This is also why we change rays and astrological horoscopes each lifetime — to create this balance. All the knowledge, information, and abilities necessary to achieve balance are already in our subconscious mind. We have probably lived out each one of these types at least thirty or forty times before. None is better than any other. They are all of equal importance to the perfect fulfillment of God's Divine Plan. This means of achieving a balanced self on all levels is already within us—all we have to do is allow it to come forward.

The following charts from Alice Bailey's two-volume work *Discipleship in the New Age* show the ray method of teaching truth and distinctive methods of service and professions.

The Rays and the Corresponding Professions

Ray I   Government and politics; international relations
Ray II   Education and teaching; writing, speaking, radio, TV
Ray III   Finance, trade, business and economics
Ray IV   Sociology; racial and cultural cooperation and conciliation; the arts
Ray V   Sciences, including medicine and psychology
Ray VI   Religion, ideology, philosophy
Ray VII   Structuring of society; ordering of power through ceremony, protocol, and ritual

In this first chart we see the well-balanced distribution of professions the seven rays give us. Look at government and politics. Why do we have so many corrupt and egotistical politicians? Because they are highly developed in first ray but not in second ray and sixth ray. Second-ray initiates are great spiritual teachers but are often dysfunctional in business, which is third ray, or have not learned how to fully own their personal power and move into leadership. Initiates on the third ray may be well developed in dealing with money and business; however, if they are not developed in second ray, they will not use love and wisdom and integrity in their dealings. If they don't have the first ray, then they won't be powerful and decisive. If they are not developed in the sixth ray, their devotion may be to man rather than to God.

The fourth-ray type may be an artist, but without the fifth-ray energy he or she is too yin. The fifth-ray type may be a great scientist, but without developing the sixth ray may be too focused on science at the expense of God. Such a person may not be able to deal with money effectively without the third ray, or may not be loving in the way he or she works and may be cruel to animals without the second ray. This type may be pushed around by his or her boss because of lack of development in the first ray.

By looking at the chart and by doing an honest self-assessment so that we know which rays we possess and which we don't, we will make great strides toward the goal of being balanced, integrated persons.

All the rays are Christ qualities in the same way all the astrological signs are. The true self-realized being is developed in all of them. All these rays need to work together like the threefold flame of love, wisdom, and power being balanced in the heart. If we are deficient in any one of these, our whole personality will become imbalanced. There is also a seven- or twelvefold flame in our hearts that we also must balance. Mastering the science of the rays, archetypes, and astrology, which all dovetail together, will help you do this. The problems that arise when these twelve aspects are not balanced are of infinite number. From health problems to relationship problems, emotional problems, spiritual problems, and blocked creative expression, all are rooted in imbalance.

The next chart reveals how each ray has a higher and lower expression. Each of the twelve rays can be used in service of the negative ego or in service of the soul. This chart lists the lower and higher expression of each of the seven rays.

Ray Methods of Teaching Truth

Ray I Higher expression: The science of statesmanship and of government
Lower expression: Modern diplomacy and politics

Ray II Higher expression: The process of initiation as taught by the Hierarchy of Masters
Lower expression: Religion

Ray III Higher expression: Communication systems, satellites, digital information systems
Lower expression: The use and spread of money

Ray IV Higher expression: The Masonic work based on the formation of the Hierarchy; related to Ray II
Lower expression: Architectural construction; modern city planning

Ray V Higher expression: The science of the soul, esoteric psychology
Lower expression: Education

Ray VI   Higher expression: Christianity and diversified religions; note relation to Ray II
Lower expression: Churches and religious organizations

Ray VII   Higher expression: All forms of white magic
Lower expression: Black magic; spiritualism in its lower aspects

THE RAYS AND THEIR DISTINCTIVE
METHODS OF SERVICE

Each ray type has a unique and distinctive method of service.

Ray I: Servants of the first ray impose the will of God upon the minds of men. They do this through the powerful impact of their ideas, and their knowledge of the principles and practices of governing. They lead the process of the death of the old form and the rebirth of the new idea. Servants on this ray are God's destroying angels in a positive sense; however, servants who still operate on the personality ray often distort and misuse this energy.

Ray II: Servants of the second ray meditate on and assimilate ideas associated with the Divine Plan. Because of the powerful attraction of love, they teach people to respond to the Divine Plan. They educate others to do the same work and carry these ideas even deeper into the consciousness of humanity.

Ray III: Servants of the third ray function to stimulate the intellect of humanity. They help the mass consciousness to achieve greater comprehension through the manipulation of ideas.

Ray IV: There are few servants of the fourth ray in incarnation at this time who fully embody this ideal; however, there are fourth-ray personalities. Their major task is to harmonize emerging ideas with older ideas to bridge that schism. They are initiates who are able to synthesize many ideas and create from them a new vision of reality.

Ray V: This ray is coming into more prominence at this time on a mass level. Servants of the fifth ray investigate forms in order to uncover their underlying meaning and power. Their job is to prove whether ideas are true or false. For that reason, they focus on concrete science.

Ray VI: This ray has been very strong in our past history; however, it is now waning in power as the seventh ray begins to pour in. Servants on this ray are focused on the art of recognizing ideals, which are the blueprints of ideas. They train humanity to seek the good, the true, and the beautiful.

Disciples on this ray are heavily influenced by the desire aspect within man. They want to see the desire aspect used correctly in service of humankind. People who are galvanized into action by an idea are usually first-ray souls. Persons galvanized into action by an ideal to which they subordinate their lives serve the sixth-ray energy. However, when the sixth ray is focused on the personality level rather than the soul level, it can be quite destructive because of the personality's fanaticism.

Sixth-ray servants also must avoid the danger of being too one-dimensional and full of personal desire. The fundamentalist Christians or Muslims come to mind as a good example of this distortion. The sixth-ray servant uses desire in a positive sense to materialize an ideal on the earthly plane. The sixth ray increases the emotional desire for the ideal to materialize, and the seventh ray uses this desire energy to manifest it.

Ray VII: This is the ray that is strongly coming into power now. Servants of the seventh ray organize the ideal and physically manifest it on the earthly plane.

All the rays are essential to the completion of the Divine Plan, and no ray is better than another. All the rays work to carry out a specific group idea of the seven Chohans or archangels of the seven rays.

This next chart offers us a deeper understanding of each ray type's distinctive methods of service. If you have never experienced a ray reading and don't know the rays of your monad, soul, personality, mind, emotions, and body, I highly recommend that you do so. Ray readings are vital to the understanding of your soul's purpose and destiny, just as a well-interpreted astrological chart is to understanding your personality. For more information about exploring your basic constitutional rays, contact the Melchizedek Light Synthesis Academy (see Appendix).

THE RAYS AND THEIR GLAMOURS

Esoteric psychology and the science of the rays is a vast and complex science much like astrology. My intention is to make it as simple, easy to understand, and practical as possible. Toward this end, let's take a deeper look at the glamours connected with each ray. The word *glamour* was used by Djwhal Khul in describing the phenomenon of delusion that occurs on the astral plane. The delusion that occurs on the mental plane he called illusion; the delusion on the etheric plane is maya.

The following chart depicts the glamours or astral delusions associated with each of the seven major rays. As you review this list, create a personal inventory and note imbalances that you feel need to be cleared. The glamours are caused by the negative ego, which distorts and misuses the seven great rays and directs them toward a lower instead of a higher expression. The following adaptation from Alice Bailey's *Esoteric Psychology* will be greatly enhanced if you understand your personal ray configuration.

The Rays and Their Glamours

Ray I *Glamours*: Love of power and authority, pride, selfish ambition, impatience and irritation, self-centeredness, separateness, aloofness.

Ray II *Glamours*: Fear, negativity, a sense of inferiority and inadequacy, depression, constant anxiety, self-pity, excessive self-effacement, inertia, ineffectiveness.

The Second ray is the ray of the World Teachers. The student on this ray is never satisfied with his highest attainments. His mind is always fixed on the unknown, on the heights to be scaled.

Normally he has tact and foresight and makes an excellent ambassador, teacher, and head of a college. The artist would produce work that is instructive.

Ray III *Glamours*: Always being busy, materialism, preoccupation with detail, efficiency and self-importance through being the one who knows, scheming and manipulation of others, deviousness, self-interest.

Ray IV *Glamours*: Diffusion of interest and energy, impracticality and glamour of imagination, changeability, vagueness and lack of objectivity, constant inner and outer conflict. Causes argument and acrimony, dissatisfaction and envy in response to beauty and that which is higher and better. The ray of struggle, Rajas (Activity) and Tamas (Inertia) are balanced so man is torn in combat which leads to the "Birth of Horus" or the Christ born from the throes of constant suffering and pain.

Ray V *Glamours*: Constant analysis and splitting of hairs, criticism, overemphasis of form, cold mental assessment and disparagement of feeling, intellectual pride, reason, proof and intellectuality are sacrosanct.

Ray VI *Glamours*: Fanaticism, possessiveness and overdevotion, bigoted narrow-mindedness, love of the past and existing forms, reluctance to change, rigidity, too much intensity of feeling.

Man on this ray is full of religious instincts and impulses and intense personal feeling. Everything is either perfect or intolerable. He must always have a personal God. The best type is a saint. The worst is a bigot, fanatic, or martyr. Religious wars and crusades all originated on the sixth-ray energy.

Ray VII *Glamours*: Rigid adherence to law and order, overemphasis of organization and love of the secret and the mysterious, psychism, the glamour of ceremony and ritual, superstitions, deep interest in omens.

This is the ray of the Court Chamberlain and High Priest, the born organizer, the perfect nurse for the sick, the perfect sculptor. Loves processions, ceremonials, military and naval reviews, genealogical trees.

MORE ON GLAMOURS OF THE RAYS

The next chart is a very concise, easy-to-read list of what can be called the archetypal negative expression of the rays or glamours. Again, I recommend going through this list as a way of doing a personal inventory, checking the ones that need clearing. Once you have done this, you can use the methods and techniques described at the end of the chapter for removing these glamours and the negative ray archetypes.

Ray I

The glamour of physical strength

The glamour of personal magnetism

The glamour of self-centeredness and personal potency

The glamour of "the one at the center"

The glamour of selfish personal ambition

The glamour of rulership, dictatorship, and wide control

The glamour of the messiah complex in the field of politics

The glamour of destruction

The glamour of isolation, of aloneness, of aloofness

The glamour of superimposed will, upon others and upon groups

Ray II

The glamour of being loved

The glamour of popularity

The glamour of personal wisdom

The glamour of selfish responsibility

The glamour of too complete an understanding, which negates right action

The glamour of self-pity, a basic glamour of this ray

The glamour of the messiah complex, in the world of religion and world need

The glamour of fear, based on undue sensitivity

The glamour of self-sacrifice

The glamour of self-satisfaction

The glamour of selfish service

Ray III

The glamour of being busy

The glamour of cooperation with the plan in an individual way, not a group way

The glamour of active scheming

The glamour of creative work without true motive

The glamour of good intentions, which are basically selfish

The glamour of the spider at the center

The glamour of God in the machine

The glamour of devious and continuous manipulation

The glamour of self-importance, from the standpoint of knowing, of efficiency

Ray IV

The glamour of harmony, aiming at personal comfort and satisfaction

The glamour of war

The glamour of conflict, with the objective of imposing righteousness and peace

The glamour of vague artistic perception

The glamour of psychic perception instead of intuition

The glamour of musical perception

The glamour of the pairs of opposites, in the higher sense

Ray V

The glamour of materiality, or overemphasis of form

The glamour of the intellect

The glamour of knowledge and of definition

The glamour of assurance, based on a narrow point of view

The glamour of the form, which hides reality

The glamour of organization

The glamour of the outer, which hides the inner

Ray VI

The glamour of devotion

The glamour of adherence to forms and persons

The glamour of idealism

The glamour of loyalties, of creeds

The glamour of emotional response

The glamour of sentimentality

The glamour of interference

The glamour of the lower pairs of opposites

The glamour of World Saviors and Teachers

The glamour of the narrow vision

The glamour of fanaticism

Ray VII

The glamour of magical work

The glamour of the relation of the opposites

The glamour of the subterranean powers

The glamour of that which brings together

The glamour of the physical body

The glamour of the mysterious and the secret

The glamour of sex magic

The glamour of the emerging manifested forms

ADVANCED INFORMATION ON THE SCIENCE OF THE RAYS

The First Ray

The six key qualities of the first ray are clear vision, dynamic power, sense of time, solitariness, detachment, and singleness of purpose. The six qualities express how the first ray affects the human kingdom. It also must be understood that the rays affect the other kingdoms as well.

The purpose of the first ray is to bring forth the death of all forms in all kingdoms in nature and on all planes. This could be the death of an insect, solar system, star, organization, religion, government, root race, or planet. The cyclical nature of life is death and rebirth, and the first ray performs this most important function. The first ray will bring forth the death of egotistical values and institutions so that we can move into the golden age of soul-inspired values and institutions.

The Second Ray

The key qualities are divine love, radiance, attraction, the power to save, wisdom, and expansion or inclusiveness.

The Third Ray

The key qualities of the third ray are the power to manifest, the power to evolve, mental illumination, the power to produce, synthesis on the physical plane, scientific investigation, and balance.

The Fourth Ray

The key qualities of the fourth ray are the dual aspects of desire, the power to reveal the path, the power to express Divinity and growth, the harmony of the spheres, and the synthesis of true beauty.

The Fifth Ray

The key qualities are emergence into form and out of form, the power to make the voice of silence heard, the power to initiate activity, revelation of the way, purification with fire, and the manifestation of the Great White Light.

The Sixth Ray

The key qualities of the sixth ray are the power to kill desire, the spurning of that which is not desired, endurance and fearlessness, the power to detach oneself, and the overcoming of the waters of the emotional nature.

The Seventh Ray

The key qualities are the power to create, the power to cooperate, the power to think, the revelation of the beauty of God, mental power, and the power to vivify.

Strength, Vice, and Virtue of Each of the Seven Rays

This following chart identifies the strength, the vice, and the virtue to be acquired from each ray. I recommend that you do your personal inventory, which will prepare you for the work to come. Return to this chart as a reference whenever necessary.

THE FIRST RAY OF WILL-POWER
Special Virtues:
Strength, Courage, Steadfastness, Truthfulness arising from absolute fearlessness, Power of ruling, Capacity to grasp great questions in a large-minded way and of handling men and measures.
Vices of Ray:
Pride, Ambition, Willfulness, Hardness, Arrogance, Desire to control others, Obstinacy, Anger.
Virtues to Be Acquired:
Tenderness, Humility, Sympathy, Tolerance, Patience.
Glamour:
Love of Power and Authority, Pride, Selfish Ambition, Impatience and irritation, Self-centeredness, Separateness, Aloofness.
Method of Healing:
Steadfast, Trust in self and others, Fearless, Devotion, Prayer.
Approach to Path:
Likes crashing choruses, Takes the Kingdom of Heaven by violence.

THE SECOND RAY OF LOVE-WISDOM
Special Virtues:
Calm, Strength, Patience and Endurance, Love of truth, Faithfulness, Intuition, Clear intelligence, Serene temper.
Vices:
Overabsorption in Study, Coldness, Indifference to others, Contempt of mental limitations in others.
Virtues to Be Acquired:
Love, Compassion, Unselfishness, Energy.
Glamours:
Fear, Necessity, A sense of Inferiority and Inadequacy, Depression, Constant anxiety, Self-pity, Excessive Self-effacement, Inertia, Ineffectiveness.
Method of Healing:
To thoroughly know the temperament of the patient and the nature of the disease so as to use willpower to best advantage.

Approach to Path:
By close and earnest study, making them more than mere intellectual knowledge.

THE THIRD RAY OF ACTIVE INTELLIGENCE—HIGHER MIND
Special Virtues:
Wide views on all abstract questions, Sincerity of purpose, Clear intellect, Capacity for concentration on philosophical studies, Patience, Caution, Absence of tendency to worry self or others over trifles.
Vices:
Intellectual pride, Coldness, Isolation, Inaccuracy in details, Absentmindedness, Obstinacy, Selfishness, Overly critical of others, Paralysis of action from too many details.
Virtues to Be Acquired:
Sympathy, Tolerance, Devotion, Accuracy, Energy and Common Sense, Good at higher mathematics.
Glamours:
Glamour of always being busy, Materialism, Preoccupation with detail, Efficiency and self-importance through being the one who knows, Scheming and manipulation of others, Deviousness, Self-interest.
Methods of Healing:
Use of drugs made of herbs and minerals belonging to the same ray as the patient under treatment.
Approach to Path:
Deep thinking and study on philosophical and metaphysical lines.

THE FOURTH RAY OF HARMONY THROUGH CONFLICT
Special Virtues:
Strong affections, Sympathy, Physical Courage, Generosity, Devotion, Quickness of intellect and perception.
Vices:
Self-centeredness, Worrying, Inaccuracy, Lack of Moral Courage, Strong passions, Indolence, Extravagance.
Virtues to Be Acquired:
Serenity, Confidence, Self-control, Purity, Unselfishness, Accuracy, Mental and Moral balance.
Glamours:
Diffusion of interest and energy, Impracticality and glamour of imagination, Changeableness, Vagueness and lack of objectivity, Constant inner and outer

conflict, causing argument and acrimony, Dissatisfaction because of sensitive response to beauty and that which is higher and better.

The ray of struggle of Rajas (activity), Tamas (Inertia) balanced so man is torn in combat which leads to the birth of Horus of the Christ from the throes of constant suffering and pain, Varies from brilliant conversations to gloomy silences, Loves color.

Method of Healing:

Massage and magnetism used with knowledge.

Approach to Path:

Self-control, thus gaining equilibrium, thus gaining balance among the warring forces of his nature, Hatha Yoga is said to be very dangerous for this ray type.

THE FIFTH RAY OF LOWER CONCRETE MIND

Special Virtues:

Strictly accurate statements, Justice without mercy, Perseverance, Common sense, Uprightness, Independence, Keen intellect.

Vices:

Harsh criticism, Narrowness, Arrogance, Unforgiving temper, Lack of sympathy and reverence, Prejudice.

Virtues to Be Acquired:

Reverence, Devotion, Sympathy, Love and wide-mindedness.

Glamours:

Constant analysis and splitting of hairs, Criticism, Overemphasis of form, Cold mental assessment and disparagement of feeling, Intellectual pride, Reason, "proof," and intellectuality are sacrosanct.

The ray of science and research, Orderly, Punctual, The ray of the great chemist, The first-rate engineer, The surgeon.

Method of Healing:

Surgery and electricity.

Approach to Path:

Research pushed to its ultimate conclusion and the acceptance of the inferences that follow.

THE SIXTH RAY OF DEVOTION

Special Virtues:

Devotion, Single-mindedness, Love, Tenderness, Intuition, Loyalty, Reverence.

Vices:

Selfish and jealous love, Leaning too much on others, Partiality, Self-deception, Sectarianism, Superstition, Prejudice, Overly rapid conclusions, Fiery anger.

Virtues to Be Acquired:

Strength, Self-sacrifice, Purity, Truth, Tolerance, Serenity, Balance and common sense.

Glamours:

Fanaticism, Possessiveness and overdevotion, Narrow-mindedness, Love of the past and existing forms, Reluctance to change, Rigidity, Too much intensity of feeling.

Man on this ray is full of religious instincts and impulses and intense personal feeling. Everything is either perfect or intolerable. He must always have a personal God. The best type is a saint. The worst is a bigot, fanatic, or martyr. Religious wars and crusades all originated on the sixth-ray energy. He is a poet of the emotions, devoted to beauty and color.

Approach to Healing:

By faith and prayer.

Approach to Path:

Prayer and meditation aimed at union with God.

THE SEVENTH RAY OF CEREMONIAL MAGIC OR ORDER

Special Virtues:

Strength, Perseverance, Courage, Courtesy, Extreme care in details, Self-reliance.

Vices:

Formalism, Bigotry, Pride, Narrowness, Superficial judgments, Self-opinion, Overindulged.

Virtues to Be Acquired:

Realization of unity, Wide-mindedness, Tolerance, Humility, Gentleness and love.

Glamours:

Rigid adherence to law and order, Overemphasis of organization and love of the secret and the mysterious, Psychism, The glamour of ceremonial and ritual, Superstitious, Deep interest in omens.

This is the ray of the Court Chamberlain and High Priest. The born organizer. The perfect nurse for the sick. The perfect sculptor. Loves processions, ceremonials, military and naval reviews, genealogical trees.

Approach to Healing:

Extreme exactness in carrying out orthodox treatments.

Approach to the Path:

Observance of the rules of practice and of ritual can easily evoke and control the elemental forces.

METHODS FOR CLEARING THE NEGATIVE RAY
GLAMOURS AND ARCHETYPES

There are a number of methods that you can employ to clear the negative ray glamours. I've listed them here with a brief explanation of each.

Self-Inquiry

Self-inquiry is always the most important tool for clearing the negative ego or the negative ray glamours. It involves monitoring your thoughts and feelings at all times, and when a negative ray quality tries to enter your consciousness or mind, you deny it entrance. Immediately focus your attention and consciousness on the positive ray quality that is its opposite. This is the process of denial and affirmation, or attitudinal healing. It requires constant vigilance, personal power, and the understanding that it takes twenty-one days to cement a new habit into the subconscious mind.

Keeping a Log

Make a list of all the glamours you checked in your personal inventory. I recommend that you create this list in a positive form by rewording the negative qualities into qualities you want to develop. In other words, if superiority was on your inventory, then you might list equality as the characteristic you are trying to develop. The idea here is to give yourself a score or grade as to how you are doing in manifesting this quality. Do this three times during the course of each day. Keeping a log such as this forces you to be conscious and is also a positive game you are playing with yourself to try to have as high a score or grade as possible. Do this for twenty-one days and these new qualities will start becoming positive habits.

RAY SYMBOLS

The following seven symbols correspond to the Seven Great Rays and can be used as a type of meditation tool to access or balance the ray energy you would like to manifest at any given moment.

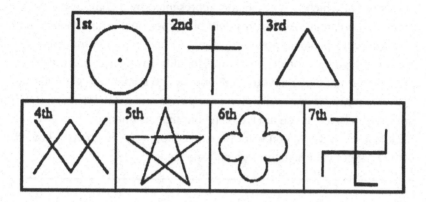

This is more a right-brain method. It is absorbing the positive arche-type by meditating on all the symbols or only one of them. These symbols trigger the positive aspect of the rays in an autosuggestive and right-brain fashion.

Ray Reading from Djwhal Khul

A qualified practitioner who can access Djwhal Khul can do a reading that will tell you the rays of your monad, soul, personality, mind, emotions, and body. During this reading you can ask how these ray areas affect you currently and where areas of ray glamour are present. Sometimes the Masters are able to see things that we aren't aware of. You can also ask how you are doing in integrating all the rays and getting rid of the negative aspects of the rays. I provide contact information in the Appendix.

Dialoguing with Glamours

Isolate a particular glamour you are trying to correct. If you use chairs, put the glamour in one chair and in the other chair put the opposite Christ-like ray quality that is the correction. Whether in a chair or a journal, let each side speak almost as if you are channeling these subpersonalities. You want to give them expression to see how they are operating within you. Sometimes it is helpful to do this with a friend who can ask questions of these parts to facilitate the gathering of information.

Once each part has fully expressed itself, move back into the conscious mind, which is symbolically represented by a chair in the center of the two polarities. As the president of the personality, talk to each part and with your personal power tell the part how you and the Ascended Masters are going to organize your personality. In essence, you are telling the glamour good-bye. If you want, you can go back to the glamour and see what it says. If you really own your power and mean business, it will not have a choice. If you are weak in your first-ray energy, it will give you back talk. However, if you want to realize God, you are going to have to take charge of your negative ego and silence it.

Chapter 15

✴

How to Clear the Negative Ego Through the
Science of the Archetypes

The study of the archetypes is fascinating and is one that many lightworkers are less familiar with than other areas of psychological understanding. One morning in meditation the Masters revealed to me that the clearing of the negative ego through the science of the archetypes needs much more exposure among spiritual seekers. As my own work has progressed I have come to understand the incredible importance of studying the archetypes, and in the future they will become a key area in the study of psychology for every person. Studying archetypes will help you gain greater clarity and self-realization.

The study of the science of archetypes from a spiritual perspective is much like the science of the rays. It falls more into the realm of esoteric psychology, which has rarely been written about for a general audience. Carl Jung first coined the term; however, the science of the archetypes from the perspective of the Ascended Masters has not reached mass consciousness yet.

Archetypes are underlying mythic themes that can be found in all races and cultures at all times. The archetypes are ageless roles or key stereotypes that exemplify different forms of behavior. In other words, the archetypes are universal personifications of perennial themes. They can often appear as the main characters in legends, fairy tales, Shakespearean dramas, and Bible stories.

Every person who has ever lived on earth, or ever will, fits into one of these twelve archetypes or mythic themes. That is why the study of this science is so important. The ultimate goal in your final incarnation on earth is to integrate all of them and be victimized by none of them. Just as each astrological sign has an evolved expression and an unevolved expression, dependent on the disciple's soul development, each of the twelve archetypes has a positive and negative side. This applies to the science of the rays, too, which also have higher and lower expressions. The goal in all spiritual sciences is to develop the highest expression of each of them. The same is true of the science of the archetypes.

The following chart lists the twelve major archetypes and some of the twelve subarchetypes that comprise them. We will examine each of these in more detail.

The Archetypes

DESTROYER	FOOL	INNOCENT	MAGICIAN
Change Maker	Risk Taker	Artist	Fairy Godmother
Enemy	Clown	Child	Merlin
Betrayer	Flake	Harmless One	Priestess
Evildoer	Lunatic	Lover	Shaman
Mischief Maker	Madman/Madwoman	Trusted One	Sorcerer
Devil		Wonderer	Trickster
Rascal	Philanderer	Youth	Warlock
Smartass	Scatterbrain		Witch
			Wizard

MARTYR	PATRIARCH/ MATRIARCH	RULER	SEDUCER/ SEDUCTRESS
Great soul	Ancestor	Aristocrat	Deceiver
Saint	Father	Emperor/ Empress	Enchanter
Savior	Mother	Judge	Lover
Loser	Old One	Prince/Princess	Philanderer
Struggler	The Great Father	Queen/King	Tempter/ Temptress
Unfortunate Victim	The Great Mother	Superior	

SEEKER	SERVANT	WARRIOR	WISE ONE
Adventurer	Assistant	Fighter	Guru
Explorer	Attendant	Gladiator	Holy One
Hermit	Person Friday	Hunter	Master
Hunter	Right-Hand Person	Knight	Mystic
Monk		Rival	Oracle
Pioneer	Slave	Soldier	Philosopher
Pursuer	Subject	Survivor	Prophet
Wanderer	Subordinate	Struggler	Sage
Wonderer	Worker		Teacher
			Thinker

What separates the science of the archetypes from other spiritual sciences is that in studying them as a psychological science, we discover that some of these major archetypes as a whole are more advanced than others. Djwhal Khul told us the least advanced archetype on this list is the Destroyer and the most advanced is the Wise One. Even the Destroyer still has a positive and negative side; however, the Wise One is a more evolved archetype.

The ultimate goal of this science is to enable you to integrate all twelve archetypes, along with all the subarchetypes, with the Wise One as the main archetypal theme during your last life. As a result, everyone may have a different focus at a certain time, such as Spiritual Teacher, Counselor, Philosopher, Prophet, or Priestess.

Incorporating the Wise One in your final incarnation before breaking the wheel of rebirth will help you to bring out the positive higher expression of all your other major and minor archetypes. Nevertheless, the Wise One archetype has its negative side, too, one that every spiritual seeker must beware of. The idea is to integrate all of them from the perspective of being the Godman or Godwoman—what Djwhal Khul called the Fair Witness or Observer.

In our past lives we all have had incarnations where we have lived out all of these roles. In some lifetimes we lived out just one archetypal theme. In other lifetimes we lived out combinations of one to four archetypes. How the archetypes combine is a fascinating aspect of this study. Many volumes could be written on this subject, much like the infinite combinations in the science of the rays and the science of astrology.

The most important thing is not to judge one's self. Living out all these themes, whether in a positive or negative manner, is all part of the process. Archetypes, past life aspects, and subpersonalities are all related. When God created us, these archetypal potentials were built into us from the start, like a psychic substructure or psychic constitution. As we went through the reincarnation process, these past life aspects began to build up as we lived out one or more of these archetypal themes.

In our present life all of our past life aspects are manifested as our subpersonalities, which can be expressed in an infinity of ways. When babies are born, they have different personalities because of all the past life aspects and archetypal themes that have been lived out in the hundreds of incarnations they have had. You can get a sense of their past lives just by looking at the programming a child comes into this world with. But whatever your programming is from past lives, you can easily change it in this life.

It is also important to remember that every archetype or role has an opposite. This is why you can't in truth identify with any single archetype, but must embrace all of them from the position of the Witness self. The Wise One archetype, because its main role is to achieve complete balance, incorporates all the archetypes within itself. However, those who overidentify with the Wise One cannot step out of the role of Guru, Teacher, Leader, or Priest/Priestess. The conscious mind is not any of the archetypes, but it chooses which role you need at any given time for the highest expression of God and service. When you integrate all the archetypes you have infinite possibilities of expression and are not stuck in any one role. You have all of them available in their positive aspects when you need them.

The negative ego always manifests the negative side of the archetype and distorts each archetype's true purpose as created by God. One might say the negative ego works through all the archetypes just as the soul and monad do. In all spiritual sciences, the goal is to reject the negative ego and lower-self expression and always attune oneself to the soul and higher-self expression. It is a good idea to become very familiar in a detached manner with these archetypes in both their negative and positive expressions. This can be done in a number of ways.

Voice Dialoguing with the Archetypes

Voice dialogue, or gestalt, as it's often called, is a useful tool that involves role playing. Use this process when you want to have a live "conversation" with various other people in your life, or parts of yourself. In this particular case, we're using it to move through the personal expressions of the twelve archetypes as they appear in your life.

It's too much to ask of yourself to dialogue with all twelve archetypes in one session. Working with one of them a week will give you time to integrate each one, and to meditate on how that particular archetype is expressing itself in your life. Never forget that you are none of the archetypes—You are God! The archetypes are merely the forms that you, as God, are using to give expression to the self on the earthly plane.

Always remember when working with the archetypes that your personal power resides in your conscious mind. When you get weak or off center, you may find yourself surrendering your power to the various aspects of the archetypes. In other words, you surrender to the negative ego, your child consciousness, your emotional body, your subconscious mind.

The idea is first to understand and then to consciously master these twelve roles. If you make a mistake, that's okay, just correct it. The science of archetypes offers an objective tool for mastering your personality and eliminating the hold of the negative ego.

• You can do a voice dialogue with a friend, a counselor, or by yourself. You can use your friend or counselor to play the role of one of the aspects of the archetype—or simply as an objective observer or questioner. However, you might want to tape whatever is being said to play back for later reference.

• Choose a quiet space and time, when there will be no outside interruptions. Set up three chairs—one in the center, the other two facing each other on either side.

—The center chair represents your conscious mind and/or choice maker.

—The other two chairs represent the positive and negative expressions of whichever archetype you wish to work with.

• You may wish to begin with the archetype that seems the closest to who you feel you are at the present time, or work through them in the order in which they appear on the list. Remember that each archetype has a positive and negative expression. It is very important to listen to both sides, and this process is set up to give each of them the opportunity to speak.

• Doing a voice dialogue may seem a bit like channeling to you, or perhaps an exercise you might have experienced in an acting class or a workshop. You begin by sitting in the middle chair, and inviting both the lower and higher energies of a particular archetype to join you. Tell them that you'd like to hear what each one of them has to say about this aspect of your self.

• Let's say you've chosen The Destroyer, who is the least developed of all the archetypes. And you're beginning with its negative aspects. Move from the center chair to the negative chair, and take a deep, relaxing breath. Then allow the negative side of The Destroyer to begin to speak through you. Simply say whatever enters your mind. Don't be judgmental or edit what's coming out, just speak what you "hear" or "think."

• When there seems to be nothing more to say, move back to the center chair and assume your role as the mediator/conscious mind. Ask the negative Destroyer if it has anything else it wishes to say, or ask any questions you might have.

• If there is more to say, move back into the negative Destroyer's seat, and allow it to speak its piece. If not, move into the positive Destroyer's seat, and again, take a deep, relaxing breath, and say whatever pops into your mind. It's amazing what comes to the surface sometimes, especially with the positive aspects of the Destroyer.

• Move back to the center chair and ask if the positive Destroyer has anything else it wishes to say, and/or ask any questions you may have. If there is more, move back to the positive seat, and answer the question.

• If you experience any conflict between the two aspects, you may need to dialogue back and forth, by moving from one chair to another. In the end, return to your mediator/conscious mind chair to resolve the conflict and integrate the result.

• When both sides have had their say, return to the center chair, and talk to both sides. Use your conscious personal power to tell both aspects of the Destroyer how you're going to manifest its energy from now on, and how you're going to express this in your life.

• End by making a vow to God that you commit yourself to avoiding the unconscious expression of the Destroyer, or any of the other archetypes.

Journal Dialoguing with the Archetypes

This is simply a variation on the voice dialogue technique, however, instead of moving into another physical chair, you will move into one of the three roles on paper in your journal, or on your computer screen.

• As always, choose a quiet place and a quiet time when you won't be interrupted to do your dialogue work. Follow your accustomed method of doing a journal dialogue, except that this time there will be three participants instead of two—your conscious mind, the negative aspect of the archetype, and its positive aspect.

• As the mediator/conscious mind, invite both aspects of your chosen archetype to join you in this dialogue.

• Begin with the negative aspect of the archetype. Let it express itself through you for the purpose of greater understanding—of yourself and what the archetype represents. Simply write down whatever enters your mind.

• When the negative aspect is done, as mediator, ask it if there's anything else it would like to add, or ask any questions that you may have.

• Either respond as the negative aspect, or move to the positive aspect, and allow it to express itself through you. Again, whatever you "hear" or "think," write down in your journal or on your computer screen.

• As mediator/conscious mind, ask if there's more, or ask questions.

• In case there's any back talk from either or both of the aspects, then feel free to dialogue back and forth until you resolve the conflict and achieve integration. Remember, your conscious mind always holds the power. You're always in charge, and all the archetypes take their orders from you. The ideal is always to have the archetypes working in the service of the soul and monad—not subjugated to the negative ego.

• Now, as mediator/conscious mind, speak to both aspects through your journaling. In your power mode, tell them what adjustments you're going to make in your personality to make the best use of this particular archetypal relationship in its highest aspects.

• End by writing out a vow to God that you plan to use the highest aspects of this archetypal relationship in the integrated expression of your personality.

SELF-INQUIRY

This is probably the most important tool of all for clearing the negative ego archetypes. Once you have gone through this book and have done one or both of the previous exercises, then the process of self-inquiry takes over your life. Sai Baba says that 70 percent of the spiritual path is self-inquiry. It means refusing to operate on automatic pilot, and it means committing to being alert, aware, and vigilant—conscious at all times of what archetype is in operation and whether at any given moment the lower expression of one of them is dominating your personality.

This is the same thing as being vigilant about when the negative ego is taking over. The science of the archetypes gives us a more refined tool for objectifying this process and getting a handle on it. Many people use astrology this way. They might say it was the Mars (anger) part of them or the Venus aspect (love) that took over at a certain time. The archetypes are a psychological system that doesn't require a lifetime of study. In truth, the science of archetypes and the science of astrology dovetail perfectly together.

The rays can be used in the same way by looking at the qualities of the twelve rays and seeing which ray is in operation. Just as we are always expressing one of the archetypes, we are also always in one of the rays and one of the twelve astrological signs and houses.

One of the purposes of self-inquiry is to catch ourselves when a negative ego archetype begins to take over. We then use our will to stop it in its tracks. We then reaffirm the positive side of the archetype, letting this be our expression in thought, word, and deed. Instead of calling this attitudinal healing, we call this process archetypal healing. By doing this for twenty-one days on this higher level of expression of any given archetype, we can form a new habit in the subconscious mind. By remaining vigilant and keeping our archetypal expression steady in the light, all our misqualified past life archetypal expressions can be reprogrammed without our even knowing what the past lives were.

THE MAJOR ARCANA IN THE TAROT DECK

The Major Arcana in the Tarot Deck
and the 22 Paths to God

Again, past lives manifest as preprogrammed subpersonality expressions in our subconscious mind. It takes some effort in the beginning to reprogram them, but after twenty-one days the old expressions will be working for us instead of against us. The most important aspect of this process is the cultivation and development of a strong will and personal power; this is the number-one key to psychological health. If we don't own our personal power, then we will give it away automatically to the negative expression of these archetypes.

These twelve archetypes could also be related to the Tree of Life, the ten Sephiroth and the lines that connect the ten Sephiroth, as well as the twenty-two major arcana tarot cards. Tarot is probably the premier system of working with the archetypes. Some of the tarot cards deal with planetary archetypes such as the Sun and Moon and are not hence listed with the twelve I have mentioned. The twelve archetypes as referenced in the tarot can be seen in the Tree of Life in the study of the Kabbalah as part of the lines that connect the tree. The diagram on page 243 is reprinted from my book *Hidden Mysteries*, which depicts this quite clearly and shows the archetypes of the major arcana from the perspective of the science of tarot.

Like other spiritual sciences, the science of the archetypes is a tool for gaining greater self-mastery over the mind, emotions, and body in service of the soul. The science of archetypes is less well known than many spiritual sciences. What is nice about it is that, as a psychological science, it is very easy to learn. Even if you do no more than thoroughly study this chapter and meditate on the chart and the overview of the positive and negative sides of each archetype, you will derive enormous benefit in terms of mastering your personality. It is also helpful to see the synthesis of these different spiritual sciences.

DEVELOPING THE OVERSOUL

In the development of one's oversoul, which is made up of twelve incarnating soul extensions, some soul extensions will be more developed in certain archetypes than others. From the perspective of the oversoul, this is okay. For example, one set of soul extensions might be more occultist, and another set might be more sensitive and mystical.

The ultimate goal of each soul extension is to integrate all twelve, especially if you are choosing to be the one who will ascend for your entire soul group. As you develop to higher levels of initiation you may begin the process of helping to clear archetypes for your twelve soul extensions and then for your 144 soul extensions. The higher and higher you go in your evolution, the more responsibility you will take in the integration and clearing process.

You have lived out many of these archetypes in past lives, so they don't have to be expressed in an extreme way in this life, although all are still available when needed. By integrating all of them, you will have the greatest possible sense of wholeness.

People who are born under one particular astrological sign may have an inclination to manifest certain archetypes. How this occurs is a whole science unto itself. Even though there may be this slight inclination, Djwhal Khul tells us that each sign can and does manifest all twelve archetypes. Nevertheless, the sun sign, astrological house, and planets you are under the influence of will have their effect.

The exact same thing is true of the science of the rays. The ray type of your monad, soul, and personality will have some influence over the archetypes you may manifest, although again, all twelve manifest through all twelve rays. An example of this might be someone who is a first-ray monad. The first ray is the will or power aspect of God. This type of person might be predisposed slightly to the Patriarch, Ruler, Magician, or Warrior archetype. The second ray, because of its focus on love-wisdom, might predispose someone to the Seducer, Seeker, or Wise One.

The combinations of the archetypes is also a science unto itself. The Wise One mixed with any of the other archetypes will bring out the positive aspect of each. A mixture of the Patriarch and the Warrior will bring out the Warrior King. If this is mixed with the Destroyer, the Warrior King will be fighting either for self-glory or for the glory of God, depending upon whether the Warrior archetype is manifesting in a negative or positive way. You can see how complicated this can get, just as a horoscope takes into consideration all of the different influences in a synergistic understanding. Exploring this aspect of combinations of archetypes could take up many volumes and is not the purpose of this chapter, but I mention this so you can begin to play with it.

Djwhal Khul tells us that the keys to mastering and integrating the twelve archetypes are the will to good, the will to God, and the will to harmonize. This intent will move you in the right direction. The science of the archetypes is really an investigation of your belief system in your conscious and subconscious mind. It is a process of being devastatingly honest with yourself and exploring your every motive to see what archetype it is stemming from and whether it is coming from the lower or higher expression of that archetype.

As we all know, it is very easy to deceive ourselves and be deluded by glamour, maya, and illusion. It is much easier to see these archetypal expressions in others than it is to see them within ourselves. We all have our blind spots. The purpose of this discussion is to help you uncover them. The negative ego is incredibly tricky in its philosophy, and is as brilliant in the use of the mind as the soul and Holy Spirit are. Most people don't realize this. The only difference is that the soul is working for God and the negative ego is working as the prime cause for glamour, maya, and illusion. Do not underestimate the negative ego.

The archetypes are the cause of all our karma throughout all our lifetimes, be it for good or for bad. Again, we are manifesting one or more of the archetypes every moment of our lives. It is a good idea to become very familiar with them, for if we don't, we are opening ourselves to be victimized by their unconscious expression. The archetypes, left to their own discretion, will attempt to monopolize our attention and expression.

It is essential to understand that archetypes don't reason. Each archetype's primary goal is to express itself. By taking control of your personality and becoming the executive director, you can make them work with you in a cooperative manner. But they must have a leader. You are that leader, but you must own your personal power and maintain absolute mastery and tough love, for the archetypes are like children. If they don't take you seriously, they will not listen to you. Your will or power is the organizing faculty of the mind, and in the ideal state is guided by intuition.

The study of archetypes can be refined even further. Nations express certain archetypal themes, as do races and religions. All of these external influences, including our past lives, have their effect on us as well. This is why it is so important to be conscious at all times and not live as if on automatic pilot. If we are not conscious, then mass consciousness, past lives, parental programming, educational programming, mass media programming, and so on will determine our archetypal expression at any given moment. We must strive to be not the effect but the cause, to be a Master in the service of God, and not a victim, to become the fully integrated Godman or Godwoman.

In our final lifetime, when we achieve our ascension and complete the seven levels of initiation, we may be an artist, athlete, politician, banker, scientist, diplomat, spiritual teacher, or channel. It doesn't matter. The Wise One archetype will work through whatever profession we are destined to have. Our ray makeup plays a large part in determining what profession and service work we get involved in. First-ray monads are usually in politics, second rays are often spiritual teachers, third rays are often economists, fourth rays artists, fifth rays scientists, sixth rays ministers, and seventh rays diplomats.

God and our particular soul destiny include a profession we will pursue. We can complete our seven levels of initiation and achieve ascension in all professions, not just in the classical healing professions. All professions are healing professions if we manifest them in our higher expression. This is very important to understand. We must be the Wise One in whatever profession we choose to serve in this lifetime. What we need to improve life on earth is more people who can synthesize all twelve archetypes, regardless of their service and professional focus, to become Godmen and Godwomen made manifest. In truth, we probably have too many counselors and not enough Godmen and Godwomen bankers, economists, artists, scientists, and politicians. Each of us must follow the path that is our soul's destiny to serve. This is the fastest path to the seven levels of initiation.

Are you letting the negative ego program your archetypal expression each moment of your life, or are you letting the soul and Holy Spirit program your archetypal expression? As *A Course in Miracle* says, "Choose whom ye shall serve."

THE POSITIVE AND NEGATIVE QUALITIES
OF THE TWELVE ARCHETYPES

The Destroyer

Some people at first may have a hard time considering that the Destroyer as an archetype has any redeeming qualities at all, but I assure you it does. The negative side of this archetype is more obvious. When the negative ego is in control, this archetype manifests as destruction, glorified violence, abuse, control, domination, negative anger, power used in service of self, and criminal behavior. I think of fraternity parties where the men get drunk and immediately start destroying things. The Los Angeles riots after the Rodney King incident are another example where the negative side of this archetype takes over.

The positive side of the Destroyer is in the positive use of the first-ray energy. The first ray is the ray of power. The Masters use this ray to destroy old forms. Our society can't change unless the old negative ego forms that have been made externalized in material form are destroyed. Their destruction leaves room for the New Age form to take its place, the form the soul and monad would make manifest.

Hinduism has the trinity of Brahma, Shiva, and Vishnu. Shiva is the Destroyer aspect of the Hindu Trinity. The other two are the Creator and Preserver. Edgar Cayce referred to this in his source channelings as positive and negative anger. He said everyone must get rid of negative anger but that it is essential for every person to own positive anger. This is the channeling of the Destroyer archetype with all its power into a positive direction. In essence, it is using the Destroyer energy to eliminate the negative ego in all its manifestations.

The Destroyer is related to the archetype of the Spiritual Warrior. The Destroyer energy is used as a force to make positive change. It is the healthy use of denial. As A Course in Miracles says, "Deny any thought that is not of God to enter your mind." The Destroyer archetype can be channeled into destroying all that is blocking us from achieving our ascension, passing our seven levels of initiation, and manifesting all our goals.

In my own life, I have not been afraid to fully own and use this Destroyer archetype against the negative ego and for the goals of my soul and monad. This archetype is very tied up with the psychological issue of owning your personal power. It is almost as though if you don't own the Destroyer, it will destroy you. It is a case of cause or effect, Master or victim. God wants us to own our power full force, for our power in conjunction with His power is an unbeatable team. God helps those who help themselves!

The Fool

The Fool archetype in its lower or negative expression is foolhardy and blind. When the Fool archetype is run by the negative ego, we become scatterbrained and prone to the use of negative control and manipulation. In the tarot deck, the Fool is jumping off a cliff. We can do this when we're on automatic pilot and it can be disastrous, or we can do it in service of the soul as the ultimate healthy surrender in any given situation and lesson.

The positive aspect of the Fool is the Risk Taker. The Risk Taker is the most advanced card in the tarot deck. The Fool in its positive aspect has detachment and uses humor in an uplifting and positive manner. The positive side is the Innovator, the one who is not afraid to try new things, even though others may think us insane. Christopher Columbus, Thomas Edison, and Louis Pasteur might be people who lived the positive side of this archetype. This same ability used by the negative ego can be manipulative and used for a selfish purpose rather than for the good of the whole. In its highest form the Fool represents superconsciousness. In its lowest form it is the Lunatic or Madman/Madwoman, subject to folly, mania, extravagance, intoxication, frenzy, negligence, absence, carelessness, apathy, and vanity.

The Innocent

The negative aspect of this archetype is being too naive and childlike and lacking in spiritual discernment. When the negative ego controls this archetype, the disciple is not able to see darkness in self or others. This, of course, is a dangerous state of affairs, and we all know people like this—they may have a Pollyanna philosophy that doesn't take into consideration the existence of the dark forces, which are quite real. Not recognizing this makes us vulnerable to them.

The positive side of this archetype is what *A Course in Miracles* calls innocent perception. It is seeing life free from past programming, fresh and untarnished. It is the positive side of being like a child. It is innocence, but with the wisdom of the Wise One archetype. When the Innocent archetype is guided by the soul and Holy Spirit, we live in purity, adopting a do-no-harm, love-all-of-life-philosophy tempered by our spiritual discernment.

The Innocent is often connected to the soul-inspired artist. The positive archetypal Innocent lives in the holy instant and sees each meeting with another human being as a holy encounter, Christ meeting Christ. The highest evolution of this archetype is seeing everything in life through our Christ vision. It is remaining in love and oneness at

all times and in perfect Christ perception and interpretation—seeing
life as God sees life!

The Magician

The negative side of this archetype is using one's Magician powers
for the purpose of manipulation. The Magician uses his abilities to seduce others to follow him. This is much more common than people
realize. These are often healers, counselors, psychologists, psychiatrists,
social workers, marriage counselors, even spiritual teachers, who are
really operating out of a fourth-dimensional consciousness and not a
fifth-dimensional consciousness (ascended state). They have brilliant
minds (the Magician part) but are not completely soul-connected.
It is amazing how many spiritual seekers get seduced by this type of
person.

These are also the false gurus and psychologists and counselors who
spout a certain theory and try to convince you to take it on even
though it is not soul-directed. I have observed a great many of them using Neuro-Linguistic Programming. They are often very charismatic
and use this appeal as part of their deception. Often they are not aware
of their own deception, and other times they actually have made pacts
with the Dark Brotherhood for the purposes of power, fame, and fortune. Until we reach the fifth dimension, ascension, and/or sixth initiation, we are all in danger of being seduced by the negative side
of this archetype. The fact that we are still in the fourth dimension
means we are not yet totally fused with our soul and spirit. This leaves
us open to the negative ego programming of this archetype. Because
these powerful figures can do either good or harm, the term "black
magician" is used to describe them.

The healers who are still using their abilities for selfish purposes,
which is extremely common, are twilight masters. In other words, they
embrace both the dark side and the light side. I am giving a very stern
warning here to watch out for them. This is the danger of going to
psychologists and counselors who have no spiritual training. They
sound absolutely brilliant, and I am sure they are, but this is true
only on the personality level, not on the soul and spiritual levels. Remember that there are three levels of self-actualization: personality
self-actualization, soul self-actualization, and spirit self-actualization.
Magicians of the negative orientation are personality self-actualized,

which is why people flock to their charisma and magnetic energy. The problem is they are still fourth-dimensional and still totally run by the negative ego. A great many of the leaders in the consciousness movement exist on this borderline. They have not cleared this negative archetype.

The positive side of this archetype is the true soul-inspired magician. The white magician is not interested in negative manipulation or self-glory but true service of humanity and love of mankind. They are the true Alchemists and Transformers. They work as healers on the energetic or etheric level, or as metaphysicians, counselors, psychologists, and spiritual teachers on the psychological or spiritual level. They are magical in the way they can create change and transformation in our physical body, etheric body, astral body, mental body, and spiritual body. They do this by understanding universal laws at each level and applying them to catalyze greater healing and fusion with the soul and monad.

The true Magician is egoless and a true servant of the divine; he or she is not interested in self-glory, fame, or fortune and uses these brilliant abilities in service of God and the Ascended Masters out of true love and humility. The Magician has great personal power and self-mastery on either side of the coin, but the white magician never misuses it for selfish egotistical gain, or the negative manipulation of others. Fairly recent examples of black magicians are Jim Jones and David Koresh. Most people on the earth don't fully own their power and mastery and don't understand the difference between negative ego and Christ thinking. As a result, they are easily seduced by the dark force's brilliance and persuasiveness. Unless our motives are clear, we can easily be turned to the dark side.

This is a very dangerous archetype and, in my opinion, one of the ones that holds the greatest potential for blind spots. Even after achieving seven levels of initiation, we can manifest the negative aspect of this archetype. It all has to do with the issue of power. Most of us don't have power, and when we finally do get it the black magician within us wants to use it for self-glorification, worldly inflation, fame, and fortune. This is truly one of the great tests of the spiritual family. Can you have this kind of power over others and still retain the Wise One archetype and the positive Innocent archetype? Here again we see how these archetypes blend and work together in the ideal state.

The Magician as discussed in the tarot classically has great skill, diplomacy, self-confidence, and will. When reversed in the tarot it becomes sickness, pain, loss, disasters, mental disease, disgrace, and disquiet.

The Martyr

The Martyr archetype in its negative aspect or lower expression sacrifices, but as a means to manipulate and control others. Martyrs often perform sacrifices as a kind of guilt trip, saying, "I did this for you, and now what will you do for me?" Often Martyrs do this because of faulty programming. Fundamentalist Christianity has programmed millions and millions of people in this manner. Women especially are taught to martyr themselves and are led to believe that spiritual selfishness is bad. This creates a total imbalance in the personality, which breeds subconscious resentment and lack of self-love. It teaches that suffering is the path to God. Nothing could be further from the truth. In essence, many Christian sects teach people to be not right with themselves as a path to being right with God. People serving from this state of consciousness are not self-actualized at any level. This eventually leads to heavy karma. Our first responsibility in life is to self-actualize before we help others.

Being a negative Martyr archetype bankrupts a person, until the inevitable breakdown and heavy karmic life lessons force him or her to learn to be selfish. Remember, there is spiritual selfishness and there is negative ego selfishness. We must develop spiritual selfishness. This is the Wise One archetype's philosophical approach. Without being spiritually selfish, we can't set healthy boundaries. The healthy approach is to at any given moment choose when it is time to be selfish and when it is time to be selfless.

When this archetype is guided by the soul and spirit he or she can become a true Saint. Saint Francis of Assisi, Mother Teresa, and Mahatma Gandhi come to mind. These are Martyrs who sacrificed themselves in the name of the Wise One and positive understanding, not out of faulty thinking. In a sense we will all become positive healthy Martyrs as we evolve. The higher we go in the ascension and initiation process, the more we realize that the main reason we are here is to serve. This is the vow of the bodhisattva in Buddhism. The more we are filled and infused with the soul and monad or spirit, the more we want to dedicate our lives to planetary world service.

I have been trying to follow the path of the bodhisattva for much of my adult life; however, I also know how to be spiritually selfish when I need to set boundaries, protect my space, or take care of my physical health. As my life has evolved I need less and less time for myself and am able to spend more time trying to help others. This is not because I have to but because I want to. Who isn't inspired by such Saints as Mother Teresa and Mahatma Gandhi? People like them touch a very deep chord in all of us and move us to dedicate our lives to aid and serve others in some capacity. The world could use more expressions of the positive aspect of the Martyr and/or Saint archetype.

The Patriarch or Matriarch

The Patriarch in its negative or lower expression manifests as either the weak father or the totalitarian, control-obsessed father. We can manifest this attitude in how we parent real children, or how we parent our own child consciousness. This applies to both men and women equally. Everyone is a Patriarch, for everyone has a child within. The key question is whether it is soul-guided or negative-ego-guided in its expression.

The weak Patriarch, who can be either a man or a woman, gives no protection to the real child or to the child within. He/she can be wishy-washy and totally controlled by the feminine, which turns the feminine into its negative aspect. Conversely, the negative aspect of the Patriarch or Matriarch can be overprotective, too militaristic, and too controlled by the masculine. This turns the masculine into its negative aspect, and therefore the negative ego is its guide.

The Patriarch or Matriarch in its positive or higher expression is strong and expresses love in proper proportion. We are open, not subject to manipulation, consistent, warm, and compassionate, yet we can still set boundaries when needed. When soul-guided, the Patriarch/Matriarch has what Djwhal Khul has called divine indifference. In other words, we have healthy detachment in proper proportion to compassion. In essence, we are the ideal father and mother every child, both inner and outer, would like to have.

Coming to proper terms with this archetype is one of the most important tasks we can undertake. It is also another of the greatest blind spots lightworkers have — especially as it applies to how we parent our child consciousness. Proper self-parenting is an important concern on the spiritual path. It deals with the proper use of personal power and unconditional love in inner and outer expression. These two qualities are the two most important factors in psychospiritual health.

We still have a long way to go before we achieve proper self-parenting. This is because the core feminine and masculine energies can be guided either by the voice of the negative ego or by the voice of the soul and Holy Spirit. Most of us don't commonly think of ourselves as a Patriarch or Matriarch, but examine yourself with devastating honesty to see how you have raised yourself and how you are raising or would raise real children. Usually the pattern is that we raise real children better than we have raised ourselves.

The most common archetypal theme in society is to be the too-critical parent or, at the opposite extreme, to be the spoiling, indulgent parent. Tough love is the highest manifestation of the Patriarch/Matriarch if we really want to make progress on our spiritual path. Without tough love, the child within us will act out or become deflated, depressed, and love-starved.

The Ruler

The negative side or lower expression of the Ruler archetype is the tyrannical, dominating, and manipulative leader. Napoleon, Genghis Khan, and Mussolini are certainly examples. The benevolent Ruler is fair, just, cooperative, and empowers all. When the Ruler archetype is guided by the soul and spirit, there is divine objectivity, stability, even-mindedness, reason, and compassion tempered with divine authority. In addition, the positive Ruler properly blends power and love, ruling with courage, magnanimity, fairness, wisdom, and conviction.

In essence, the Ruler is the benevolent king or queen who stands for divine principles. The prime example is Camelot's King Arthur. King Arthur set up the Round Table, whose knights saw serving others as their highest goal. The search for the Holy Grail and the story of Parsifal are examples of the Ruler taken to its highest archetypal expression. The divine law applies to all, including the king.

In its negative expression the Ruler has become drunk with power. This may manifest as a superiority complex, as with the pharaohs, who were looked at as God, or the infallible pope, who can do no wrong. They take advantage of their ability to rule others, which is a gift from God, and practice hedonism, self-centeredness, and narcissism, all used for self-interest and self-glory.

As we progress on our spiritual paths, all of us will at some point be put into positions of power and leadership over others. The truth is that all of us are in that position right now—for example, in terms of how we treat the person who cleans our house or pumps our gas, or in terms of the power we have over our children. The key question when we are in this position, which we can never avoid once we begin to own our power and self-mastery, is which kind of Ruler will we be. All of us rule our thoughts, emotions, body, subpersonalities, archetypes, instincts, sensations, and intuition. Will we be guided by the negative ego's voice in our rulership, or by the voice of the soul and spirit in how we rule others and our own personalities?

How does an unconscious man of military background rule his own personality? Probably in the same way he rules his troops. How does a housewife who has been dependent on her husband most of her life and not learned to own her masculine side rule her energies? She doesn't; she is victimized by them. We all must become the divine Rulers over ourselves and over others.

The ultimate example we should strive to emulate is Sanat Kumara, our Planetary Logos, or Lord Maitreya, the Planetary Christ. They wield awesome power, the likes of which we can only dream about, and yet their love, respect, admiration, compassion, harmlessness, and support know no bounds. Melchizedek is the shining example of this type of ruler in our entire universe. God is the ultimate example of this type of ruler in the infinite universe.

These Masters rule with complete egolessness through the perfect blending of feminine and masculine, heaven and earth, oneness and group consciousness. Let us now aspire together to raise this Ruler archetype within us to such heights. Let us aspire to rule with inclusiveness rather than exclusiveness, with oneness and group consciousness rather than elitism, with love and innocent perception seeing the divine in all regardless of appearance, wealth, or status. Let us not be swayed by impermanent, materialistic values but rather set our sights high on those values and ideals that are permanent, eternal, and treasured by the soul and Mighty I Am Presence!

The Seducer/Salesman

The negative or lower expression of this archetype is negative manipulation, bribery, molestation, a narcissistic love of self, self-indulgence, and corruption. When the Seducer is guided by the negative ego, it

manifests as the Deceiver, the con man, the fast talker, the unscrupu-
lous used-car salesman, the Tempter or Temptress, or the greatly
amoral businessperson. The negative Seducer archetype uses everyone and everything to manipulate and seduce to meet its own selfish
needs. At its worst it is sociopathic, with no concern for others. All
methods and means are used to entice others to get what it wants, even
if this is on the emotional level—as when trying to make up for a lack
of self-love by using others.

The positive and higher expression of this archetype is the "spiritual
salesperson." Many of you may not have ever thought of such a thing.
I consider myself a kind of spiritual salesperson. What I am selling is
God, love, the teachings of the Ascended Masters, egolessness, forgiveness, unity, integrity, and so on. I use all of my persuasive abilities in
my books and workshops to persuade spiritual seekers to give up the
life of the lower self and negative ego, which offers only a one-way
ticket to pain and suffering.

The difference between this type of salesmanship and less savory
kinds is that my motive is pure and not contaminated by self-interest.
The Seducer archetype, when guided by the soul and spirit, is a teacher
and instrument of God. Every person on this planet stands for and believes in something, and it is part of our purpose to set this more divine
example. It doesn't have to be through words; it may be through actions or in silence.

The term salesperson has a stigma attached to it. Let go of this.
Salesperson is a neutral term. Whether the Salesman is guided by the
negative ego or soul and spirit is the key question. It is possible to have
an honest car salesman who really has integrity and who really wants
to serve. Remember, you're selling your children on your philosophy,
which is good. When you counsel others you are selling them on the
value of your suggestions. This is good as long as it is not egotistically
motivated and your focus is truly to help others and not yourself.

The positive expression of the Seducer/Salesman archetype helps
to bring awareness and invites people into equality, empowerment,
self-mastery, and clarity. As a parent, you can use this quality to help
your children realize their highest potential. The positive Seducer/
Salesman is even applied to self, for often you must seduce or coax
parts of your subpersonalities to cooperate. This is the positive use of
self-talk. We must tell ourselves that we are powerful, that we love ourselves, and that we are happy. The use of all affirmations, creative visu-

alization, self-talk, and even prayer is the positive use of the Seducer archetype.

The problem here is that the word *seducer* has a negative connotation, too. This is why Salesperson is a good alternative name for this archetype. When I was just finishing high school I took vocational tests and scored high on sales ability, which surprised me. I hated the negative aspect of sales, but I'd always known I was a good communicator and storyteller. I could never be a salesperson unless I believed in what I was selling. The only thing I could ever truly believe in and get behind is God.

One good way to check whether you are a Seducer or Salesperson is by examining how motivated you are to get paid for your service. Are you willing to do it for free? This is not the only check, for the negative Seducer can have many other self-interests, such as power and fame. Another check is to do your service and not tell anybody about it. This is called humility. The trick here is to again merge the Wise One archetype with the Seducer archetype to get the ideal combination of humility and assertiveness.

If you are weak in this area, then cultivate the positive Destroyer archetype with the Spiritual Warrior archetype into the Seducer under the guidance of the Wise One and you will have the power to put yourself out there. The lives of great Masters such as Jesus, Buddha, Sai Baba, Mohammed, Moses, Confucius, Lao-tzu, and Yogananda are prime examples of great souls selling and preaching and teaching their philosophies, which were so effective that great religions formed around them. Don't be afraid to truly own your power in this regard, for the success you seek in your service work and prosperity consciousness is intimately related to the proper integration of this archetype.

The Seducer archetype in its highest expression helps to bring out the best in all the people it meets. The Seducer is the ultimate motivational speaker, and when tied to the positive Wise One archetype is the ultimate spiritual teacher and planetary world service representative. The positive Seducer archetype holds the spiritual carrot to inspire others to focus their energies and achieve their highest potential and excellence. Cupid is the ultimate example of the Seducer in a positive sense. Lord Maitreya and Sai Baba are the ultimate enticers toward self-realization.

The Seeker

The negative side or lower expression of the Seeker archetype is the person who seeks materialistic goals and gains and not the path of ascension or self-realization. This can manifest on a number of levels. On a purely physical level the seeker's whole life is dedicated to accruing money and material things. On the emotional level it may manifest as seeking hedonistic pleasure and experiences. On the mental level the negative ego influence of this archetype may manifest as the seeking of intellectual development of the concrete mind and not of the higher mind. This type of seeking could manifest as personality-level self-actualization, but not as soul or monadic self-actualization. There could also be a fourth-dimensional seeking, as in the case of a famous psychologist, healer, or even psychic who does not believe in God or spiritual things. The negative ego archetype also manifests as people seeking a marriage partner or relationships, power, or worldly fame. The seeking is usually governed by the desire body and the threefold personality.

Other examples of this Seeker influence on the material level may be seen in the Adventurer, Explorer, Pioneer, and Wanderer. This in time is refined and focused on higher-mind and Inner-Plane exploration and pioneering as the disciple evolves. The outer traveling may still continue, but the new inclination is spiritual sights, such as the pyramids, or key physical-spiritual spots on the planet.

The positive or higher expression of this archetype is, of course, guided by the soul and spirit, which provides the inspiration to seek the inner rather than the outer, to seek the permanent rather than the impermanent. The refined level of this archetype seeks the Kingdom of God. In seeking this goal, material desires are still strived for, but under the umbrella of heavenly pursuits. As the Bible says, "Set your mind on God's Kingdom and his justice before everything else, and all the rest will come to you as well" (Matthew 6:33). The evolved expression of the Seeker archetype realizes the best of both worlds.

The Servant

The negative or lower expression of this archetype is the Servant of others from an unevolved state of consciousness. This can manifest on an inner or outer level. An example on the outer level might be a wife who serves the demands of a selfish husband out of fear, lack of self-

love and self-worth, or lack of personal power and spiritual attunement. This may also be caused by the negative Martyr archetype from
fundamentalist Christian doctrine, which throws her into servitude.

I once had a client who was a Mormon with twelve kids. She served
her husband and wasn't allowed to enjoy the higher spiritual benefits
of the Mormon Church because these were reserved for men. The
same has been true in the Jewish religion in the study of the Kabbalah.
The caste system in India in the past created servants and masters.
Even though slavery was abolished in the United States around the
time of the Civil War, psychological slavery still exists.

On an inner level we can be slaves to drugs, alcohol, bad habits,
obsessive thoughts, feelings, archetypes, sexuality, food, the physical
body, the negative ego, the desire body, the concrete mind, the child
consciousness, or the subconscious mind. We are being influenced by
the negative ego's interpretation of this archetype when we are a victim of self or others. At every moment of our lives we are either a Master or a victim, a cause or an effect, a Servant or the served!

The positive or higher expression of this archetype is the Servant of
God, Servant of the Masters, and Servant of Humanity. The soul expression of the Servant archetype serves the Most High God. This type
of person is right with self and right with God as the two most important relationships in his or her life. Such people serve from wholeness
instead of emptiness. They serve from personal power, self-love, self-
actualization, egolessness, and attunement to God. They serve out of
true love and compassion for their brothers and sisters, without any
self-interest. They recognize that the only reason they are on this earth
is to achieve ascension—to break the wheel of reincarnation and to
serve.

To this more evolved understanding of the Servant archetype, true
pleasure is found in serving God. The highest example of this archetype is the person who has taken the Vow of the Bodhisattva. This is
the vow to forgo one's personal or cosmic evolution and to instead
help all sentient beings on earth. Another ultimate manifestation is
the initiate who has transcended all victim consciousness and is the
complete master of his or her mind, emotions, and body, in sub-
servience to the wishes of the soul and monad. The true servant is a
willing, conscious bondslave of Christ who daily dies to the machina-
tions of the negative ego. It is only through serving our brothers and
sisters that we can realize God.

Our brothers and sisters are the Eternal Self who share an identity with us. Each person you meet during your day, whether you know him or not, is really God visiting you in physical form! If only people realized this on a mass scale, what a different world we would have. Instead the negative ego would have you look on your brother as a stranger and judge him by his physical, emotional, and mental appearance, which is nothing more than a set of inner clothes he has put on that day. As Sai Baba has said, if you wish to know Him, see Him in every brother and sister you meet. Christ said the same thing. By serving our brothers and sisters, we are not doing them a favor; rather, we are doing ourselves the favor. How we treat our brothers and sisters is literally how we treat ourselves. Do anything but serve your brothers and sisters and you have separated yourself from self and God. The key to this archetype is to understand that you are always serving—this cannot be helped. The question is, who and what are you serving? This archetype is another one that is very tricky and prone to blind spots among lightworkers. As Djwhal Khul would say, "Ponder on this."

The Warrior

The negative or lower expression of this archetype deals with the unevolved soul who is run by the negative ego and looks at life as a war, with himself battling the egos of millions of others. In its worst-case scenario it manifests as criminal behavior. This state of consciousness may for some be sublimated slightly and channeled into military service, which is an outlet for the negative ego interpretation of the Warrior archetype. We see the glorified violence of this archetype manifested in movies and television.

On an emotional level the negative Warrior archetype is pervasive in terms of negative anger or many types of abusive behaviors directed toward other people, animals, or even the environment. On an inner level it can very commonly manifest as abuse of self. On the mental level it manifests as what A Course in Miracles says are "attack thoughts" toward self or others, which ideally we are to replace with "love thoughts."

When this Warrior archetype is raised in its expression to the soul, we have the Spiritual Warrior. The disciple and initiate are indeed still warriors, but they are fighting for love, oneness, harmlessness, Christ consciousness, ascension, and enlightenment of self and others. They are fighting for the good of the whole. This is another one of these confusing archetypes for many lightworkers. Their belief is that all war is bad; they therefore believe they must reject it and so don't see the value of the Spiritual Warrior. I am here to tell you that if you do not own the positive aspect of this archetype, you will be extremely ineffective in your life.

Becoming a Spiritual Warrior means owning your power. They are really one and the same thing. To reject this is to make yourself powerless. Christianity understands this in its discussion of the battle of Armageddon. We are all in our own personal battle of Armageddon. This battle is being waged on the inner plane and in our own consciousness. It is the battle between the negative ego and the soul. It is the battle between the lower self and the higher self. It is the battle between the Dark Brotherhood and the Great White Brotherhood.

People who do not own the Spiritual Warrior have a totally naive understanding of life. Yogananda said, "Life is a battlefield." Krishna said to Arjuna on the battlefield, when Arjuna was falling apart emotionally, "Get up now, and give up your unmanliness. Get up and fight. This self-pity and self-indulgence is unbecoming of the great soul that you are." We are all in God's army, and our weapons are love, prayer, affirmations, visualization, japa (the constant repetition of the name of God), chanting, meditation, spiritual reading, service, forgiveness, harmlessness, defenselessness, egolessness, and Christ consciousness.

The full owning of the Spiritual Warrior makes you relentless in your focus, commitment, self-discipline, and self-mastery. My experience in actualizing the positive aspect of Spiritual Warrior and Destroyer archetype in service of the Wise One archetype has allowed me to fully own my personal power. I use this power in the service of God and the Divine Plan. People who do not own the Destroyer and Spiritual Warrior are afraid of their power, and this applies to a significant number of spiritual seekers.

Earth is a very tough classroom, and if we don't own these two archetypes, we are going to get beaten up by people and life. When we own these two archetypes, they enhance all the others enormously, for there is first-ray energy at full tilt supporting them. When we own our full power in conjunction with God's full power and the tremendous power of the subconscious mind, we are unbeatable.

This combination, undertaken with a pure heart, gives you the Midas touch, and the strength of ten. You become absolutely unstoppable! Sai Baba is the ultimate example of this on our planet. As he has said, there is no force in this universe that can stop his mission. The Knights of the Round Table and the fellowship of the Three Musketeers were built upon such a concept. It was the Spiritual Warrior archetype that during World War II stopped Hitler's Germany. Gandhi and Mother Teresa were ultimate Spiritual Warriors in the struggle against violence and suffering.

We must use our full power at maximum drive to achieve self-mastery of our energies. The opposing forces of the subconscious mind, desire body, emotional body, negative ego, and lower self are very strong. We must master our energies or they will master us. There is really no middle ground. If we fully own the two archetypes of the Destroyer and Spiritual Warrior in service of the Wise One, we will easily achieve this goal, and many will be served in the process.

Those misguided souls who reject such a concept are emotional and psychological victims. We must not fall prey to their faulty thinking, for our ascension and breaking the wheel of reincarnation depend on this. We must become as strong as steel in our pursuit of God-realization and service to humanity!

The Wise One

The Wise One in its negative or lower expression uses its wisdom to control others. You have heard the expression "Knowledge is power." The key question is, how will we use this power? The scientists who created the atomic bomb were wise, but was this a good use of their wisdom? This is an interesting philosophical question. When the negative ego controls this archetype, the Wise One can be on an ego trip, acting superior, judgmental, or self-righteous. The Wise One here may focus all of his or her energies to become wise, but for what purpose? If it is to control, manipulate, or demean, or to gain fame, power, money, praise, or special status, the Wise One has been taken over by the dark side.

The positive or higher expression of the Wise One archetype is the embodiment of the Ascended Masters we revere, such as Buddha, Lord Maitreya, Jesus/Sananda, Mother Mary, and Quan Yin. These are our guides and examples. Their wisdom is completely infused by soul and spirit, the Mighty I Am Presence, and love. The Wise One is the true guru, not the power-hungry one. The true guru seeks nothing more than to empower his or her students and make them equals, rendering him unnecessary.

The Wise One may manifest in many forms, such as Spiritual

Teacher, divine Psychologist, Healer, or Philosopher. As mentioned previously, this archetype manifests into all professions and no profession. It is the guide and teacher of all other archetypes. It lifts all other archetypes into a higher and soul-directed expression. The true self-realized being uses this archetype as its main theme but is not identified with it; such a self-realized being lives in a state of consciousness as the Fair Witness or Observer, free of all archetypes.

The true Ascended Master consciousness identifies itself as God, who is beyond the balancing of all archetypes. To overidentify with any archetype is to see ourselves as a role instead of as the Master, who has all roles integrated and available. All archetypes are mythic roles and thus have an opposite. To overidentify with one keeps us locked in a limiting duality and polarity. The Wise One is more important than the other eleven only in the sense that it sees this and guides us to integrate all twelve equally to their highest potential.

In its positive expression the wise one has the wisdom to know that even it should not be overidentified. To overidentify with any archetype is to limit yourself. The ideal is to have infinite potentialities and roles to play as needed in any given moment for highest service potential with you as God in total charge. The most important thing is that you are in charge of these archetypes. They are not in charge of you. When great obstacles come into your life, call on your Destroyer, Spiritual Warrior, and Wise One to help you. When you need to market yourself, call on the positive Seducer/Salesman and Wise One to help you. When positive parenting is needed, whether inwardly or outwardly, call on your positive Patriarch and Wise One. When you are in a position to rule others, call on your positive Ruler archetype and the Wise One. Call on your positive servant archetype and the Wise One when involved in your service work.

The Wise One turns all twelve archetypes into healers and helps you to wield the power of the universe in service of God and humanity. Study and befriend these archetypes, and call upon them as needed. They are more than just principles. They have a life of their own, each bringing a whole philosophy surrounding the unique focus they embody. With all twelve working as a team in your service and God's service, you will have all the tools you need to master self, master life, and complete your service mission. *Namaste!*

Chapter 16

✳

The Fifteen Major Tests of the Spiritual Path

Being alert to the dangers of the negative ego is but one of many steps along the spiritual path. Many lightworkers face a variety of struggles and challenges. I have found that the most common major tests are the following:

1. Power	9. Selfishness
2. Money	10. False Pride
3. Fame	11. Greed
4. Attachment	12. Duality
5. Sexuality	13. Jealousy
6. Desire	14. Vanity
7. Anger	15. Egotism
8. Fear	

POWER

The first major spiritual test every lightworker faces is the issue of power. The lesson to learn here is how to own it without abusing it. Personal power is the fundamental first key to psychological health and spiritual growth. The ideal is to own it all the time in a considerate, unwavering manner. It is through owning our personal power that we will attain self-mastery over our energies. We either own our power or give it to other people and/or the subconscious mind or negative ego.

On the other hand, we must not repress the yin aspect of our self. We must properly balance the masculine and feminine sides so that they work together in a beautiful dance. The real test of power comes when we move into leadership. Do we use our power in total service of the Christ consciousness and love, or do we allow the negative ego to use it to control others? In essence, does our power over others go to our head? Many spiritual teachers, gurus, and psychics fail this first and most fundamental test. One way to test yourself is to see if you treat people exactly the same as you did before you got the power you now hold.

MONEY

The next great test of the spiritual path is dealing with money. Each of these tests is like a false god and idol, in a metaphysical sense. The key question is whether lightworkers will always put the true presence of God first and put these other, lesser gods on the altar of sacrifice. This is the real test of a self-realized being.

How attached are you to money? I am amazed to see lightworkers claim to be living from Christ consciousness—except when it come to money. Then, mysteriously, their Christ consciousness goes right out the window. Manifesting Christ consciousness only as long as doing so remains profitable is not true spirituality.

What happens to you when someone takes advantage of you financially? How do you respond? I am not saying that money is not important, for it is. It is not more important than God and the Christ consciousness. If all your money and material possessions were stripped away, how would you respond? Would you retain your faith and righteousness in God? When lightworkers move into the position of having a lot of money, the key question is, does their personality change? Do they still treat people in the same loving manner? How do they look at people who do not have any money? Do we judge them or love them as we would God? If we don't, then the negative ego's interpretation of money has a hold on them.

God wants every person to have an abundant amount of money. It is not good to be poor. Being poor is often a product of the negative ego's poverty consciousness. There is no judgment in being poor, but God would like everyone to be millionaires. The reason is so that all His millionaires can give their money and lives to help those still in need. What does having a lot of money do to your personality? How does this dovetail with the issue of power? You will pass or fail on the spiritual path with such issues.

FAME

The next great test on the spiritual path is fame. The three great tests of power, money, and fame are all very interconnected. The question here is what happens to our personality when we achieve fame and worldly recognition. Does this change our personality? Do we start treating others differently? Do we start treating others like second-class citizens? Does the fame just inflate our ego? How do we use the fame—for self-glory, or as an opportunity to be of greater service? Does the fame create an opening for the negative ego?

One problem with earth life is that most people who move into fame and worldly recognition are not equipped psychologically to deal with it. This applies both to earthly personages and to a great many spiritual leaders, who often are highly developed spiritually or psychically but not as developed psychologically and so lack control over the negative ego. The key with all these tests is to remain exactly the same as you were before power, money, and fame were achieved. These blessings by God should be used for His purposes. Know that they are on loan, and if they are misused, they will be taken away.

ATTACHMENT

To achieve self-realization, happiness, inner peace, success, good relationships, and God-realization we must let go of all attachments and addictions. As Buddha said, "All suffering comes from attachment." It is amazing how many things we get attached to. All negative emotions can be traced to attachment. All failed relationships can be traced to attachment. To pass the fourth initiation, in its fullest sense of the term, we must become a renunciate, which means being *in* this world but not *of* this world. We must learn to have strong preferences in life but not attachments. The nature of preferences is that we go after them with all our heart and soul and mind and might, but if we don't get them, we are still happy.

In matters of love, that which we share and then let go of will come back if it is meant to be. If it doesn't come back, it is not God's will. This is the law of life. That which we try to hold on to, we lose. This is one of the key principles in understanding the laws of manifestation.

Whatever we are attached or addicted to in life, no matter what it is—people, material things, future events, sex, money—we need to change them to preferences. We may go too far in the other direction and become totally detached, with no preferences. This is not good, either, for then we are not involved in life. It is important to have a total passion for life and for all our goals, preferences, and priorities, but the key is to be happy and have inner peace regardless of what happens. We shouldn't fight life.

SEXUALITY

Are we the masters of our sexuality, or is it the master of us? Does the flow of our sexuality serve the lower self or the higher self? Which comes first, God or sexuality? Are we moderate in our sexual practices? Does our sexuality serve love and intimacy or just materialistic animal pleasure? Does our sexuality serve a selfish purpose or a selfless purpose? Is our sexuality used also for the raising of our kundalini and brain illumination, or just for a second-chakra release?

These are all key questions lightworkers need to ask themselves with devastating honesty. We need to avoid making a judgment if our sexuality is being misused. As we become aware of this tendency, we can make the appropriate adjustment and spiritual vow to correct the imbalance. Life is nothing more than making continual adjustments and attitudinal and physical corrections to bring ourselves constantly back to inner peace. Mistakes are not bad; only uncorrected conscious mistakes become a problem. The idea is to learn by grace instead of karma, to learn the easy way instead of in the school of hard knocks.

Sexuality is a wonderful thing. God created it for us to enjoy as a communication device in the service of love. Sexuality is not bad. It becomes negative, however, when it is used by the lower self, or carnal self, or negative ego. Use it in service of the higher self and love, and it becomes a most sacred consecration.

One of the great tests of the spiritual path in regard to sexuality also comes when we achieve power, money, and fame. How do we deal with our sexuality then? A great many spiritual teachers have fallen when confronted with this lesson. They use their position of power to have sex with their students and/or devotees. We have all heard stories of well-known New Age and Eastern masters who have degraded their standing in this regard. We have also seen several Christian ministers fall in this way. Let this be a lesson to us all!

DESIRE

The next great test of the spiritual path is the transcendence of desire. This is the main precept of Buddhism. Many lightworkers are confused by this. What we must transcend are our lower-self desires, for they are the mother of all negative ego qualities. All lower-self desires should be transformed to higher-self desires. Many lightworkers mistakenly block all desire, which is neither appropriate nor good. We should have a desire to ascend, or a desire to achieve liberation, or to be of service. Even Melchizedek and all the Inner Plane Ascended Masters continue to strive for greater and greater levels of spiritual growth. Transform lower-self desire into desire for God-realization. This is the ticket to paradise!

ANGER

Anger is the lack of control and the attempt to regain it. The misuse of anger deals with the misuse of power. Everyone needs positive anger. This is like being the Spiritual Warrior in life or manifesting tough love with self or others when needed. Anger is ego, so instead of getting rid of anger, we should channel it properly, for there is enormous power in anger. This is what is meant by positive anger. It is anger channeled in Christ consciousness directions.

When not used in a completely and unconditionally loving manner, anger is a means of attack and therefore wrong. It is never appropriate or right to attack a brother or sister. To hurt another is to hurt God and ourselves. People who are angry all the time demonstrate lack of true personal power and consistent self-mastery. Anger creates separation. The purpose of life is to retain oneness at all times, not separation. Cultivate personal power, a Spiritual Warrior's attitude, and toughness but not anger. Chronic anger will debilitate your liver function, among other things. Anger stems from our attachment and from not looking at experiences as lessons in life. It also stems from our inability to transcend duality.

When things bother us in our relationships, we should most definitely share them, but only in a loving and respectful manner. There is no such thing as righteous anger. Righteous anger is a delusion of the negative ego. Anger is such a critical lesson in life, for it comes up every time life doesn't go the way we want it to go. We all know how often this occurs. Our anger results from what Buddha calls "wrong points of view." It is not in life, it is in our attitude toward life. Someone who is angry all the time is angry because they are fighting life instead of working with life and learning from it. Anger is caused by faulty thinking, as all negative emotions are.

When we move into positions of power, fame, and money the proper control of this energy is even more important, for a great many people are in our spiritual care. When anger arises, we can channel it into things like cleaning the house, exercising, transformative journal writing, and meditating. We can use the enormous power in anger as an alchemical process to create God-realization. We must not judge ourselves when anger arises, but rather take responsibility for creating it. We must not take it out on others or ourselves, or karma will be incurred!

FEAR

In many ways this lesson should have been first on the list. If there had to be one word that describes negative ego more than any other, it is *fear*. If there is one word that describes the Christ consciousness more than any other, it is *love*. There are in truth only two emotions in life: love and fear. All other positive and negative emotions have these at their core. To understand fear is to see that it is projected attack. When we attack others we live in fear of the Law of Karma operating in our own mind. This is why *A Course in Miracles* says to give up all our attack thoughts. Probably the greatest test of the spiritual path is to learn to release all core fear and to replace it with core love. When we have released all fear, we have released and transcended negative ego consciousness. The releasing of fear is also tied to having faith in God and self. This is why Edgar Cayce said, "Why worry when you can pray?"

A *Course in Miracles* says there are no neutral thoughts. All thoughts are either fear-based or love-based. This is why it is of the utmost importance not to allow any thoughts that are not of God to enter your mind, and to affirm and visualize only thoughts of God and the Christ consciousness.

One of the great dispensations of the twentieth century given to us by the Ascended Masters has been the Core Fear Matrix Removal Program. With the Ascended Masters' help, this advanced technology can remove all the core fear programs from this life and all your past lives in a matter of months if you will work with this tool on a regular basis. I will explain how this program works in the next chapter. No lesson in life or the spiritual path is more important than transcending negative ego consciousness and replacing it with the Christ consciousness. The transcending of fear is the great work of the spiritual path!

SELFISHNESS

Selfishness is truly the scourge of the earth. It is amazing to me how many prominent spiritual teachers and very high-level seekers still see life through the lens of selfishness. This stems from their high level of spiritual development but weak development on the psychological level. They often have not learned to parent their child consciousness properly. When we allow ourselves to be run by the child consciousness, we are going to be very selfish. This also stems from not ever being trained in the difference between negative ego thinking and Christ thinking. Very often lightworkers are extremely weak in this area. This is not a judgment, just a clarion call to encourage dedicated seekers to develop themselves to become as selfless as possible within self and then to train others to do the same. We don't have enough spiritual counselors doing this kind of work.

We all must learn to let go of our own selfish viewpoint and see the bigger picture. We must learn to wear the moccasins of our brothers and sisters. We must learn to embrace the opposite of selfishness, which is selflessness and helping others. The quality of total and complete selflessness is the sign of the true spiritual Master. This doesn't mean that at times the true spiritual Master isn't spiritually selfish. The key principle here is that they are *spiritually* selfish, not negative ego selfish. This may come into play in terms of having proper boundaries, or the need to be impersonally loving at times, or just taking care of the physical body so that we don't burn ourselves out in doing service work. The true spiritual Master's consciousness sees everything out of the group body and not out of the point of view of the child consciousness, negative ego, and physical body.

FALSE PRIDE

The lesson here can be summed up in the biblical statement "Pride comes before disaster, and arrogance before a fall" (Proverbs 16:18). This is one of the great tests that comes with power, fame, and money. Will the ego become inflated? Will the personality fill itself with self-aggrandizement and self-glorification? Excessive pride is the number-one problem of all fallen lightworkers. It is a danger no matter what your level of initiation, and is something every lightworker on the planet must be constantly vigilant against.

The other side of false pride is false humility. It is just as bad as false pride. More spiritual seekers are caught up in the bottom side of the negative ego than the top side. This results in an inferiority complex, low self-esteem, lack of self-worth, poor self-concept, feeling undeserving, and so on. These are as much an illusion as false pride is. The key to inner peace is to transcend duality in this regard. Both superiority and inferiority must be transcended to release oneself from the negative ego's grasp. To be stuck in either one is to stay stuck in both of them.

Transcending duality is one of the least-understood concepts of the spiritual path. There is another way of thinking beyond the duality of ego — it is called Christ consciousness. It is so unfortunate to see on this earth incredible psychospiritual teachers taken over by self-aggrandizement and self-glorification. No matter how great their teachings or books, false pride and inflation completely poison the work and create a push-pull dynamic between such gifted teachers and their students. These great spiritual teachers, who are bringing through some incredible energies and information, become synonymous with ego instead of the glory of God, and that's tragic. We all need to learn from their example, and we all need to constantly be on guard against succumbing to it. The negative ego is incredibly tricky and seductive and can enter in the briefest moment of nonvigilance.

GREED

Greed is truly a vile quality. Instead of being satisfied with the piece of the larger whole that God has for us, the negative ego quality of greed would have us try to acquire other people's pieces in God's Divine Plan. Greed generally refers to money, but in truth it goes far beyond just money or material things. It can be greed for power, fame—even greed for spiritual growth. The Buddhist Lama Chogyam Trungpa addressed this topic in *Spiritual Materialism*. The negative ego and the spoiled child consciousness always has desires, because they are run by the negative ego or astral body.

Instead of focusing on what we can give, the negative ego focuses on what it can get. This can even apply to spiritual information. We sometimes try to greedily save it for ourselves and not share it with others. It usually connects with competition, jealousy, and envy. In truth, what we greedily hold on to we will ultimately lose. We retain only what we give away. This is the law of life!

DUALITY

Transcending duality goes far beyond just transcending the top dog/underdog complex. It applies to all aspects of life. The key here is to see that lower forms of consciousness focus on duality and polarity. When we move into fully realized consciousness, we use our Christ consciousness or Buddha consciousness, and this can help us transcend dualistic thinking while we remain fully involved with life. Negative ego expression always has two side to it. This can be seen and most clearly understood in the Eastern teachings of such Masters as Sai Baba, Parmahansa, Yogananda, and Lord Krishna. In the Bhagavad Gita Krishna states that when we have profit or loss, pleasure or pain, sickness or heath, victory or defeat, success or failure—that is, duality—we remain the same.

In learning to transcend duality, we don't have to be tossed around on a continual roller coaster of emotional highs and lows. The Christ consciousness allows us to be unceasingly the same, always in our power, always loving, always happy, always even-minded, always with equanimity, and always forgiving, regardless of the fluctuation of the dualities of life. This is the consciousness of the God self. This allows us to remain the same whether people praise us or vilify us.

This is possible because the negative ego does not become engaged. The storms and fluctuations of outer life do not affect the stability and even-mindedness of our thinking process. It is not what is going on outside life that should be our concern, but rather our inner attitude toward what is going on.

Everything in life is perception, interpretation, and our belief system. The whole purpose of soul psychology is attitudinal healing—to shift our thinking from fear-based thought and emotions to love-based thoughts and emotions. Our salvation is not up to God, it's up to us. God has given us everything from the beginning. The question is whether we will give ourselves salvation by releasing our negative ego completely and fully embracing Christ consciousness.

JEALOUSY

Jealousy stems from insecurity and attachment and hence the need to compete with others instead of cooperate. Jealousy is completely a part of the negative ego and should be released at all cost, for it is not of God. Jealousy is connected also with the negative ego quality of envy. We have all heard the term "green with envy," which means we are filled with greed and selfishness. The main point here is to connect with all creation and transcend the illusion of separation. Our true identity is the Eternal Self, not the physical body and personality. In realizing this truth, every happiness and benefit another achieves is our happiness, too. Every suffering of another is our suffering, and vice versa. Our identity is God rather than self. This is a great lesson of the spiritual path.

The spiritual path is really quite easy to understand. If you want to be with God in heaven, then act like Him. Would God be jealous if another had more leadership, power, fame, or money? Can you see the absurdity of such thoughts and emotions? Would God compete with another over a relationship? As I said earlier, learn to state your preferences in life and then let go. If it is meant to be, it will come back, and if it isn't meant to be, then so much the better. Be happy for another person's joy. The key to life is to recognize your puzzle piece, for God created each person differently and for a different function.

VANITY

There is nothing wrong with taking care of our physical body and wanting to look nice and attractive. The key lesson here is whether this desire to present an attractive appearance is governed by the soul or by the negative ego. We must truly examine our deepest motivations and intent in this regard. It is important to have good grooming habits, to be clean, to present a nice appearance, and to wear appropriate clothes. Ask yourself if you are doing this simply to stand out and be better than others. Are you involved in a seduction of some kind? Do we spend too much time looking in the mirror and other vain pursuits? Some people don't spend enough time on these matters, and others spend too much time. They are mistakes of both omission and commission. Be moderate in this regard. Be clear on what you are trying to present. Are you presenting Godliness in your appearance, or slovenliness, or glamour in the extreme? Be honest with yourself in this regard, with no judgment, and make appropriate adjustments where needed.

EGOTISM

Egotism goes beyond even pride to really encompass all negative ego qualities and emotions. There really is only one problem in life for all incarnated souls, and that is fear-based egotism. There is only one answer to all the problems of humanity, and that is the Christ/Buddha consciousness. If we want to realize God, we must transcend the negative ego with all its negative attributes, qualities, and emotions.

The ego is the source of all life's spiritual tests. It is the source of all lower-self desire. It is the source of all separation, fear, and selfishness. It is the source of all disease. It is the premier lesson every soul must learn. The key to inner peace is not to allow any thought that is of the negative ego, that is not of God, to enter your mind. Affirm and place your attention on every thought and emotion that is Christ/Buddha consciousness. It is through this practice of attitudinal healing that the subconscious mind and conscious thinking will be reprogrammed and form a new habit. Remember, the subconscious mind does not reason. It is as happy to be programmed with the Christ/Buddha consciousness as with the negative ego consciousness. It is your job as the programmer of the conscious mind to reprogram your subconscious mind in this manner.

Many lightworkers spend too much time focusing on the spiritual glamours and do not spend enough time cleansing their mind and emotions of psychological or negative ego thoughts, emotions, and attributes. The Ascended Masters and angels will not get rid of your negative ego. That is your job. It is done very simply by not giving your attention to it. You don't need to get mad at the negative ego, for it doesn't really exist. You just think it does. It is nothing more than a bad dream. It manifests on the mental plane as illusion. It manifests on the astral plane as glamour and on the etheric plane as maya.

The negative ego has been called many things. In some schools of thought it is called the lower self. In other schools of thought it is called the "dweller on the threshold." In still other schools of thought it is regarded as just "ego," as opposed to "negative ego." One term that describes the negative ego well is "separation consciousness." A *Course in Miracles* states that there is only one problem in life—separation from God. In truth, we have never been or will ever be separate. This is illusion. The law of the mind, however, is that whatever we think is the reality we live in. The world is living in a mass negative hypnosis of separation that does not exist in reality. In this moment, wake up from the bad dream and nightmare you have lived in for many lifetimes and realize the truth that passeth all understanding.

Chapter 17

❋

How to Clear Negative Psychic Energies

Nothing real can be threatened, nothing unreal exists.
Herein lies the peace of God.
—A COURSE IN MIRACLES

Earlier in this book, we explored the psychological level of Soul Psychology in great detail. Now we are going to address the final piece in the puzzle—the psychic level of soul psychology. Both of these aspects of spiritual psychology are of equal importance. The people of earth cannot achieve ascension and self-realization without addressing both of these aspects. The psychic level of soul psychology deals with the principles of esoteric psychology that most people are not aware of. This arena is completely ignored by traditional psychology, and it is often ignored or deeply misunderstood in most spiritual practices.

We can do all the psychological clearing work in the world, but if we don't address this psychic level of soul psychology we will never fully recover from our physical or psychological problems. On the other hand, we can work at the psychic level of soul psychology and clear all these negative aspects, but if we don't do the integrative psychological work as well, we cannot recover fully or achieve full self-realization. In other words, these two approaches must be united.

What I am about to present is a method by which you can clear both levels yourself without having to rely on other humans to "fix" you—although you will be calling on the higher beings for their help. The purpose of this chapter is to give you the tools and information to clear and heal your psychic imbalances. Most people rely on other practitioners to help them on this level, which is fine. The ultimate goal, however, is to be able to clear ourselves of all negative implants, negative elementals, astral entities, etheric mucus, parasites, negative imprints, toxic astral energies, gray fields, and holes in the aura. This is an area of work that is usually addressed by psychic healers and/or those who are clairvoyant. But many of these practitioners lack an in-depth understanding of how to effectively deal with such negative forces.

Beginning the Psychic Healing and Clearing Process

The first step is to call for protection from the Ascended Masters, such as Djwhal Khul and Vywamus, who are dedicated to assisting our efforts on the earthly plane. Create a golden seal or golden bubble dome of protection whenever you do this work. Step two is to ask Djwhal Khul, Vywamus, and your own Mighty I Am Presence to set up a corridor between you and the Interdimensional Synthesis Ashram of Djwhal Khul. Step three is to ask them to take you in your spiritual body into the ashram for healing, clearing, and ascension activation work.

Step four is to request at each session the specific type of clearing and purification you require. This chapter will describe in great detail all the different negative psychic debris that must be cleared from your psychical, etheric, astral, mental, and spiritual bodies. In one session you might request that your negative extraterrestrial implants be cleared. In another session, you may request removal of any astral entities. In a third, ask Djwhal Khul and Vywamus to clear your negative elementals and/or parasites. In other sessions, you may request that they remove all negative imprints from past lives.

It's a very good idea to request this clear process as you're going to bed every night. This will allow the Masters to work on you while you sleep.

You don't need to be the least clairvoyant, clairaudient, or psychic to do any of the work described in this chapter. If you are clairvoyant or clairaudient that's wonderful, but it's completely unnecessary for this clearing process. This is because all you have to do is allow the

Masters to do the work for you upon your request. All they need is an invitation. Everyone can feel energy. You will feel lots of energy sensations going on in your head and throughout your bodies as you begin this process.

What I am sharing with you now is a new dispensation that has been given to mankind in recent times. You don't even have to completely understand the process to take advantage of it. The main point is to get rid of these unwanted negative aspects, and get purified and cleaned out. It's a lot less expensive than traditional therapy or going to a psychic healer. I'm not putting down spiritual counseling or psychic healers, for I am one myself. I just want to emphasize the classic concept that it's better to teach a person how to fish than to give them one. This is the first time in my entire life I have come across a method by which lightworkers can clear in the psychic realm as well as the psychical, mental, and emotional.

All physical diseases and psychological problems have negative implants, negative elementals, parasites, negative astral energies, or etheric damage connected to them. In the future, medical doctors will work with psychic spiritual healers as a team. Psychologists and spiritual counselors will be trained in this work as well or work with a specialist in this area to achieve a complete healing. I must emphasize again that you can obtain mastery of your mind, emotions, and body and still be plagued by negative implants, astral entities, parasites, negative imprints, and negative elementals in your auric field. This potential vulnerability applies to all spiritual seekers.

The amazing thing, however, is that these energetic imbalances can be gotten rid of. Later, I will discuss how you can do this work with other people, such as students, family, friends, and even people who are not consciously open to this level of understanding.

WHERE THE PSYCHIC ENTITIES ORIGINATE

Much of this toxic psychic energy was implanted in childhood and in past lives. These negative implants exist in all your bodies—physical, etheric, astral, and mental—and are the result of past life traumas. For example, you may have been stabbed by a sword in a past life. On a psychic level that sword is still stuck in you and needs to be removed.

This process can become complicated as you move toward the third initiation and merge with your soul, for then you begin to connect with the eleven other soul extensions from your soul family. Sometimes you will find yourself clearing your soul extensions' past life imprints, which are like parallel lives. And then, as you move higher in the initiation process into the monadic level or spirit level, which exists beyond the soul level, you will begin to clear imprints from your monadic family of 144 soul extensions' parallel lives. But you will also have all the help you need from the higher realms.

The physical interface of all this astral and psychic debris appears as the core cause of many viruses and bacterial infections. Most medical doctors deal only with the physical or material level. But the true origins of disease begin when we are implanted by negative extraterrestrials, usually during a traumatic event like an accident, depression, divorce, drug use, surgery—any physical or psychological imbalance. This period of weakness also allows the negative elementals, or parasites, to wreak more havoc in your system. The negative elementals are negative thought forms that attach themselves to different parts of our physical and metaphysical bodies.

They create pathways for viruses and bacteria to first enter the etheric body, then the emotional body, and eventually the physical body. Have you ever noticed how often a physical illness is preceded by a downswing in your mood? The physical body has a natural defense mechanism that fights disease, but the metaphysical body does not. The parasites or negative elementals slip through the openings in the molecules and attach themselves to the places in the body that are the most vulnerable.

Any area of weakness that you have in your physical, emotional, and/or mental bodies is guaranteed to have parasites and negative extraterrestrial implants. This is nothing to be afraid of since everyone on earth has them—and we have had them throughout all of our past lives. However, as we move upward on our path of initiation it is important to clear them. This process of going to the Interdimensional Synthesis Ashram of Djwhal Khul is a very effective way to clear yourself on a daily or weekly basis.

It is important for spiritual seekers to understand that even if you have cleared your implants and invaders, they can and do come back. I used to operate under the assumption that once they were cleared I was free. I know for absolute fact now that this is not true. All these things can and do at times get back in, although not to the same degree they once did. That is why it is essential for you to have a tool and method for constantly reclearing yourself that does not cost thousands of dollars. We all need to learn to do this for ourselves.

PROTECTION AS PREVENTION

Make it a habit to place protection around yourself religiously three times a day: every morning upon getting up; every afternoon; and before bed. If you do this, the negative invasion can be avoided to a great extent, though not necessarily completely. Weekly clearing, regardless of your level of initiation, is standard procedure for living in this world.

PSYCHIC HOLES IN THE AURA

Wherever we have psychic holes in our aura, it creates an opening for unwanted astral energies to enter. Years ago, I saw a psychic healer who told me there was a small torpedolike hole in my aura in the front my body. She said it had entered when I was a child. I was able to trace it to when my parents were having a major fight and about to split up. It was the worst fight my parents ever had. Even though I was in the other room, the negative energy from this fight blasted a hole in my aura that I carried with me for thirty-five years. The psychic healer repaired the damage. You can request the Masters and the etheric healing team to repair any holes or leaks in your aura.

RAISING THE ENERGIES INTO THE LIGHT

How do the Masters deal with all of these negative vibrations? They take negative psychic energies and bring them into the light, dissolve them, raise them into the light, and back into the Central Sun. Then they return that same energy, newly cleaned and restructured, back into your four-body system. It's fascinating! No energy is wasted. The same energy that was causing illness and weaknesses is transformed and brought back for healing purposes. As the different negative psychic energies are removed, the etheric body returns to its perfected form. Most people don't realize that the etheric body, or blueprint body, can be damaged. This is why many people who have chronic illness never get better no matter what they do. If you are operating out of a cracked mold, so to speak, how can you possibly heal?

In your work with the Masters, once all the negative psychic aspects have been removed, ask them to repair your etheric body.

SENSING IMPLANTS

Negative implants can be seen clairvoyantly. However, there are hundreds of levels and degrees of clairvoyance, and your clairvoyance must be tuned to them. Just because a person is clairvoyant doesn't mean he or she will see the implants. Some see certain kinds and don't see others. One way to help in this process is by calling forth the Universal White Light from Vywamus. This Light helps us to see them. The implants often look like pods or swollen seeds or spidery forms. They tend to pulsate and feel warm to those who are more clairsentient.

There are specific places in the body where implants can usually be found. The throat and glands are very common, and in the lymph nodes. Any growths on the physical body will contain implants, along with elementals. The third eye is a common place for implants, as well as the sinuses, and the heart, where the implants tend to block the functioning of the immune system. The upper chest is another place, along with the underarms. The solar plexus is where negative elementals (parasites) are often found, as well as the glands, nerves, and genitals. Usually the more abuse a person experiences in childhood, the more implants and parasites will be found in the body.

AIDS AND PSYCHIC ATTACHMENTS

Djwhal Khul has taught in his training that parasite removal and this type of overall clearing can have an enormous benefit for those with AIDS. The key here, as with all disease, is to determine to what extent the psychic attachments have damaged the physical vehicle. If you can catch it early enough, profound shifts can take place. Physical regeneration is still possible no matter what the stage. However, as we all know, the physical body is the slowest to recover once damage has occurred. Regardless of the stage, clearing should be done immediately. Even if the person dies from AIDS or cancer, the clearing achieved will allow the soul to attain a much higher level on the inner plane.

No matter what kind of disease you are dealing with—be it schizophrenia, cancer, anorexia, heart disease—it will be connected to parasites and probably negative implants. Where there is a physical, emotional, or mental weakness or vulnerability, these psychic infestations will be there.

GRAY FIELD

People who suffer from chronic neuroses or phobias often have a "gray field" around them. This is a by-product of chronic attack from these types of implants, elementals, astral entities, or negative astral aspects. For a complete healing, every person on earth must be cleared not just physically and psychologically, but also etherically and astrally. All disease begins first at the astral level, and then moves to the other bodies.

PSYCHOLOGICAL BLOCKS AND
NEGATIVE ELEMENTALS

Problems occur when we don't do our psychological work of clearing the negative ego, and all negative emotions and qualities of judgment, anger, superiority or inferiority, or violence. These negative qualities, especially the emotionally loaded ones, attract negative elementals, and this is why both the psychological and psychic astral levels must be cleared simultaneously, or one will defeat the other.

These clearings and cleansings make more space for the positive elementals of love, joy, and inner peace to enter and work with us. Their beneficial nature helps us to build positive habits.

One of our basic requests when doing a healing with ourselves or others should be to ask that the physical, emotional, and mental bodies return to the light of the soul. For it is in the soul, or higher self, that all healing work is done. It may sound foolish to make such a simple request, but I assure you it isn't. Until we take the third initiation—the soul merge initiation—we are not completely connected with the soul and/or higher self. And it is not until the fourth initiation that this merger is complete. The higher self basically does not pay attention to the incarnated personality until the incarnated personality pays close attention to the soul. This is why we find criminals and sociopaths doing things a person who is connected to his or her soul can't possibly understand.

THE RAYS AND THE PURIFICATION PROCESS

Another way of clearing astral and etheric debris is to work with the rays. The seventh ray of Saint Germain is the violet transmuting flame, and it can be of great help in this work. Another ray that is extremely helpful is the eighth ray, the violet and green flame, which is especially used for "cleansing purposes."

THE LOVE FEAR MATRIX REMOVAL PROGRAM

One of the keys to removing all of the psychic attachments is the Love Fear Matrix Removal Program. Call upon Djwhal Khul and Vywamus to do this work. It will appear as a network of golden-white light strands that superimpose themselves over a person's light grid and through all the chakras. This light makes all irregular etheric parts visible. The Matrix Removal Program not only removes the core fear from your four-body system, it also removes implants and parasites.

Next, focus on removing all alien implants. This can take up to an hour or longer. Your first meditation should begin with core fear removal. This can take awhile because you are removing fear not only from this life but from all your past lives, and even your soul extensions. Then move to removing parasites or negative elementals. Now follow the rest of the list on pages 296–297, and remove negative imprints, etheric mucus, etheric damage, astral entities, and so on.

This three-stage process could be done in one session, but only if it is done with a team of healers. If it is being done by one healer or by yourself, it is better to break it up into three sessions.

YOUR NEW MONADIC BLUEPRINT BODY

As mentioned earlier, most people's etheric body has been tainted by traumas in this life or past lives. It is good to have it repaired, but it is even better to request the anchoring and activation of your new monadic blueprint body by Djwhal Khul and Vywamus. This is much like your mayavirupa body, which is a perfect blueprint body of your Mighty I Am Presence and it will assure you that you will be working with a perfect mold prior to ascension.

SELF-INQUIRY

On the psychological level you always want to be vigilant about every thought you think, for it is your thoughts that create your reality. It is your thoughts that create your feelings, emotions, behavior, physical body, and whatever you attract or repel in your life. Lightworkers are not vigilant enough in this regard; they tend to go on automatic pilot too easily. They forget that negative thoughts lead to negative feelings and emotions, and thus the attention of negative elementals, parasites, and lower astral entities. Sai Baba has called this process the process of becoming aware of and transmuting negative thinking, "self-inquiry." He says this work is 75 percent of what we must deal with on the spiritual path.

NEGATIVE EMOTIONS

Practice self-inquiry with your negative emotions, as you also practice attitudinal healing.

When a negative emotion comes up, immediately reinterpret the situation with your Christ mind, which will instantly release the negative emotion. There is also a time and place for catharsis—for giving it expression as a form of release. As you acquire mastery of the process of attitudinal healing, you will need to rely on catharsis less and less. Your capacity to remain in a state conscious of love, joy, even-mindedness, inner peace, and forgiveness will increase over time.

PHYSICAL ILLNESS

Do not give physicality your power. Know in truth that it is an illusion, for Christ cannot be sick. As Yogananda said, even on your deathbed you should be affirming that you are in perfect, radiant health. Whatever you think programs your subconscious to create that thought form in your physical body.

Work with homeopathics, herbs, good nutrition, fresh air, sunshine, and daily exercise. Drink lots of pure water to flush out as many of the physical toxins as you can. Removing physical toxins helps you strengthen your immune system on the physical level, just as removing all the psychological and psychic toxins strengthens your psychological immune system.

Just as you need rest to recover from a physical illness, when your initial psychic clearing meditations are over, it is a good idea to rest. Much of this work is like psychic surgery and you need time to recover. So don't ask the Masters to remove all your implants and then go to a wild party. Also remember that much of the work being done in this chapter now takes only hours to accomplish, but in the past, disciples took many lifetimes to accomplish the same thing.

RELEASING ASTRAL ENTITIES

Astral entities are attracted though gross traumas we may have experienced—such as catastrophic illness, loss of spouse or children, involvement in war, psychological shock, and the like. These terrible occurrences have misaligned our energy field and left entry points for negative astral entities. They are also attracted by the negativity we produce when we think from the lower self rather than the positive approach of the higher self. A person living a lower self-existence will attract low-life entities. Drug addiction is another guaranteed way to attract them, as well as alcohol abuse. Sometimes these negative entities have been carried over from past lifetimes, which may occur when a soul chooses to reincarnate too quickly. Such extreme cases usually manifest massive holes in the aura that contain many negative elementals. Some entities are of a psychic nature, and some are confused souls.

In working with yourself or another person in this process, it is very important to request that the full force of Djwhal Khul, Kuthumi, and Lord Maitreya's ashram surround the entity and dissolve it, consume it, and/or remove it immediately. All negative energies associated with this process are transformed into light and brought back cleansed and purified. When you work with another person, invite them to come to the Synthesis Ashram with you. Always get their permission, either directly or on a spiritual level, for this work to be done.

Whenever you work with another person, be sure to first seal yourself in the golden bubble of light. In extreme cases, when you need more assistance, call upon the Karmic Board for consultation and help.

ANIMALS AND ASTRAL ENERGIES

Animals also have a spiritual mission in this lifetime. Our pets will often take on the problems of their owners in an attempt to burn off karma for them. There is very often a clear mirroring process between your pet's health and your health.

Some animals' missions are to act as a sacrificial karma clearer, while others act to transmute the negative energy. For this reason you should do healing work with your animals just as you would with yourself. Again, call upon the Inner Plane Healing Masters to keep your pets healthy, and to remove implants, astral entities, and negative elementals.

DJWHAL KHUL'S LIGHT PROFILES

Even though Djwhal Khul is a second-ray Ascended Master, most students of all seven rays spend time training in his ashram because of his unique second-ray focus on spiritual education. To keep track of his students, Djwhal Khul maintains light profiles of all the lightworkers he works with. It is like a computer data retrieval system in which he can call up on the screen the aura and overall development of each of his students. Through these light profiles he studies brainwaves, thinking, emotional life, physical health, service work, initiation level, light quotient level, and the ascension readiness of everyone he meets to better help them when they call upon him for assistance.

THE PRANA WIND CLEARING DEVICE

One other very useful tool given to Djwhal Khul's ashram by the Arcturians is the Prana Wind Clearing Device. It is like a fan anchored in your solar plexus that removes all the negative etheric mucus gumming up your psychic body by blowing energy through all the meridians and nadir to clear your whole field.

Use this tool every day when you come home from work or whenever you sense contamination. Just request that it be anchored by Djwhal Khul, Vywamus and/or the Arcturians, and it will instantly be done. Even if you can't clairvoyantly see the fan, you will feel it.

CORE LOVE

Core love is the opposite of core fear. Anytime you give in to fear it tends to feed the implants, negative elementals, and negative astral entities. Core love feeds your positive energies and patterns, for perfect love casts out fear. The first step is to call on the Core Matrix Fear Removal Program, to release any fear that comes up for you. The Masters just suck it out like a vacuum cleaner—it's quite extraordinary! In the case of implants, the Matrix Removal Program will surround the implant with a very fine filament of golden white light and simply dissolve it along with any negative elementals.

The second step is to call in core love to fill the space you have just created with Christ energy and God's external love.

ASTRAL DISEASE

All physical or psychological disease appears first in the astral or emotional body before moving into the physical body. Call upon the Masters to remove all astral or etheric disease from your four-body system, and to deny it entrance into your physical body. Imagine what would happen if this was taught in school, and all schoolchildren practiced this every day, through all grade levels. This is true, preventive medicine. All forms of disease, cancer, tumors, growths, and malignancies could be dissolved before manifesting into the physical as adults.

SELF-LOVE

If there is one thing that might be called a universal panacea in this life, it is self-love. If we don't develop a healthy self-concept and self-love, much of what we've been talking about is in danger of returning. Try it—you'll find that it's just as easy to love oneself as it is to hate oneself. Perhaps it's easier—it's certainly more enjoyable. It's just a matter of programming your internal computer in a different way than the way your parents or society programmed you. Don't forget, any new pattern can be put in place in the first twenty-one days.

SOUL FRAGMENTS

Occasionally fragments of the self, sometimes called fragments of the soul, or personality parts that the soul builds through the lifetime, can scatter because of trauma and become attached to another individual and be carried along in a piggyback fashion. Djwhal Khul said that sometimes this is carried in the form of another personality, and if it is severe enough, it creates a psychosis or multiple personality disorder. Ask Djwhal Khul and Vywamus to remove all soul fragments that don't belong to you, and to help you call back all soul fragments that do belong to you in Divine Order under the guidance of your monad and Mighty I Am Presence.

MORE ON EXTRATERRESTRIAL IMPLANTS

Negative extraterrestrials use the implants for many reasons. One is that the energy from your body can be siphoned off at night while you sleep. This can be used to access your energy. Another function of these negative implants is as a tracking and/or monitoring device. Additionally, they are used to gather information and to block the work of the light forces. There are a great many on this planet who are almost completely taken over by these devices.

One of the other consequences of negative extraterrestrial implants is that they drain energy, which causes the weave of the etheric body in that spot to collapse. This makes a person prone to disease in that particular area of the body. It also serves to disrupt the proper chemistry in the body as well as in that area. This causes a general weakening of the entire immune system. It also tends to tax the liver and lungs because of the greater toxicity that is created. Astral parasites and/or negative elementals are attracted, which creates a whole complex of additional problems. This complex web creates etheric mucus that literally squeezes out the life force.

Eventually this whole process moves into the physical tissue, which is one reason why there is so much physical disease in our culture. Add to this negative thinking, negative emotions, stress, bad relationships, bad nutrition, pollution, and environmental toxicity and you see why there is such a massive breakdown of the immune system in our culture. It is amazing, actually, that we do as well as we do.

The good news is that much of this etheric damage can be transformed. The second piece of good news is that you can learn to purify and cleanse yourself on a daily or weekly basis. The third piece of good news is that you can bring your friends and family, even your pets, with you. You can do this consciously with another person, or you can do it without their conscious permission. However, if you do it without their conscious permission, you must get permission from their higher self to do the work. This is helpful, for example, if you have a mate who is not open to these practices but you want him or her to be cleared anyway. Most of the time the higher self will say yes. However there are times when it won't. Make the request and ask the Masters to do the work if it is okay with their higher self and then just let go. Even if you are unclear what the answer is, just put the whole affair into the Masters' hands and trust them to do what is appropriate.

MORE ON ATTACHED ASTRAL ENTITIES

I want to make it clear that astral entities are not just confused or earthbound souls. There are a great many other kinds of astral entities of a more psychic nature that are not incarnated.

The initial occurrence most often takes place in your childhood if your parents are disturbed, in a rage, alcoholic, or sexually abusive. Some aspect of the parental energy field will attach itself as an entity to the child. An energy that the parent is carrying will transfer partially or wholly to the child. This is a type of possession, and it will cause the child's behavior to change dramatically.

An entity of this sort most probably comes from the elemental kingdom and is an etheric form that bonds with the mineral-based body as well as the etheric body of a child or adult. It then begins to form a negative system of psychological response, and it interferes with normal development and growth. Most violent criminals have these attached entities.

There are other types of elemental entities that are not earth-based, but rather are psychologically based. They can attach to the brain, mind, and nervous system of a child or adult. They mimic whatever they receive as stimulation. If they are given the example of mistreatment, they will mimic it. This will increase the harmful messages going through the individual's consciousness. This forms a tape loop that screens out all positive messages. In extreme cases, it can also screen out all positive emotions. We've all seen individuals who are in such a sorry state and have wondered how they got so fouled up. Understanding that some of these mechanisms were installed in childhood can give us greater compassion for those tragic souls.

Often, a disturbing form of codependency develops between the individual and these entities. Some people would rather stay in negativity than change, for change is scary. They have no experiences of positive support, so negative support is better than the unknown. It seems to me that many people stay in bad marriages for the same reason.

A third type of astral entity is an extraterrestrial attachment of a lower nature. This extraterrestrial astral entity has lost connection with its own source and rides piggyback on another source in a vain attempt to keep itself alive. Again, the connection is often made during some kind of trauma, such as a life-threatening illness, car accident, or emotional separation, where the individual on earth feels afraid and wants company. So, he or she reaches out without conscious discrimination, and connects to the first being encountered.

Djwhal Khul has suggested that all parents need to teach their children from the earliest possible age to understand prayer, and to talk to their guardian angel and to angels in general. The earlier a child can form this spiritual connection, the better.

We could also be carrying entities from other lifetimes, and entities who jumped into our energy field when we died during a war. Even worse would be a combination of several or all of these astral entity possessions. The most important thing here is that all these entities can be removed through dedicated practice in Djwhal Khul's Interdimensional Synthesis Ashram.

IRRITATIONS, SPOTS, AND LEAKS

One other thing you might ask Djwhal Khul and Vywamus to do is repair and heal any spots or irritations in your etheric, astral, and/or mental body. Such requests for help can also be addressed to the Inner Plane Healing Masters. Also make certain that all leaks in your four-body system are examined and repaired on a regular basis.

FATIGUE

Fatigue is another factor that makes us vulnerable to implantation. This is a lesson we all deal with at times and it is why it is a good idea to keep clearing ourselves once a week. If you are overtired, run down, or sick, request extra protection from the Archangel Michael.

After you have been cleared of implants, core fear, negative elements, astral entities, negative imprints, and etheric mucus, you will feel and see your etheric grid reconnecting and coming back into proper alignment. All ingredients are now in place for the perfect unfolding of your personal Divine Plan and service mission, and the way is made clear for the completion of your seven levels of initiation.

REPATTERNING

This is the perfect follow-up to the clearing work with a positive repatterning process that aligns us with our Divine Plan. It works much the way bringing in core love does. Once you remove core fear, you must replace it with something or there is a void. The opposite of core fear is core love. Whenever you remove a negative pattern, reprogram its opposite into your consciousness by putting yourself on an affirmation and prayer program for twenty-one days. Use the affirmations, meditations, and prayers offered earlier in the book, especially the Core Fear Matrix Removal meditation. This always helps to cement the new habit.

MOTIVES

One other golden key is to examine with devastating honesty what your motives are for doing all that you do. Are your motives coming from the negative ego or from your Christ consciousness and soul? The negative ego can be very tricky and very selfish. Really be honest with yourself in this regard. Clearing negative ego motives may be the single hardest lesson on the entire spiritual path. It is very easy to pass this off with, "Oh, I mastered that in the Spring of '72." Clarifying our motivations is an area we all need to be constantly vigilant about!

Requesting Dispensations from the Lords of Karma

If you work with other people regularly as part of doing your form of healing work in service of the Divine Plan, occasionally you will come across certain clients that are more difficult than others. When this happens, call upon the Lords of Karma for special assistance or dispensations on their behalf.

For example, after clearing all their negative implants, elementals, and astral entities, you might offer this prayer request: "Lords of Karma, if this prayer is in harmony with God's will, please create a greater merger between the client's personality, soul, and monad. Please provide a special dispensation that will help this person disengage from the lower self."

The Golden Cylinder

Yet another phenomenal method for removing implants, elementals, and a varied assortment of negative energies is the Golden Cylinder of Lord Arcturus. I would recommend that you not use this until you have done a massive matrix removal clearing. Once you have been cleared, the Golden Cylinder can be used as a very quick method of clearing. This is one of the most phenomenal tools I have ever shared and I use it every day or so to purify and refine my field. The subtle body energy technologies of the Arcturians are so fabulous they are beyond description.

To use it, all you have to do is call upon the Lord of Arcturus and the Arcturians and ask them to anchor the Golden Cylinder, just as you would the Prana Wind Clearing Device. You can ask for implants, negative elementals, and negative energy to be removed, and the Golden Cylinder will suck it all out. It is a very efficient way to clear your field whenever you need help.

The Crystal Light Technology of the Arcturians and Melchizedek

This crystal light technology is another road to healing on many, many levels. Melchizedek told us that liquid crystal has the effect of "neutraliz-ing" all imbalanced energies within the physical, etheric, astral, men-tal, and spiritual bodies.

This technology is a two-step process. All of the various Arcturian technologies can be divided into two aspects: the first is the "neutraliz-ing" effect, and the second is activational.

Prepare yourself as usual to enter a visualization. See yourself entering a cave, walking fearlessly down into it. You are surprised to discover that the cave is not dark. Rather, it is filled with a million sparkling pinpoints of light, for this is a crystal cave. You find a rough-hewn bench of rock crystal and you sit down. Sense the powerful energies around you and ask the Arcturians and Melchizedek to focus this energy directly on you. Now look up and see that you are sitting right underneath a large, faceted, clear quartz shaped like a feeding tube as liquid crystal is being siphoned into your crown chakra, and you are receiving a treatment of crystal energies. Drink this in. Feel it knitting bones into the perfect body you need to carry the light. The liquid crystal is creating a physical struc-ture and foundation for your light body.

Melchizedek recommends that, after you sit for a while in the crystal cave absorbing the liquid crystal, ask for the Golden Cylinder of the Arc-turians to pull out and vacuum up all the negative energy that has now been neutralized.

You can also use the Arcturian crystal light technology to neutralize all alien implants. Again, when you are done, ask for the Golden Cylinder to remove the neutralized energy. This is very important.

Next, call upon the Lord of Arcturus to place a crystal in each of your chakras. Breathe deeply and allow this process to take place. Now ask him to activate these crystals. You will feel them begin to spin in each chakra in a clockwise manner. Feel the chakras expanding and reaching toward each other until they become one unified chakra. Breathe deeply and allow this unified energy to be incorporated through your whole body system. These crystals are very light, but very powerful. They are gifts from the Masters, who ask that you go out into the world and share the light they help to intensify with as many other people as you can. You are now a living crystal, a light body.

Crystal Technology for Healing Etheric Wounds

Return to your crystal cave visualization.

Ask the Lord of Arcturus and the Arcturians to use their liquid crystal technology to cauterize any etheric wound you may have. Feel the healing energy starting from the furthest reaches within, and traveling outward until all the wounds are cleared and closed.

Now ask Vywamus to reweave your etheric webbing. This creates a true healing, for the etheric wound will no longer be present—all your bodies will have returned to their original state.

Crystalline Protection for Children

This tool is specifically for children. It is a new technology designed to help New Age children, who are very vulnerable when young, and it is available to any and all children of your own or children you work with. Use this tool to provide extra protection as their healing progresses. Ask Djwhal Khul, Lord Maitreya, Vywamus, and the Lord of Arcturus to place a crystalline web of golden screening protection around the field of the child, enfolding it, and creating a barrier until the child is able to hold the healing itself.

Ascended Master Healing Beam for Ailing Organs

When you are working on healing a weak organ, such as the heart or liver, ask the Ascended Masters to send an energy beam directly into that organ for five days to strengthen it.

The Spiritual Faucet

One of the healing techniques you might request if you are having weakness with an organ such as the liver, pancreas, spleen, gallbladder, or kidneys is the Spiritual Faucet or Spiritual Spigot technique.

Usually there is a cloud of etheric mucus surrounding an organ having trouble. Ask the Inner Plane Healing Masters to install a faucet in the organ on an etheric level. Whenever the etheric mucus starts to build up, this faucet will automatically drain it. When you are feeling symptomatic in that organ, you can also ask the Masters and your etheric body to open the faucet to that organ to drain the negative energy.

Bach Flower Remedies

Bach Flower Remedies are wonderful tools for healing emotions on a subtle energy level. The remedies can be purchased at health food stores, which usually carry books describing their use.

Also, the Futureplex line has three flower essence products—biofield protection, anger release, and fear release—which really work.

Aromatherapy

Aromatherapy is another extremely helpful tool for your overall healing. Healing can come through smell, taste, touch, sight, hearing, the mind, emotions, physical body, or spirit.

Etheric Needles, Bullets, and Darts

In the process of living on earth, each of us encounters the anger of other people. This may be a spouse, family member, child, business partner, friend, or acquaintance. What most people don't realize is that when a person is angry, this sends etheric needles, bullets, and darts into the other person's field. These become lodged in the etheric body.

Many years ago, I was involved with a lady who did not have a great deal of control over her emotional body and negative ego, even though she was considered to be a major lightworker. When we ended our relationship, she was creating a great deal of anger within her own consciousness, and at that moment I seemed to be the point of her focus. After our breakup, I was doing a "spring cleaning" on my four-body system, and the Masters told me that my liver and my pancreas were so filled with needles or darts from the anger of this person that I looked like a porcupine. A lot of this had occurred on the psychic or inner plane level and not overtly. But I had been having liver symptoms and now I knew that her anger was poisoning my liver.

This, of course, is a universal phenomenon, and is something that all lightworkers should ask the Inner Plane Healing Masters to remove. In my case, they had to pull these darts and needles out of my liver and pancreas one by one, being careful not to poison my system in the process. I felt much better after having them removed.

The main lesson here is to not attack even if attacked.

Lesson number two is that if you are being attacked or have been attacked in the past, ask the Masters to remove this poison from your etheric body wherever it may be lodged. Most of the time we don't realize that we have been carrying these needles, darts, pins, and bullets for many, many years—sometimes many lifetimes. It's never too late to be rid of them.

Entity, Imprint, and Implant Removal List:

Alien Implants
Astral Entities
Negative Elementals
Parasites
Core Fear
Imprint Removal
Physical Illness
Etheric Damage
Etheric Mucus
Gray Fields
Irritations, Spots, and Leaks in the Auric Field of the Four-Body System
Negative Thoughts
Negative Emotions
All Negative Ego Programming
Removal of Improper Soul Fragments That Belong to You
Body Repair

Clearing and Repairing of Chakras
Clearing Archetypes

REVIEW OF THE PROCESS FOR
CLEARING NEGATIVE PSYCHIC ENERGY

1. Prepare as usual for a visualization. However, you may either sit up or lie down, especially if you're ready for bed.

2. Ask for the Golden Dome of Protection to be placed around you.

3. Ask to be taken to the Synthesis Ashram of Djwhal Khul.

4. Ask for the help of Djwhal Khul and Vywamus in installing the Matrix Removal Program.

5. One by one, request the removal of the negative psychic attachments mentioned in the list, as well as the subsequent healing processes. Or, choose to do a separate session for each one.

6. Relax and become passive and allow the Masters to work on you as you remain still and quiet.

7. When the clearing is done, meditate on each psychic attachment on the list to gain insight into what effect it had on your life.

8. Ask the Masters to help you do a repatterning to replace the negative energies with new healthy positive energies. Repeat this clearing once a week or every couple of weeks— or whenever you feel the need.

9. Clear your family and your pets simultaneously, for the Masters can work on many people and animals at the same time. If you feel it necessary, call in other Masters to help. Always remember to call in friends and relatives and students once you are accustomed to the process; however, always ask permission of the person's higher self and the Masters when working with others.

An Even Deeper Body Cleansing

When you complete this process I recommend an even deeper physical body cleansing.

For example, ask to have your liver cleansed and cleared by Djwhal Khul, Vywamus, and the Inner Plane Healing Masters. The liver may have dark spots in it from past life or present life abuse. Any area of weakness can be cleared and cleansed.

Other organs and systems to clear might be:

Liver	Heart
Pancreas	Lungs
Kidneys	Genital System
Gallbladder	Muscular System
Lymph System	Stomach
Bloodstream	Colon
Brain	Small and Large Intestines
Nervous System	All Obstructions
Bones	All Toxins
Glandular Systems	Upgrading the Immune System
Spleen	

It is probably best here to call on the help of the Inner Plane Healing Masters. Go to the Synthesis Ashram healing seat for a truly preventive form of healing. This clears the dark etheric spots that could eventually manifest in the physical tissue.

A Complete Clearing

Once you've become accustomed to being worked on in the Synthesis Ashram and have made it part of your regular routine, you can eventually shorten the process by just going into the ashram and asking Djwhal and Vywamus and/or the Inner Plane Healing to install the Matrix Removal Program for a complete clearing. At first you might want to read the list through quickly. But after the routine is established, you can just say you want a complete clearing.

This is a lot like taking your car in for its 50,000-mile overhaul and tune-up. Call up the Matrix Removal Program in the Synthesis Ashram anytime you feel your fields getting contaminated and run down by the lessons of earth life. I think we all agree that the planetary mystery school called earth life can be a tough one.

The Synthesis Ashram of Djwhal Khul and the Matrix Removal Program is an invaluable tool for keeping yourself clear. Perhaps now you can see why I said at the beginning of the chapter that the healing seat in Djwhal Khul's ashram is as important as the ascension seats. See you in the ashram. Namaste!

Chapter 18

✴

Transcendence of Negative Ego and the Living Bardo

From the soul's perspective, death and dying are very different from the accepted concept of death in most Western cultures. Since much of Western thought is based on a scientific-rationalistic point of view, in which reality is limited to what can be perceived through the physical senses, most people view the death of the physical body as the death of the person. They don't take into account the soul's existence.

Others believe in conditional immortality. This theory holds that immortality is possible only under certain conditions. For example, you have to espouse a certain dogma, or join a particular church; you have to accept Jesus as your savior, or be absolved of all sins. If you don't do this, then you go to hell, or you discover that there is no existence after the death of the physical body.

The third theory is reincarnation. Even though the majority of the people in the world believe in reincarnation, it's not a popular way of thinking in the West. However, there's a growing body of evidence showing that the early Christian church suppressed this belief. In fact, the church sanctioned the removal of all references to reincarnation from the Bible during the Second Council of Constantinople in 533 A.D.

But no matter how uncomfortable this may make Westerners, reincarnation is a fact. Death is simply an illusion created by the negative ego. We are continually reincarnated as we journey on our quest to realize our true identities as sons and daughters of God. It's only when we get trapped into thinking that we are exclusively our physical bodies that death becomes real for us. Many of us fear death, when in fact it is the ultimate liberation and release. Death is nothing more than our transformation from one form of consciousness to another.

Death frees us from illusion and facilitates our return to our spiritual home. It is being incarnated in a physical body that is truly limiting, especially if we allow ourselves to overidentify with our physical consciousness. When we die, we experience the true reality of who we are. But then, when we reincarnate back into matter, we overidentify with the physical, fall back asleep, and lose conscious awareness of our true identity once again.

Ascension is the process of waking up, and staying awake, while progressively moving forward to reestablish our identity as the sons and daughters of God. In the past, I've found strong parallels between the ascension process and the experience of merging with the Clear Light of God in the bardo experience after death. The only difference is that, in the bardo, one merges with the Clear Light of God after leaving the physical body. But in the ascension process, one merges with the Clear Light of God, or monad, or Mighty I Am Presence, while still in the physical body.

The amazing news I have received from the Masters is that now, once we have moved through at least half of our seventh initiation, every Ascended Master candidate will go through the bardo experience while still living in a physical body on earth. This totally new and critical stage of the ascension process is an astounding development in human history, and it offers us an unparalleled opportunity for accelerated spiritual transformation.

To understand this gift we have been given, we must first examine the actual bardo experience.

The concept of the bardo we are most familiar with comes from Tibetan Buddhist beliefs concerning the journey every human soul moves through in the three to four days following the death of the body. The classic English translation of the ancient *Tibetan Book of the Dead*, or the *Bardo Thodol*, "The Great Doctrine of Liberation by Hearing and Seeing," was first published by W. Y. Evans-Wentz, an Oxford Don and dedicated spiritual seeker, in 1927.

He describes the soul's passage through the three after-death bardic journeys that we all face—their purpose being to forcefully wake us up to the true nature of reality. The first bardo offers us the opportunity to walk directly and consciously into the Clear Light of God, which frees us of all karmic ties and longings, as we merge with the Mighty I Am presence.

However, the Tibetans believe that only those souls capable of maintaining total conscious awareness through life, through the process of dying, and through the after-death state manage to achieve this. Most of us go to the next bardic state in which we begin to wake up to the fact that we are dead and no longer have a body. This realization offers us our first small glimpse of the true reality.

The third bardic state is the three-day, total wake-up call life review of the *Bardo Thodol*. During this period, every single thought-form we have ever created moves before our eyes like a movie, or perhaps more like virtual reality, for we actually interact with them.

While each of us sees the imagery in our own familiar mind-set, beliefs, and cultural programming, the experience is universal to all humans. Slowly, over the three days, we wake up more and more to the fact that these are simply illusions created by our negative ego.

The *Bardo Thodal* is read continuously to the dying and the newly dead to help them remember who they truly are. It offers them prayers and reminders to support them and to ease their passage. The ultimate reminder being:

> O Nobly Born, when thy body and mind were separating, thou must have experienced a glimpse of the Pure Truth, subtle, sparkling, bright, dazzling, glorious, and radiantly awesome, in appearance like a mirage moving across a landscape in springtime in one continuous stream of vibrations. Be not daunted thereby, nor terrified, nor awed. That is the radiance of thine own true nature. Recognize it.

However, since very few of us seem to be able to recognize our own true natures, we next encounter all the Peaceful Deities that emerged from our hearts, and the often much more numerous Wrathful Deities that our negative egos concocted. This is where the *Bardo Thodol* offers us one of the most powerful affirmations in all spiritual literature:

Alas! When the Uncertain Experiencing of Reality is dawning upon me here
With every thought of fear or terror or awe for all (apparitional appearances] set aside,

May I recognize whatever [visions] appear, as the reflections of mine
own consciousness . . .
When at this all-important moment [of opportunity] of achieving a
great end,
May I not fear the bands of Peaceful and Wrathful [Deities], mine
own thought-forms.

—W. Y. Evans-Wentz
The Tibetan Book of the Dead
(New York: Oxford University Press
1973, pp. 103–104)

From a more Western perspective, in the after-death bardo experience we review and relive all our thoughts, words, and deeds through
the eyes of the higher self and Mighty I Am presence. The point is to
see whether we lived our life from the perspective of the soul and
Christ consciousness, or from the lower self and negative ego. This is
where the process of transcending the negative ego comes into play.

Going though the bardo, we see clearly the effect our thoughts,
words, and deeds have had on our brothers and sisters on earth. We
discover for the first time the true extent to which the negative ego has
controlled our life. One of the great benefits of the bardo is that it
opens us up to a greater sense of compassion and empathy, for we
deeply feel the emotions of others. Painful though this may be, it gives
us the opportunity not only to relive but to actually correct some of the
mistakes we made.

The bardo is something every lightworker goes through after physically dying, although some go through this process faster than others.
One of the main purposes of the bardo is to help us merge with the
Clear Light of God, and this opportunity is offered to us immediately
in the first stage of our bardo experience. Walking into the light at
that point is a choice that every person on this planet has to make for
themselves. Most of us lose the opportunity for a number of reasons—
frequently because of fear, but also because of a poor self-image and
other negative ego thinking.

THE LIVING BARDO

Since merging with the Light of God — consciously — is the whole purpose of life, why should we have to wait until we die to come to a more mature understanding of our birthright? The whole point is that we're here to develop this maturity, compassion, empathy, oneness, and clarity WHILE WE'RE STILL IN A PHYSICAL BODY, SERVING ON EARTH! This is how we become Ascended Masters.

The Masters seem to have come to the same conclusion. And they have now given us an amazing new dispensation that is completely different from anything any lightworker on earth has ever experienced before, no matter what their level of inner work and study.

In the past the bardo was always done without the physical body. But the new dispensation we have been given now is to do the bardo IN the physical body, ON the material plane. This is the final stage of discovering the truth that there is no separation between the personality, the soul, the Mighty I Am presence, and the physical body.

The Living Bardo is a tremendous opportunity for us all because it allows us to move from the kindergarten level of Ascended Master to a fully mature Ascended Master. It makes sense if you think about it. If we're going to merge with the light of our monad and Mighty I Am presence, then we need to do this not only with the light at the spiritual level, but also with our four bodies to fully integrate spirit and soul on all levels.

In the past, most souls who took their sixth and seventh initiation in the ascension and initiation process immediately passed on to the inner plane. In this new dispensation, 90 percent of all high-level initiates and ascended beings will remain on earth and continue their service work. And, in fact, only those who are planning to stay will be given the opportunity to do the Living Bardo work. Those who choose to leave the earth will go through their bardo on the inner plane.

How does the Living Bardo work? Basically, through some mysterious process known only to God and the Mighty I Am presence, all this material will be processed through our subconscious mind, our emotions, and our physical body over a period of two to three years.

Speaking from experience, since I've been going through this process myself, I've discovered that this "crash course" in spiritual growth can be quite intense. This is why it's imperative that all lightworkers have a firm grasp on how to think with the Christ mind rather than the negative ego mind. Don't kid yourself on this point, for many, many lightworkers are ill prepared for this experience.

Knowing that each of us has 144 soul extensions in our monad or Mighty I Am presence, you may wonder how many lives you're actually processing when you go through your bardo. Speaking firsthand, I can tell you that we're not only working through all our experiences in this life, but we're also processing all the past lives this particular soul extension has experienced on earth. However, each of our other eleven soul extensions and their incarnated personalities must go through their own personal bardos—we are not responsible for them.

The Living Bardo offers us a tremendous opportunity for accelerated spiritual growth, but there's no doubt it will entail an intense period of training. Some of us will go through it more easily than others, depending on the psychodynamic structure of our four bodies and three minds. However, in the process, some of us will develop serious health problems. Others may go through emotional upheaval. Still others may experience mental difficulties. There's no dodging and weaving once we're in it—you might say "The buck stops here."

One thing I will promise you is that the more you learn to clear your negative ego on an ongoing basis every day, the easier your bardo experience will be, whether you're on this side or the other. Remember, it's the negative ego that is the cause of all physical disease, negative emotions, negative thoughts, and all karma with other people. The bardo gives us the opportunity to reexperience our stuck places from a more compassionate, clear-eyed perspective, and to make corrections in our thinking, emotions, and behavior.

Never doubt that this experience is worth whatever it costs us. For ultimately, going through the Living Bardo consciously on earth represents the final transcendence of death.

This is what prepares us for the final stage of the planetary ascension process—the universal planetary realization of the twelfth dimension of reality. The Living Bardo helps us to integrate the consciousness of God not only in terms of our ability to carry the light, but also in terms of proper Christ thinking, Christ feeling, and Christed physical health. It is the true completion process of the seven levels of initiation.

We are all pioneers on earth now, doing what has never been done on this planet before—moving toward becoming fully realized twelfth-dimensional beings in our present incarnations. For it is in the twelfth dimension that we achieve integration, activation, and actualization of universal energies, not just galactic and solar.

Lightworkers need to let go of the idea that ascension is a fifth-dimension manifestation. This is now outdated, for attaining the fifth dimension is only the very beginning of the ascension process. Full maturation as a planetary Ascended Master now comes at the twelfth-dimensional level of reality.

The Masters tell us that all Ascended Beings still go through a type of bardo and merging with the Clear Light of God. This may sound contradictory, considering that they've already merged with it. But the point is that there is always another higher level of the light available to us.

Jesus' life and crucifixion were the only exceptions to the rule because of his unique mission. Jesus experienced his bardo on the cross, and he took on the sins of humanity in order to become the Avatar of the Piscean Age. His resurrection of the physical body proved that the belief in the separation between the monad, soul, personality, and physical body were merely illusion.

Now, each one of us going through the Living Bardo in our physical body is demonstrating the same lesson! Experiencing the bardo consciously on earth means that we are being raised to a level where we are able to think with God's mind, to feel with God's heart, and to function on earth with God's physical body.

Afterword

Soul psychology is intricately woven into the fabric of every aspect of our lives. This is because it teaches us that every aspect of life is a part of God and so a part of ourselves. Soul psychology sees that every event in our lives happens for a reason. It also sees everything as positive. This is so because soul psychology recognizes everything that happens in life is there to teach us something our souls need to learn. Mistakes are positive because there is always a golden nugget of wisdom to be learned and in the psychology of the soul, everything is forgiven.

By working with this book and the tools it contains, we have been able to clear an enormous amount of negative ego programming. The beauty of this process is that you, too, now have the techniques you need to continue clearing the negative ego and reprogramming your subconscious mind. You also know that you must remain vigilant in this process and not fall back to automatic pilot and become a victim of your own or other people's energies. You are now capable of fully owning your personal power and becoming the master of your life, serving God in unconditional love in a balanced and integrated manner.

Once you gain psychological mastery and complete your seven levels of initiation, or self-realization, it is your spiritual responsibility to move into expanded areas of planetary world service and spiritual leadership. How you do this is up to you, although it has a lot to do with your ray structure, astrological configuration, and the puzzle piece in the Divine Plan that God created you to fulfill.

My hopes are high for all of you reading this book and for the future of the earth and all life on earth. It is my sincere hope and desire that you continue to work with the understanding, ideals, and tools that I offered. Remember that psychological and spiritual self-realization is not achieved in one day. In truth, it is a lifelong process. Even though this book will accelerate your psychological and spiritual evolution and help you avoid years of searching and getting caught in forms of psychology and spirituality that do not see life from a full-spectrum prism spiritual path, it is still a process. And even when you master your psychological self, you will need to develop new levels of refinement and vigilance no matter how high you climb on the spiritual ladder of evolution.

For once planetary ascension is achieved, the process of cosmic ascension begins. In terms of fully realizing God on the highest cosmic level planetary ascension is like moving up one inch on a ten-inch ruler. Becoming a full-fledged Ascended Master and self-realized being is a wonderful thing, and so is achieving liberation from the wheel of rebirth. But there is always another step—and another.

Since the path of God realization is a long process, please remember to take time to have fun and enjoy life. Although life has a very definite purpose, try not to lose your sense of humor. Most of all, never forget that highest and most advanced spiritual practice of all—unconditional love. If you do nothing else but this, you will be on the right path. As the Master Jesus said, the whole law could be summed up in these words: "Love the Lord, thy God, with all thy heart and soul and might, and love your neighbor as you love yourself." The law of unconditional love is what the Buddha, Mohammed, Moses, Krishna, Zoroaster, and all the Masters of the Cosmic and Planetary Hierarchy teach. It is this ideal above all that we need to aspire to. Work to prevent the negative ego and its negative thinking from interfering with this process.

It is my great hope that the science of soul psychology will now begin to be integrated into the field of traditional psychology, religion, psychiatry, medicine, and every other aspect of our society and civilization.

Peace in our world will not happen until we develop peace within ourselves. This only can come about through the integration of soul and spiritual psychology, for this is the key to inner peace, happiness, right relationships, success, liberation, self-realization, and enlightenment on a personal level. On a planetary level, it is the key to resolving all the problems and challenges now facing all life on earth.

We cannot continue separating church from state. This is like saying let's keep God and Christ/Buddha/spiritual consciousness out of our earthly civilization. This is a prescription for letting the negative ego continue to conduct business as usual on planet earth. When soul psychology is integrated, we will all be striving to unconditionally love, to be egoless, to perform selfless service, to be generous, and not attached to money and material things.

If Christ consciousness were taught in our schools, churches, and temples, and by parents, television, movies, the print media, counselors, psychologists, social workers, medical doctors, healers, and all the rest of us, the world would change so quickly it would make our collective heads spin. Think about it!

If we all thought with our Christ/Buddha/spiritual mind and not with the negative ego mind, would there be violence, abuse, greed, materialism, misuse of power, lack of love, or lack of wisdom? Would there be hunger, poverty, or homelessness? Of course not! We would see everyone as an aspect of God and, practicing soul psychology, they would be working for God, not their selfish, self-centered, hedonistic negative egos. They would recognize that helping their brothers and sisters is literally helping themselves, for we all share the same identity in God as the eternal self.

There are a great many people who have read prophecies and predictions of a coming axis shift or pole shift, as predicted by Edgar Cayce, Nostradamus and other prophets, and even scientists. I am here to tell you, my friends, that although there was a time when these prophecies were true, the people of the earth have evolved to a point that these catastrophic events are not going to happen. The only axis shift that is going to happen is the shift all over the planet from negative ego thinking to Christ/Buddha/spiritual thinking. I am happy to say that this shift has begun. This book is one of many signposts that the new millennium is upon us, and that it is time for us to move into the Seventh Golden Age.

It is my sincere hope and prayer that this book will serve to not only help each of you, my beloved readers, to attain inner peace, happiness, success, liberation, ascension, self-realization, and enlightenment but that it will also pave the way for the transformation of our society and civilization that is our true destiny. If each of us simply does our own part in God's Divine Plan, success is ensured!

Namaste!

Appendix

✶

Melchizedek Synthesis Light Academy

For a free information packet about all Dr. Stone's workshops, books, audiotapes, academy membership program, and global outreach program, please call or write.

Dr. Joshua David Stone
Melchizedek Synthesis Light Academy
28951 Malibu Rancho Rd.
Agoura, California 91301
Website: http://www.drjoshuadavidstone.com
Tel: (818) 706-8458
Fax: (818) 706-8540
e-mail: drstone@best.com

Books Published
by Dr. Joshua David Stone

The Complete Ascension Manual
Soul Psychology
Beyond Ascension
Hidden Mysteries
The Ascended Masters Light the Way

Books Now Completed and Available through the Melchizedek Synthesis Light Academy

Cosmic Ascension
How to Clear the Negative Ego
How to Teach Ascension Classes

Revelations of Sai Baba and the Ascended Masters
Manual for Planetary Leadership
Ascension and Romantic Relationships
A Beginner's Guide to Ascension
Revelations of a Melchizedek Initiate
Your Ascension Mission: Embracing Your Puzzle Piece
Integrated Ascension—Revelation for the New Millennium
Divine Mother and the Lady Masters
How to Celebrate Wesak (booklet)

Books Soon to be Published

Ascending with the Angels and the Elohim
Mahatma, Melchizedek, and Metatron Revealed
Ascension for Children
The Global Divine Blueprint for the Golden Age
The Golden Book of Melchizedek
The Light Revelations of Metatron
Revelations of the Great Pyramid, Sphinx, and the Hall of Records
The New Dispensation of Teachings of St. Germain
Steps Within the Great White Lodge

Index

Abandonment, feelings of, 85
Acting "as if," 123–124
Action plan, 115–117
Active Type, 214–215
Adam and Eve, 15
Adlerian therapy, 204
Adult development theory, 8
Adventurer archetype, 258
Affirmations, 173
   cards, 121
   defined, 120
   disidentification, 31
   of faith, trust, and patience,
      134–135
   favorite, 135–136
   Golden Bubble, 52–53, 64,
      129–130
   to higher self, 117
   for reprogramming subconscious
      mind, 121
   self-love, 42–43
   spiritual, 31
   tape recording, 122
   walks, 121–122
   writing down, 174

Aging process, 66
AIDS, 281–282
Alcoholics Anonymous, 194–195
Altars, 118–119
Analytical thinking, 50
Anger, 268–269, 295–296
   versus peace of mind, 81
   positive, 30, 73, 81
Animals, 286
Aquarian cycle, 54, 150
Archetypes, 8, 204, 212, 218,
      235–263
   chart of, 236–237
   defined, 235
   journal dialoguing with, 241
   positive and negative qualities of
      twelve, 247–263
   self-inquiry and, 242, 244
   voice dialoguing with, 239–240
Arcturian crystal light technology,
      293–294
Arjuna, 73–74, 77–78, 261
Aromatherapy, 295
Arthur, King, 254
Artwork, as affirmations, 125

Ascended Masters, 7, 15, 56, 66, 68, 72, 168, 199, 263, 268, 270, 275, 305
Ascension Handbook, The (Stone), 7
Assagiolo, Roberto, 7–8
Astral (emotional) aura, 143
Astral body, 137, 139–140
Astral disease, 287, 289
Astral entities, releasing, 285–286, 289–291
Astral projection, 139
Astrology, 216, 218
Atlantis, 54, 150
Atmic body, 137, 143
Atonement, 72
Attachment, 266–267
  versus preference, 76
Attack thoughts, 70, 260, 269
Attenborough, Sir Richard, 206
Attitudinal healing, 17–18, 59, 110, 199–200
  process of accomplishing, 64
Aumakua, 48
Aura, 143–146
  psychic holes in, 280
Auras (Cayce), 145
Authority problem, 63–64
Autosuggestions, 124

Bach Flower Remedies, 295
Bailey, Alice A., 66, 140, 143, 147, 159, 185, 217, 221
Balance, concept of, 10, 18–19
Bardo experience, 300–302
Beesley, Ronald, 137
Behavioristic psychology, 204
Bhagavad Gita, 73–74, 78, 196, 272
Blessing method, 16
Bodenburg, Dorothy, 148
Bodhisattva, 252–253, 259
Brahma, 48, 248
Branden, Nathaniel, 189
Brennan, Barbara, 151
Bubble of protection, 25–26, 29
Buddha, 11, 12, 47, 63, 76, 197, 200, 257, 262, 266, 308
Buddhic body, 47, 137, 141
Buddhism, 139, 180, 252, 268

Cards, affirmation, 121
Caste system, 259
Causal (soul) body, 47, 137, 141, 182
Cause and Effect, Law of, 185
Cayce, Edgar, 29, 30, 72, 73, 75, 81, 145, 179, 184, 248, 270, 309
Celestial bodies, 137
Chakra system, 11, 17, 19, 144, 147–158
  basic configuration, 147
  chart of, 149
  colors, 151–152
  fifth-dimensional chakras, 156–158
  fourth-dimensional chakras, 153–156, 191
  perception and, 190–192
  third-dimensional chakras, 149–152, 191
Child consciousness, 17, 19, 37–39
Christ consciousness, 11–12, 59–89, 155, 199, 260, 271–275, 308–309
  accomplishing attitudinal healing, 64
  anger versus peace of mind, 81
  attachment versus preference, 76
  authority problem, 63–64
  death versus eternal life, 80
  gratitude versus taking life for granted, 82
  guilt versus innocence, 83
  holy encounter, 67–68
  Job initiation, 77–78
  loneliness versus being alone, 85
  optimism versus pessimism, 78
  poverty versus prosperity consciousness, 79–80
  Psychological Centering Model, 85–86
  security versus insecurity, 84
  sickness as defense against truth, 66–67
  sin versus mistakes, 69
  spiritually centered attitudes, 87–89
  top dog/underdog versus equality, 70–71
  transcendence of duality, 76–77
  unconditional versus conditional love, 69–70
Clairaudience, 24, 277

Clairvoyance, 24, 167, 277, 281
Cognitive psychology, 204
Collective unconscious, 8, 24, 173
Colors
  chakra, 151–152
  in human aura, 144–145
Colossians, 20
Columbus, Christopher, 249
Complete Ascension Manual, The
  (Stone), 210
Conditional love, 34, 69–70
Confucius, 66, 200, 257
Conscious mind, 20, 21, 168, 169
  balancing, 47–50
  functioning of, 24–25
Core Fear Matrix Removal Program,
  270, 287, 291
Core love, 287
Cosmic healing visualization, 207–209
Course in Miracles, A, 11, 15, 16,
  59–61, 63, 64, 67, 69–72, 74, 79,
  83, 93, 120, 172, 195, 247–249,
  260, 269, 270, 275, 276
Creative visualization, 121
Crown chakra, 151, 152
Crucifixion, meaning of, 71
Crystal light technology, 293–294

Daily routine, 115
Dalai Lama, 200
Death versus eternal life, 80
Deceiver archetype, 256
Decisiveness, 28
Decrees, 121
Deductive reasoning, 50
Denial, process of, 66
Depression, 11
  versus peace of mind, 81
Depth psychology, 8
Desire, 268
Destroyer archetype, 237, 245,
  247–248, 257, 261, 262
Devotee Type, 215
Dialoguing, 39, 101–103, 123
  with archetypes, 239–241
  with glamours, 233–234
Diet, 138, 139
Discipleship in the New Age (Bailey),
  217

Diseases, 50, 139
Disidentification affirmations, 31
Djwhal Khul, 12, 65, 66, 140, 143,
  147, 152, 159, 182, 185, 197, 213,
  220–221, 233, 237, 245, 253,
  260, 277, 281, 283, 284,
  286–288, 290, 291, 294, 297,
  298
Dreams, 8, 16, 23, 36
Duality, 18
  transcendence of, 76–77,
  271–273

Edison, Thomas, 249
Education of Oversoul Seven, The
  (Roberts), 182
Ego, Hunger, and Aggression (Perls),
  71
Egotism, 274–275
Eighteenth chakra, 157
Eighth chakra, 153
Eighth ray, 283
Eleventh chakra, 155
El Morya, 213
Emerson, Ralph Waldo, 64
Emotional body, 279
  balancing, 47, 49–54
Emotional healing, tools for, 93–119
  contacting higher self, 117–119
  dialoguing, 101–103
  journal writing (*see* Journal
  writing)
  negative emotions log, 103
  prayer versus meditation, 117
  six-step process for spiritualizing
  emotions, 93–95
  writing letter to subconscious mind,
  100–101
  Yin Approach, 96–99
Emotional invulnerability
  visualizations, 42–43
Enthusiasm, 173
Equality, top dog/underdog versus,
  70–71
Esoteric Psychology (Bailey), 221
Etheric body, 137, 138–139, 279–281,
  284
Etheric body aura, 143
Evans-Wentz, W.Y., 300–302

Explorer archetype, 258
Extroversion, 8

False pride, 11, 271–272
False Sense of Balance Theory, 10, 11
Fame, 266
Fatigue, 291
Fault finder, 71–72
Fear, 12, 16, 62, 74, 269–270
Feminine energy, 192
Fifteenth chakra, 156
Fifth-dimensional chakras, 156–158
Fifth Ray, 215, 221, 225, 227, 230,
    283
First Golden Key (*see* Personal power)
First Ray, 214, 221–223, 226, 228
Fitness program, 138
Fool archetype, 248–249
Forgiveness, 41, 69, 71, 173, 181
Four-body system, 11, 12, 17, 19
    balancing, 47, 49–58
Fourteenth chakra, 155–156
Fourth-dimensional chakras, 153–156
Fourth Golden Key (*see* Christ
    consciousness_
Fourth Ray, 215, 221, 224, 227,
    229–230
Francis of Assisi, Saint, 252
Freud, Sigmund, 8
Freudian psychology, 203
Fundamentalist Christianity, 252
Future, 74–75

Gandhi, Mahatma, 200, 252, 253, 262
Genghis Khan, 254
Germain, Saint, 66, 213, 283
Gestalt therapy, 204
Glamours, and science of the rays,
    220–226
Glorified light body, 137, 143
Goals and priorities in journal, 111
Golden Bubble visualization, 52–53,
    64, 129–130
Golden Cylinder of Lord Arcturus,
    292–293
Gratitude, 172
    versus taking life for granted, 82
Gray field, 282
Greed, 272

Group karma, 179–180
Guilt versus innocence, 83

Habit mind, 23
Hands of Light (Brennan), 151
Harmonic Convergence of August,
    1987, 149
Heart chakra, 150, 152, 191
Hidden Mysteries (Stone), 244
Hierarchy of needs, 8
Hilarion, 213
Hinduism, 48, 139, 248
Hitler, Adolf, 69, 202–203
Holy encounter, 67–68
Holy Spirit, 16, 48, 59, 72, 246, 247
Homeostasis, 8
Human aura, 143–146
Humanistic psychology, 203–204
Humility, 82
Huna teachings, 39, 48
Hypnogogic state, 174
Hypnosis, 22, 66, 122–123, 183

I Ching, 81
Identity visualization, 46
Implants, 281, 288–289
Inferiority complex, 11
Inner bubble, 25–26
Inner parenting skills, 38–39
Inner senses, 24
Innocence versus guilt, 83
Innocent archetype, 249–250
Insecurity versus security, 84
Inspiration section of journal, 117
Introversion, 8

Jealousy, 85, 273–274
Jesus, 15, 16, 19, 30, 35, 59–61, 66, 68,
    71, 72, 79, 83–84, 120, 179, 200,
    213, 257, 262, 305, 308
Job initiation, 77–78
Jones, Jim, 251
Journal writing, 105–110
    action plan, 115–117
    with archetypes, 241
    cycles, 112
    daily routine, 115
    goals and priorities, 111
    inspiration section, 117

life plan and design, 111–112
Major Lessons of the Day section, 110
reprogramming subconscious mind and, 121
weekly routine, 112–114
Jung, Carl, 7, 8, 24, 173, 201–202, 235
Jungian psychology, 201–202

Kabbalah, 244, 259
Kahunas of Hawaii, 48, 175
Kanaloa, 48
Kane, 48
Karma, 18, 141
laws of, 178, 179–186, 269
King, Rodney, 201
Knights of the Round Table, 254, 261
Koresh, David, 251
Krishna, 73–74, 78, 196, 200, 261, 272, 308
Ku, 48
Kuthumi, 213, 286

Lao-tzu, 200, 257
Law of Magnetism and Attraction, 23
Lemuria, 54, 150
Letter-writing
to higher self, 117
subconscious mind, 100–101
Levitation, 19
Life plan and design, 111–112
Light body, 47
Lincoln, Abraham, 64
Living Bardo, 303–305
Logic, 50
Logs, types of, 104
Loneliness versus being alone, 85
Lord Maitreya, 213, 255, 257, 262, 286, 294
Love Fear Matrix Removal Program, 283
Love finder, 71–72
Love Type, 214
Ludig gland, 150
Luke, 179
Lunatic archetype, 249

Madman/Madwoman archetype, 249
Magician archetype, 245, 250–252

Mahabharata, 73
Major Lessons of the Day section of journal, 110
Manifestation, laws of, 166–178
Martyr archetype, 252–253, 259
Masculine energy, 192
Maslow, Abraham, 7, 8, 204
Materialism, 12
Materialization, 19
Matriarch archetype, 253–254
Matthew, 176, 179, 258
Meditation, 117, 140, 174
Melchizedek, 255, 268, 293
Menendez brothers, 200–201
Mental aura, 143
Mental body, 137, 140–141
balancing, 47, 49–51, 54–55
Mighty I Am Presence, 49, 143, 255, 284, 288, 300–302
Mirror, affirmations and, 122
Mistakes, 9, 40–41, 69, 180–181
Mohammed, 200, 257, 308
Monadic level of self-actualization, 7
Monadic merge, 49
Money, 126–128, 265–266
Moses, 257, 308
Mother Mary, 262
Mother Teresa, 82, 200, 252, 253, 262
Mozart, Wolfgang Amadeus, 184
Mussolini, Benito, 254

Nadis, 138
Napoleon, 254
National karma, 179–180
Needs, hierarchy of, 8
Negative ego, 9, 11–18, 59
Negative emotions log, 103
Nineteenth chakra, 157
Ninth chakra, 154
Non-reasoning mind, 21
Nostradamus, 309

Observer self, 45
Optimism versus pessimism, 78
Organizer Type, 215–216
Oversoul, development of, 244–247

Parasite removal, 281–282
Parent consciousness, 19

Parenting, 37–39
Past, 74–75
Pasteur, Louis, 249
Patriarch archetype, 245, 253–254
Paul the Venetian, 213
Perfection, 170, 181
Perls, Fritz, 71, 197
Perseverance, 140–141, 171
Personality level of self-actualization,
 7, 8, 10, 202, 258
Personal power, 20–33, 264–265
 affirmations, 31–33
 claiming, 30
 defined, 30
 development of, 28–30
 versus powerlessness, 73–74
 visualizations, 42–43
Pessimism versus optimism, 78
Philosophy, 205–206
Physical body, 137–138, 279
 balancing, 47, 49–51, 55–57
Physical health aura, 143
Physical illness, 281–282, 285
Pineal gland, 151
Pioneer archetype, 258
Pitfalls and traps, 159–165
Planetary karma, 179–180
Poetry, as affirmations, 125
Ponder on This (Bailey), 143
Positive anger, 30, 73, 81
Positive mental attitude, 27
Positive-negative clearing, 122
Poverty consciousness, 79–80
Power, 264–265 (*see also* personal
 power)
Power Type, 214
Prana Wind Clearing Device, 287,
 292
Prayer, 117, 168–171, 174–178
Preference versus attachment, 76
Prosperity consciousness, 79–80
Psychic energies, clearing negative,
 276–298
 aromatherapy, 295
 Bach Flower Remedies, 295
 Core Fear Matrix Removal
  Program, 270, 287, 291
 crystal light technology, 293–294
 deeper body cleansing, 297–298

Djwhal Khul's light profiles, 286
Golden Cylinder of Lord Arcturus,
 292–293
gray field, 282
implants, 281, 288–289
Love Fear Matrix Removal
 Program, 283
motives, 292
origination of psychic entities,
 278–280
Prana Wind Clearing Device, 287,
 292
psychic holes in aura, 280
psychological blocks and negative
 elementals, 282–283
raising energies into light,
 280–281
releasing astral entities, 285–286,
 289–291
repatterning, 291
review of process, 297
Spiritual Faucet, 295
Psychic healers, 277, 278
Psychoanalytic theory, 8
Psychoepistemology, 189–209
 attitudinal healing, 199–200
 chakra system, 190–192
 defined, 189–190
 masculine and feminine energies,
  192
 other sources of imbalance,
  193–199
 psychological lenses, 201–207
Psychological Centering Model,
 85–86
Psychology training, 6–7
Psychosynthesis, 7–8

Quan Yin, 262

Rajneesh (Osho), 194
Ramana Maharishi, 61
Rand, Ayn, 205
Rays, 144, 145, 210–234
 advanced information on, 226–231
 being a Renaissance person,
  216–217
 and corresponding professions,
  217–218

and distinctive methods of service,
219–220
methods for clearing negative,
232–234
methods of teaching truth, 218–219
seven rays and seven human
temperaments, 214–216
symbols, 232–233
and their glamours, 220–226
Reappearance of the Christ, The
(Bailey), 185
Reasoning mind, 21
Rebirth, Law of, 185–186
Red Ladder visualization, 52
Reincarnation, 8
Rhythmic repetition, 122
Risk Taker, 249
Roberts, Jane, 182
Root chakra, 149, 152
Ruler archetype, 245, 254–255

Sai Baba, 5, 9, 11, 12, 15, 17, 63, 67,
167, 183, 197, 242, 257, 260, 261,
272, 284
Sananda, 213, 262
Sanat Kumara, 255
Schulman, Helen, 15
Scientific Type, 215
Second chakra, 150, 152
Second Ray, 214, 221, 223, 227–229
Security versus insecurity, 84
Seducer/Salesman archetype, 245,
255–257, 263
Seeker archetype, 245, 258
Self, relationship to, 75–76
Self-actualization
levels of, 7
Maslow and, 8
Self-centeredness, 16
Self-discipline, 73, 177, 178
Self-esteem, low, 11
Self-hypnosis, 124
Self-inquiry, 232, 242, 244, 284
Selfishness, 12, 62, 270–271
Selfish-selfless balance, 37
Self-love, unconditional, 34–46, 173,
288
affirmations, 42–43
child consciousness, 37–39

dialoguing, 39–40
forgiveness, 41
inner parenting skills, 38–39
making big mistakes, 40–41
selfish-selfless balance, 37
victory log, 40
visualizations, 42–43
Self-parenting, 253–254
Self-Realization Fellowship
Organization, 194
Self-Realized Masters, 11
Self-talk, as affirmations, 125
Separation, 12, 16
Separation consciousness, 275
Sephiroth, 244
Serapis Bey, 213
Servant archetype, 258–260
Seven bodies, 137–143
Seventeenth chakra, 156–157, 191
Seventh Ray, 215–216, 222, 226, 227,
231
Sexuality, 267–268
Shadow psychology, 201–203
Shiva, 48, 248
Sickness, as defense against truth,
66–67
Simpson, O.J., 201
Sin versus mistakes, 69, 180
Sixteenth chakra, 156
Sixth Ray, 215, 221–222, 225, 227,
230–231
Slavery, 259
Sleeping habits, 138
Solar plexus chakra, 150, 152, 155
Solomon, Paul, 34, 72, 81
Songs, as affirmations, 125
Soul (causal) body, 47, 137, 141, 182
Soul extensions, 181–183, 244–245,
279
Soul fragments, 288
Spangler, David, 166
Spiritual affirmations, 31
Spiritual body, balancing, 47, 49–51,
57–58
Spiritual Faucet, 295
Spiritually centered attitudes, 87–89
Spiritual mind, 21
Spiritual tests, 264–273
anger, 268–269

Spiritual tests (*cont.*)
    attachment, 266–267
    desire, 268
    duality, 272–273
    egotism, 274–275
    false pride, 271–272
    fame, 266
    fear, 269–270
    greed, 272
    jealousy, 273–274
    money, 265–266
    power, 264–265
    selfishness, 270–271
    sexuality, 267–268
    vanity, 274
Spiritual Warrior archetype, 257,
    260–263, 268, 269
Subconscious mind, 14, 20–22, 168,
    169
    balancing, 47–50
    intelligence factor of, 22–24
    reprogramming, 65, 66, 120–136
    writing letter to, 100–101
Subliminal tapes, 124–125
Sunshine, 138, 139
Superconscious mind, 20, 21, 168,
    169
    balancing, 47–50
Synchronicity, 8

Taking life for granted versus
    gratitude, 82
Tape recording affirmations, 122
Tarantino, Quentin, 206
Tarot, 243, 244, 251–252
Teleportation, 19, 155
Tenth chakra, 154–155
Third-dimensional chakras,
    149–152
Third eye chakra, 150, 152
Third Golden Key–balancing three
    minds and four bodies, 47–58
Third Ray, 214–215, 221, 224, 227,
    229
Thirteenth chakra, 155
Three-mind system, 11, 14, 17, 19
    balancing, 47–50
Three Musketeers, 261–262
Throat chakra, 150, 152, 191

Tibetan Book of the Dead (*Bardo
    Thodol*), 300–302
Tibetan Foundation, 148
Top dog/underdog versus equality,
    70–71
Traditional psychology, 6–10, 13, 193,
    197, 199
Transcendence of duality, 76–77
Transpersonal psychology, 7–8
Tree of Life, 244
Twelfth chakra, 155
Twentieth chakra, 157
Twenty-First chakra, 158
Twenty-Second chakra, 157–158

Unconditional love, 34, 69–70
Unconditional self-love (*see* Self-love,
    unconditional)
Universal Mind, 72
Universal White Light, 281

Vanity, 274
Vicious circle, 10
Victim consciousness, 10, 78,
    200–201
Victory log, 40
Vishnu, 48, 248
Visualizations, 125–134
    attracting money, 126–128
    cosmic healing, 207–209
    emotional body, 52–53
    emotional invulnerability, 42–43
    Golden Bubble, 52–53, 64,
        129–130
    to higher self, 117
    identity, 46
    personal power, 42–43
    reprogramming subconscious mind
        and, 132–134
    self-empowerment trip, 128–129
    self-love, 44–45
Vywamus, 148, 158, 277, 281, 283,
    284, 288, 291, 294, 297, 298

Walks, affirmation, 121–122
Wanderer archetype, 258
Warrior archetype, 245, 260–262
Warrior King archetype, 245
Water dowsing, 24

Weekly routine, 112–114
Willpower (*see* Personal power)
Wise One archetype, 237, 238, 245,
    247, 252, 257, 261–263

Yin Acceptance Method, 96–97
Yin Catharsis Method, 97–98
Yin Indulgence Method, 98

Yin Secondary Communication
    Method, 98–99
Yin Self-Control Method, 96
Yoga, 29
Yogananda, Paramahansa, 29, 68, 197,
    200, 257, 261, 272, 285

Zoroaster, 200, 308

A Special Thank-You

I would like to give a special thank-you to Zandria Louise Fossa for her wonderful help in putting my books on computer and helping out with many of the computer graphics. Her dedicated and devoted help in this area has allowed me to continue my creative flow of writing new books without getting bogged down in the time-consuming details of authorship.

✳

Dr. Joshua David Stone has a Ph.D. in transpersonal psychology and is also a licensed marriage, family, and child counselor in Los Angeles, California. On a spiritual level, he anchors what is called the "Melchizedek Synthesis Light Academy and Ashram," which is an integrated inner- and outer-plane ashram representing all paths to God. Serving as a spokesperson for the Planetary Ascension movement, Dr. Stone's spiritual lineage is directly linked to Djwhal Khul, Sananda, Kuthumi, Lord Maitreya, Lord Melchizedek, the Mahatma, and Metatron. He also feels a very close connection with the Divine Mother and Lord Buddha, as well as a deep devotion to Sathya Sai Baba.